Withdrawn

Ancient Life of the
Great Lakes Basin

D0916170

GREAT LAKES ENVIRONMENT

Matthew M. Douglas and Warren H. Wagner, Jr., Series Editors

Ancient Life of the Great Lakes Basin

Precambrian to Pleistocene

J. Alan Holman

Ann Arbor

The University of Michigan Press

Copyright © by the University of Michigan 1995
All rights reserved
Published in the United States of America by
The University of Michigan Press
Manufactured in the United States of America
⊗ Printed on acid-free paper
1998   1997   1996   1995   4   3   2   1

A CIP catalogue record for this book is available from the British Library.

Library of Congress Cataloging-in-Publication Data

Holman, J. Alan, 1931–
     Ancient life of the Great Lakes Basin : Precambrian to Pleistocene
/ J. Alan Holman.
         p.   cm. (Great Lakes environment)
     Includes bibliographical references and index.
     ISBN 0-472-09534-X (alk. paper). — ISBN 0-472-06534-3 (pbk. :
alk. paper)
     1. Fossils—Great Lakes Region.   I. Title.
QE745.H65   1995
560.977—dc20   94-41060
                                                                        CIP

This book is dedicated to the memory of my mother,
Catherine Pennington Holman,
who encouraged my natural history interests
when I was very young.

Preface

The purpose of this book is to provide an overview of the ancient life of the Great Lakes Basin from the Precambrian era through the Ice Age. It is written for the layperson, but it should be of value to professionals with a biological or geological interest in the Great Lakes Basin. This volume is not meant to be a textbook or a field guide for the identification of fossils, but it should lead the reader to pathways of deeper study, and for this reason a list of references for each chapter occurs at the end of the book.

Beginning with a review of some basic biological and geological principles and terms, the book provides a brief account of the geology of the Great Lakes Basin. The reader is then introduced to the important subgroups of the five great biological kingdoms, an introduction that serves as a framework for the study of the fossil record. Next there is a discussion of the nature of fossils and how they are preserved; paleoecological principles; and methods of collection, preservation, and maintenance of fossils, with emphasis on the Great Lakes region.

Three large sections follow that deal with the simple organism and plant fossils, invertebrate fossils, and vertebrate fossils of the region. Here the more common fossils are discussed and figured. Finally, to bring together the previous sections of the book, there is a chronological account of the fossil communities of the region.

I have attempted to write simply and with a little trace of humor, and I apologize for any scientific buzz words or jargon that inevitably creep into such writings.

Acknowledgments

I wish to express deep thanks to Mary C. Erwin and Christina L. Milton of the University of Michigan Press for editing and producing this book. I also wish to thank Matthew M. Douglas for reading and editing the manuscript. I am grateful to Elizabeth Merritt of the Cincinnati Museum of Natural History for allowing me to view the Indian Trail Caverns, Ohio, late Pleistocene fossils and Kevin Seymour of the Royal Ontario Museum for allowing me to view the late Pleistocene fossils from near Port Huron, Michigan.

I deeply appreciate the talents of the principal artists of this book, Gijsbert (Nick) van Frankenhuyzen and Teresa Petersen. Merald Clark, Barbara Gudgeon, and James Harding produced the art adapted for this book from Michigan State University Museum publications. I thank these individuals as well as the other artists and photographers recognized in the figure legends in the text.

Contents

Chapter 1

Introduction

The Great Lakes region is a good place to live if you like freshwater lakes, but it is also a fine place to study ancient life. The area has yielded evidence of simple organisms that lived 2 billion years ago. Millions of years later, ancient sea life was preserved when the area was part of a depressed ocean basin. Later still, fossil assemblages reflected the life of ancient coal-swamp forests. When the Great Lakes region was subsequently uplifted, there was a great "lost interval" of time when the land was high and erosion wiped away the fossil record.

Finally, the glacially derived sediments of the Pleistocene Ice Age shaped the most recent scene in the region, when giant mastodonts and mammoths and ultimately humans invaded the area. The Great Lakes region is now a microcosm for the study of the recolonization of deglaciated habitats by plants and animals, the great extinction of the mammalian megafauna at the end of the Ice Age, and the appearance of humankind in the New World.

Before we launch into our discussion of the ancient life of the Great Lakes region, we need to review some terms and concepts preliminary to the study of ancient life.

Evolution, the Unifying Concept

Evolution is the concept that unifies the sciences, especially the geological and biological sciences, which together reflect upon ancient life. More than any other field, *paleontology,* the study of ancient life, illustrates the pathways of the evolution of ancient life-forms that gave rise to present-day life. Evolution, as a unifying scientific principle, has been tested from many different directions over the years by thousands of highly trained scientists. Evolutionary theory indicates that life originated from simple aggregates of large organic molecules and that these simple early living things evolved into more and more complex living things over countless millions of years.

Perhaps no other idea has changed the course of human thinking as much as Charles Darwin's concept of *natural selection* as outlined in his *Origin of Species,* published in 1859. Darwin pointed out that in nature, more offspring are produced than will survive and that the environment will weed out the least-adapted organisms and will select for those that are best adapted for existing conditions. Since the best-adapted organisms are most likely to survive to reproduce, succeeding generations are likely to become better and better adapted to existing conditions. But if the environment changes, it may produce further evolutionary change by selecting for those organisms best adapted to those changes.

The genetic basis of organic evolution was unknown to Darwin, but shortly after the turn of the nineteenth century, the work of several scientists shed new light on the nature of the hereditary material. Genes were found to be the units of inheritance present on strandlike bodies in the cells called chromosomes. These units of inheritance then are passed on from generation to generation; and it follows that if organisms are going to change in a lasting way, the units of inheritance must change or *mutate.* Today, the study of genetics is proceeding rapidly at the molecular level and fully supports the concept of evolution.

Paleontology

The science of paleontology deals with ancient life through the study of fossils. Fossils may be defined broadly as any recognizable evidence of prehistoric life. The main subdivisions of paleontology are as follows.

Invertebrate Paleontology: fossils of invertebrates (animals without backbones), consisting mainly of the external shells of the animals that bore them

Vertebrate Paleontology: fossils of vertebrates (animals with back-bones), consisting mainly of bones and teeth
Paleobotany: the study of fossil plants
Micropaleontology: the study of fossil organisms that must be viewed with the aid of a microscope
Palynology: the study of pollen and spores

All of these subbranches of paleontology come into play in research on the ancient life of the Great Lakes Basin.

Invertebrate paleontologists usually are trained in geology departments. This is because the science had its foundation in the studies of William "Strata" Smith, an engineering geologist, who found that fossils were useful in the identification of the layers of rocks that bore them. In contrast, vertebrate paleontologists are often trained in zoology departments because vertebrate paleontology had its origin in the studies of the zoologist Georges Cuvier, who was a comparative anatomist.

Paleobotanists and palynologists must also have strong training in plant biology. The subject matter of paleobotanists is often associated with the coal fields of the world, and palynological studies are often extremely valuable in working out the paleoclimatic relationships of various deposits. The term *micropaleontology* has historically been associated with the study of tiny fossil organisms such as ostracods and foraminifera that are associated with petroleum exploration.

Some additional basic concepts and terms are necessary for the reader before this overview of the paleontology of the Great Lakes Basin is complete.

Adaptive radiation, convergence, and parallelism. Most large land masses support quite a variety of living things. These organisms exist together in natural biotic communities and fill the various *ecological niches* or "modes of life" open to them. When a new land mass, such as a large volcanic island, becomes available for colonization by living things, typically many ecological niches are available for occupancy. Usually, only a few species reach these land masses—based on luck or chance—and these few species may evolve into many species in a relatively short interval of geological time, thus filling the available niches. Such events produce one type of *adaptive radiation.*

Another type of adaptive radiation (which makes more of an impact on the fossil record) occurs when a group of animals or plants achieves an *evolutionary breakthrough,* allowing the group to exploit new eco-logical niches. The origin of jaws in fishes was an extraordinary eco-logical breakthrough that set the stage for the great radiation of fishes in the Devonian period.

When an adaptive radiation takes place in one group of animals or plants, some of them may take on the external appearance of totally unrelated forms. For instance, the adaptive radiation of sea reptiles in the Mesozoic era produced reptiles that took on the appearance of present-day porpoises, which, of course, are mammals. This evolution-ary process is called *convergence.* In contrast, when rather closely related animals living in different geographic areas tend to maintain resemblances to one another, it is because they occupy the same kinds of ecological niches, and such a situation is called evolutionary *paral-lelism.* Two living groups of lizards, the teiids of the New World and the lacertids of the old one, have certain structural and behavioral resemblances to each other because they have been evolving in parallel fashion in different continents.

Homology and analogy. The concept of *homology* relates to struc-tures being inherited from a common ancestor. Thus, the bones of the forelimbs of all living four-legged vertebrates are primitively homolo-gous to one another because they have all evolved from a common four-legged ancestor. The concept of *analogy* relates to structures of different evolutionary origins having similar functions. Thus the fore-limb of a human and the wing of a bird are homologous structures in that both evolved from the ancestral tetrapod limb; but the two struc-tures have different functions. On the other hand, the wings of a bird and the wings of a butterfly are analogous: they have similar func-tions—flight—but have different evolutionary origins. These concepts are important when it comes time to classify vertebrates.

Linnaean system of classification. The present worldwide method of classifying organisms was developed about the middle of the eighteenth century by the Swedish naturalist Linnaeus, who wandered all over Europe for years, collecting plants and trying to figure out ways of arranging them in an orderly manner.

This system tends to put organisms in larger and larger groups as their structural and biological resemblances become less and less. Each group, no matter how large or small, is called a *taxon* (plural taxa). The names for these taxa are usually derived from Latin or Greek words.

We can use ourselves—humans—as an example to show how the system works.

Humans are placed in the phylum Chordata because we share a notochord (albeit mainly in the embryonic state) with other members of the phylum. We are then lumped into the subphylum Vertebrata with all those chordates with a backbone. We are arranged in the class Mammalia with all of the warm-blooded creatures with hair and mammary glands; and in the order Primates on the basis of characters we share with the monkeylike and apelike mammals. We are placed in the family Hominidae based on characters such as our big-brained skull, teeth, bipedal form of locomotion, and other skeletal characters; and in the genus *Homo* with those hominids with the biggest and most convoluted brains. Finally, after reaching the pinnacle (we think) of primate evolution, we are classified as the species *Homo sapiens* ("wise man"). We are the only surviving species in the genus *Homo*.

Phylum Chordata
  Subphylum Vertebrata
    Class Mammalia
      Order Primates
        Family Hominidae
          Genus *Homo*
            Species *Homo sapiens*

We will use the Linnaean system of classification in this book because it allows us to easily arrange the groups we will discuss and because it generally reflects their evolutionary relationships. Another system of classification based on shared, but derived evolutionary characters, called phylogenetic systematics (cladistics), now supplements the practical Linnaean system in many studies of classification.

Modern *species* are classified using many biological criteria—soft parts, for example—that are not always available in fossils. Moreover, modern species are usually described on the basis of large numbers of individuals. Fossils are mainly known on the basis of individual parts of organisms, and many times fossil species are named on the basis of very few specimens. Thus, many *paleontological species* are the result of educated guesses. On the other hand, *paleontological genera* are usually based on more complete material and a larger number of specimens. For these reasons we will concentrate on paleontological genera in this book.

Body Plans

Some types of organisms, such as amoebas, are *asymmetrical,* meaning that the body shape is constantly changing. The one-celled amoebas move about in their aquatic environments engulfing pieces of organic material and are able to change their shape more or less to fit the situation that they encounter.

Other simple forms, such as the protist, *Volvox,* occur in *spherically symmetrical* colonies of cells. These ball-shaped clusters of cells tumble through the water as the result of the movement of whiplike flagella on the individual cells. The spherical shape allows the colony to have a maximum exposure to its environment, facilitating the absorption of the organic particles and gases necessary for its well-being.

Animals that are attached to the bottom, such as the sea anemone, have a *radial symmetry* whereby the parts of the body are arranged around a central *oral* (mouth)–*aboral* (away from the mouth) *axis,* like the spokes of a wheel. In these animals the tiny food bits in the environment are equally distributed around the oral-aboral axis; thus the body parts tend to be arranged radially.

Active animals, such as marine worms, arthropods, and vertebrates, have *bilateral symmetry,* where each half of the animal tends to be a mirror image of the other. Bilaterally symmetrical animals usually have a *head* at the front end of the body that contains the brain and major sense organs. This condition is called *cephalization.*

Fossils

Fossils of entire organisms are rare in the Great Lakes region; fossils usually consist of various individual hard parts of plants and animals (fig. 1). Plant fossils may consist of fossilized wood, roots and root casts, seeds, nuts, cones, and leaves. Fossil invertebrates usually consist of the external calcareous, siliceous, or chitinous hard parts of animals, such as shells of mollusks or elytra (hard, modified wing covers) of beetles. Fossil vertebrates usually consist of bones and teeth.

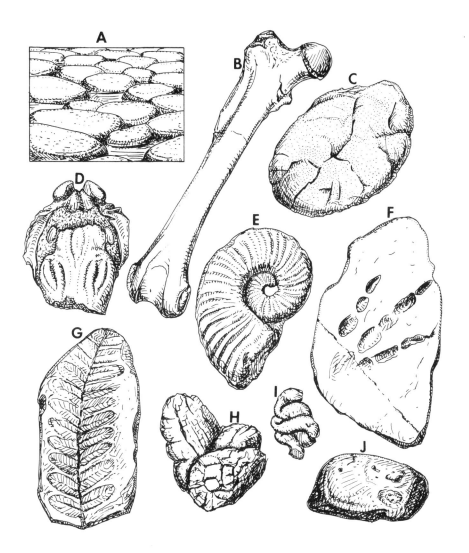

Fig. 1. Kinds of fossils. *A,* a group of large blocks of Precambrian stromatolites. *B,* femur (upper leg bone) of an Oligocene cat. *C,* artificial cast of a dinosaur egg. *D,* natural cast of an Oligocene mammal (oreodont) brain that formed inside an oreodont skull. *E,* internal natural cast of Cretaceous nautiloid shell. *F,* footprint of a small dinosaur. *G,* impression of a Paleozoic fern leaf. *H,* coprolite (fossilized fecal mass) of extinct Oligocene doglike carnivore. *I,* coprolite of a Permian shark. *J,* gastrolith (stomach stone) of a dinosaur.

Less common kinds of fossils include natural molds and casts; carbonized replicas of plants and animals; imprints and impressions; footprints, tracks, and trails; coprolites (fossilized feces); and gastroliths (fossilized stomach or gizzard stones). The organic by-products of metabolic processes or of photosynthesis are also considered to be fossils.

Geology

Classes of rocks. There are three main classes of rocks. *Igneous* rocks form by the solidification of gaseous or molten material. These may form by cooling at great depths in the earth; or they may gush out on the surface in a liquid state (lava) and then solidify; or they may be blasted into the air as gas or fragments of molten material. Common kinds of igneous rocks are granite, basalt, obsidian, and volcanic ash. Some important vertebrate fossils have been found in large ash fall deposits, but not in the Great Lakes region.

Sedimentary rocks are formed when older rocks are broken up by the action of wind, water, and ice (*clastic* rocks) or by organic or chemical agents. Some common clastic sedimentary rocks are sandstones, mudstones, shales, and conglomerates (cemented masses of pebbles and/or rocks). Organically or chemically produced sedimentary rocks include limestones, chalk, coal, salt, and gypsum. Most Great Lakes region fossils, and indeed most fossils everywhere, are to be found in sedimentary rocks (table 1).

Metamorphic rocks form when igneous or sedimentary rocks are changed by great heat or intense pressures or by infiltration of other

TABLE 1. Some Common Rocks of the Great Lakes Region

Igneous	Sedimentary	Metamorphic
Andesite	Clastic rocks:	Gneiss
Basalt	Clay and shale	Marble
Diorite	Sand and sandstone	Phyllite
Felsite	Silt and siltstone	Schist
Gabbro	Biological/chemical rocks:	Slate
Granite	Chert and flint	Quartzite
	Coal	
	Gypsum	
	Limestone and dolomite	
	Salt	

materials at great depths below the earth's surface. Metamorphic rocks tend to be either flaky like slate, schist, or gneiss; or nonflaky kinds such as marble (metamorphosed limestone). Fossils that are occasionally found in metamorphic rocks are usually distorted and difficult to interpret.

The geological cycle. The geological cycle of *uplift, erosion,* and *deposition* have been repeated endlessly throughout geological time, and these processes are recorded in rock strata throughout the world. If we begin by considering the uplift of rock strata as a starting point for the cycle (fig. 2), erosional processes move material from the uplifted highlands or mountain ranges to the lowlands or basins. In these basins deposition of sediments occurs until processes beneath the surface of the earth cause uplift to occur.

In nature breaks may occur between rock strata because of erosional intervals. These are called *unconformities.* If a great deal of time has passed between the deposition of one layer of rocks upon another, the fossils in the two layers are likely to be quite different. In the Great Lakes region a vast unconformity exists between the Pleistocene sediments that lie directly upon ancient Paleozoic bedrock. This unconformity is called the *Lost Interval* in the Great Lakes Basin and was caused by a long period of erosion of uplifted sediments.

Moving continents. The continents of the earth are composed mainly of granitic (igneous) materials that float on the heavier basaltic (igneous) material of the crust. Most paleontologists believe that the six large continents of today were once coalesced as a supercontinent called Pangea during the Triassic period, between 250 and 210 million years ago. The subsequent breaking up of Pangea and the movement of the resulting continents has been instrumental in the changes in the world climate during geological time as well as the zoogeographic relationships of plants and animals on these continents, not to mention organic evolutionary changes.

The mechanisms that run the "internal engine" of the earth are partly, but not completely, understood. Are the forces released within the bowels of the earth that cause continental movements regular or random? How important have these regular (or random) forces been in the mass extinctions that have occurred over geological time? Certainly, we know that the massive forces responsible for the ancient uplifting of the Great Lakes area were part of the forces that caused continental movements as well.

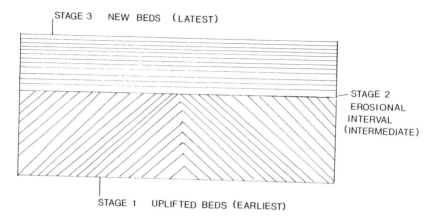

STAGE 3   NEW BEDS (LATEST)

STAGE 2
EROSIONAL
INTERVAL
(INTERMEDIATE)

STAGE 1   UPLIFTED BEDS (EARLIEST)

Fig. 2. Schematic representation of the geological processes of uplift, erosion, and deposition. Stage 2 represents an erosional unconformity between sedimentary events.

External impacts. There are also extraterrestrial forces that impact the earth's surface. It has been suggested that the collision of large objects such as asteroids and comets with the earth could inject enough dust into the air to reduce photosynthesis in plants and lead to mass extinctions in animals. The importance of these impacts has been argued recently in the continual controversy surrounding the rapid, total extinction of the dinosaurs at the end of the Mesozoic. Because the Lost Interval in the geological history of the Great Lakes area includes the Mesozoic, it is impossible to say much about the possible effect of extraterrestrial impacts in the area during the time of the extinction of the dinosaurs.

Uniformitarianism. The concept of *uniformitarianism* holds that explanations of past events may be based on observations that can be made on processes going on in the present. Obviously there have been more violent and wide-ranging changes in the earth's crust in the past than have been recorded during the brief sojourn of humans, but that does not mean that the study of processes working in the earth today cannot be useful in the explanation of the great crustal disturbances of the past. Uniformitarian principles were very important in establishing the chronology and relationships of rock strata in the Great Lakes Basin.

The geological formation. The *formation* is the basic rock unit that the geologist maps; thus it will be frequently referred to when we discuss the occurrence of Great Lakes region fossils. A formation usually results from a sedimentary event such as the filling of a basin or the building up of a coral reef. A formation has characteristics by which different instances of the formation may be identified from place to place and distinguished from other formations. However, formations may occasionally transcend established time units.

Formations are named after the geographic locality where they are characteristically exposed and where they were first adequately described. Thus the Munising Formation was named for the stratigraphic exposure at Munising, Michigan. When a formation consists of a single kind of rock, the rock type is indicated in the name. Thus, the Schoolcraft Dolomite is a dolomite formation that was named for the exposure in the town of Schoolcraft in the Upper Peninsula of Michigan. If a formation consists of different kinds of rocks, no rock type is included in the designation, as is the case in the Munising Formation.

The geological time scale. The geological time scale (fig. 3) was originally set up in Europe, mainly in England and Wales, on the basis of relative chronology discussed below. There has been an attempt to include all of the rock strata in the world in this system.

Two kinds of methods that have been used to relate geological events to one another in a temporal way are *relative* chronological methods and *absolute* chronological methods. Relative chronology is based on the relationship of rock beds to one another and upon the fact that fossil assemblages change from one bed to another. Establishing a relative chronology is based on the geological principle of *superposition*—that is, that younger beds lie upon older beds; and on the geological principle of *faunal succession*—that fossil assemblages change from older to younger beds (fig. 4).

Absolute chronology is mainly based on the fixed rate of loss of radioactive materials from natural substances. For beds over about 50,000 years old, most dating is based on the constant radioactive decay that occurs in some minerals in igneous rocks after they solidify. If the rate of radioactive decay is known, then the ratio between the original substance and the product of that decay will tell how long the radioactive clock has been ticking away.

For beds under 50,000 years old the carbon 14 method has usually been employed. This isotope of carbon reduces itself by one-half in fixed periods of time, but the half-lives are so short that accuracy is largely impossible after 50,000 or so years. Modern carbon 14 studies are usually done on the protein substance collagen that may be ex-

TIME IN MILLIONS OF YEARS BEFORE PRESENT	ERAS	PERIODS	EPOCHS
— .1 —	CENOZOIC	QUATERNARY	HOLOCENE
— 1.9 —			PLEISTOCENE
— 5 —			PLIOCENE
— 25 —		TERTIARY	MIOCENE
— 35 —			OLIGOCENE
— 55 —			EOCENE
— 65 —			PALEOCENE
— 140 —	MESOZOIC	CRETACEOUS	
— 210 —		JURASSIC	
— 250 —		TRIASSIC	
— 290 —	PALEOZOIC	PERMIAN	
— 320 —		PENNSYLVANIAN	
— 360 —		MISSISSIPPIAN	
— 410 —		DEVONIAN	
— 440 —		SILURIAN	
— 500 —		ORDOVICIAN	
— 550 —		CAMBRIAN	
— 4550 —	PRECAMBRIAN		

Fig. 3. The geological time scale

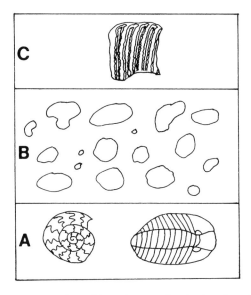

Fig. 4. Schematic representation of faunal succession in the Great Lakes region. *A, left,* ammonoid and *right,* trilobite fossils in ancient Paleozoic beds. *B,* unconformable bed of clastic rocks left by the Wisconsinan glaciation. *C,* Mammoth tooth fragment from the postglacial Wisconsinan.

tracted from plant fiber, wood, seeds, cones, shells, bones, and teeth of late Pleistocene plants and animals.

Eras are the largest divisions of the geological time scale. All four eras include the remains of fossils, but the *Precambrian* has the least number of fossils. All of the following era names come from the Greek language. The *Paleozoic* era means ancient life, the *Mesozoic* era means middle life, and the *Cenozoic* era means recent life.

The eras are divided into lesser units called *periods.* The periods of the Paleozoic era are six or seven in number, depending on whether one is an American or a European. The Cambrian is derived from Cambria, a Latin term for Wales. The Ordovician was named for the Ordovices, an ancient Welsh tribe. The Silurian is named for an ancient tribe, the Silures, that lived in the Welsh borderland. The Devonian is named for Devonshire, a county in England. The Mississippian was proposed by the famous Michigan geologist, Alexander Winchell in 1869. The Pennsylvanian was named by the American geologist H. S. Williams in 1891. Much of the Mississippian consists of limestones, whereas the Pennsylvanian is known for its numerous coal deposits.

The European term Carboniferous includes both the Mississippian and the Pennsylvanian. The last period of the Paleozoic, the Permian, is named after rocks in the Russian province of Perm.

The three periods of the Mesozoic era are the Triassic, named for a three-fold division of rocks in Germany; the Jurassic named in reference to the Jura Alps of Switzerland; and the Cretaceous, derived from the Latin *creta,* meaning chalk.

The Cenozoic era is divided into one very long period, the Tertiary, and a much shorter one, the Quaternary. The Tertiary has five epochs, the Quaternary only two, the Pleistocene (Ice Age) and the Holocene (Recent). The Pleistocene of North America has four glacial and three interglacial ages.

In the Great Lakes region we have fossils from the following units of the geologic time scale:

Precambrian
Paleozoic
   Cambrian
   Ordovician
   Silurian
   Devonian
   Mississippian
   Pennsylvanian
Mesozoic
   Jurassic (pollen only)
Cenozoic
   Quaternary
      ?Illinoian glacial age
      Sangamonian interglacial age
      Wisconsinan glacial age

With these introductory concepts and terms in mind, we are now ready to examine the geological history of the Great Lakes Basin as an introduction to the fossil forms.

Chapter 2

Geological History of
the Great Lakes Basin

The Great Lakes Basin was created by the scouring activity of glacial erosion during the Ice Age. The individual Great Lakes were also formed by this process and were filled by glacial meltwater. Previous to the Ice Age, the region was a plateau of ancient bedrock that had been eroding away for countless millions of years after the uplift of a basin containing ancient seas.

Thus, to understand the history of life in the Great Lakes region, one must first become familiar with the basic geological history of the area, as both subjects are closely linked. It will be important for the reader to constantly refer to the geological time scale (fig. 3) and the geologic map of the Great Lakes region (fig. 5) to follow this chapter.

Bedrock and Surficial Sediments

Figure 5 depicts the distribution of bedrock in the Great Lakes Basin. These rocks mainly consist of consolidated materials that are very ancient. The bedrock is mainly covered by unconsolidated sediments in the Great Lakes Basin. These materials consist mainly of silts, sands, and gravels that were the result of glacial activity in the Pleistocene (Ice Age). These sediments usually range from about 20 to 100 feet thick. Bedrock is usually exposed in areas where the surficial sediments have been eroded away by natural causes or by excavations by humans

15

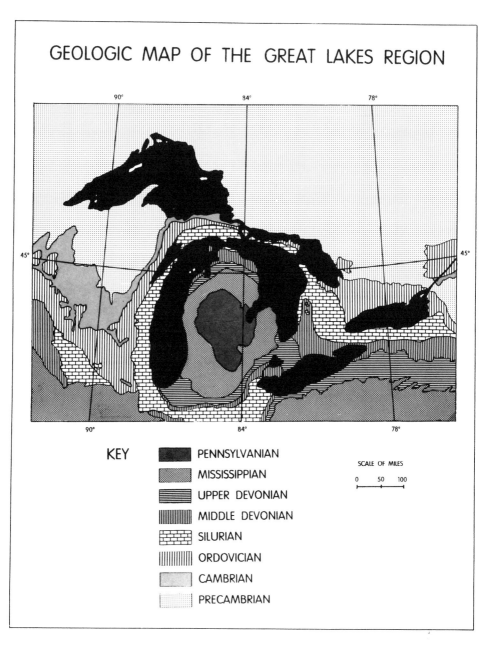

Fig. 5. Geologic map of bedrock of the Great Lakes Basin showing where rocks of the various periods occur near the surface

Fig. 6. Precambrian granitic outcrop in Dickenson County in the Upper Peninsula of Michigan. The surficial sediments that lay over and around these rocks were eroded away by natural causes. (Photo courtesy of James H. Harding.)

(figs. 6, 7). These sites mainly include eroded river and stream valleys, some lakeshores, rock quarries, and some road cuts. Other evidences of bedrock exposures are found in the cores brought up by oil well–drilling activities.

Fig. 7. Silurian limestone formation in a quarry in Schoolcraft County in the Upper Peninsula of Michigan. Limestone forms in shallow sea basins and often contains marine fossils. (Photo courtesy of James H. Harding.)

Precambrian Era

The Precambrian era includes all of the time between the origin of the earth and the Cambrian period, when life first became abundant. The Precambrian represents a vast, almost unimaginable span of time from about 4.5 billion years ago to about 550 million years ago. During this interval countless great geological events repeated themselves through the eons. Life was first recorded in the Precambrian about 3.5 billion years ago, but life-forms remained relatively simple for the next 2 billion years.

Precambrian rocks have been difficult to interpret in the Great Lakes region because much of the original structure of the rocks has been changed by metamorphic processes and because for billions of years erosion has removed huge amounts of material. Precambrian rocks are mainly igneous and metamorphic ones, but some sedimentary rocks have survived the ages. Granites (fig. 6) characteristically occur among other Precambrian rocks as younger rocks called *intrusives* that have wedged themselves into the older rocks (fig. 8).

In the Great Lakes Basin Precambrian rocks nearly enclose the area around Lake Superior and extend over a vast area north of Lake Huron and Lake Ontario. There is no worldwide system of naming Precambrian rocks, so it has been common to refer to Precambrian rocks as representing early, middle, and late Cambrian times. Within each of these intervals igneous rocks were intruded and extruded, sedimentary rocks were formed and deposited, folding and metamorphosis took place, and uplift and sometimes mountain building occurred. Divisions between the early, middle, and late Precambrian occur because of massive uplifts and eons of subsequent erosion.

During an interval in the middle Precambrian called the Huronian System (fig. 8), iron ores formed in Minnesota, northern Wisconsin, and the Upper Peninsula of Michigan. These ores were mined and carried by Great Lakes ships to the steel mills in the Chicago and Pittsburgh areas. Also in the Huronian System is evidence of an ancient ice age: glacial scratches on boulders and on materials interpreted as glacial tills. Moreover, the earliest evidences of life in the Great Lakes region are found in Precambrian rocks of the Huronian System. These fossils mainly represent lime-secreting organisms, remnants of simple microscopic organisms, and there is some evidence of photosynthesis. These fossils are among the very earliest known life-forms, and they will be discussed in other chapters of this book.

Paleozoic Era

The Paleozoic era lasted from about 550 million to about 250 million years ago. Fossils were abundant at the beginning of the era, and by the end of the era most of the important groups of plants and animals (with the exception of flowering plants, dinosaurs, birds, and mammals) had evolved.

During the Paleozoic, the interior of North America stood high on an ancient land that was composed of rocks that had been through billions of years of geological cycling. During the Paleozoic this central region was generally very stable compared to both coastal regions (fig.

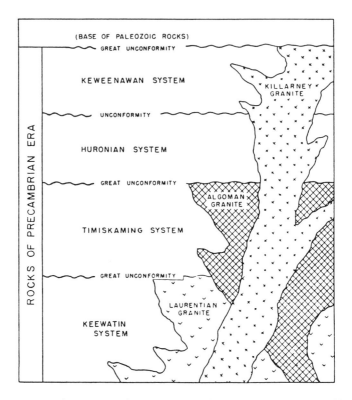

Fig. 8. Diagram of intrusions of younger Precambrian granitic rocks into older ones in the Lake Superior area of Michigan. The Killarney granite has intruded the younger Algoman granite, which has in turn intruded the Laurentian granite. (From J. L. Hough, *Geology of the Great Lakes* [Urbana: University of Illinois Press, 1958]. Copyright 1958 by the Board of Trustees of the University of Illinois.)

9). Nevertheless, this central stable interior region, or *craton,* subsided from time to time; and shallow seas moved inland into the basins that were formed. Sedimentary layers then developed in these sea basins.

During the Paleozoic the Great Lakes region was dominated by high areas called positive areas that were eroded and supplied sediments to the lowlands, and sinking areas called negative areas that accumulated these sediments. Positive areas that were important suppliers for Paleozoic seas in the Great Lakes region included the Ozark Dome; the Wisconsin and LaSalle Highlands; the Kankakee, Cincinnati, and Findlay Arches; and the Adirondack Highlands.

The basin that accumulated these sediments for most of the Paleo-

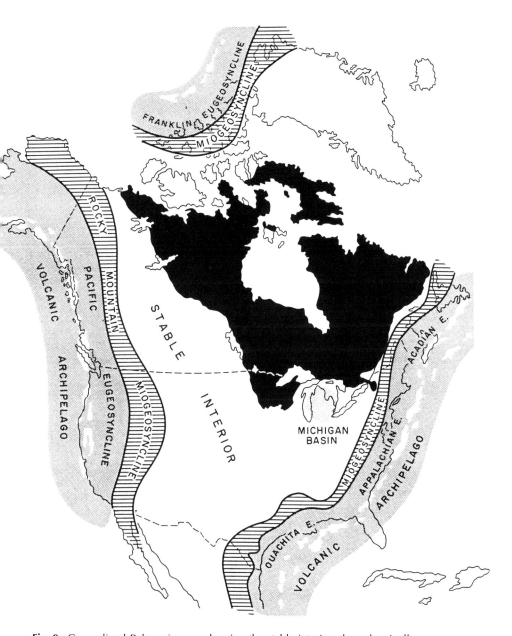

Fig. 9. Generalized Paleozoic map showing the stable interior, the volcanically active coastal areas, and the location of the Michigan Basin. The Michigan Basin formed when a part of the stable interior subsided. (From J. A. Dorr, Jr., and D. F. Eschman, *Geology of Michigan* [Ann Arbor: University of Michigan Press, 1970].)

zoic era is called the *Michigan Basin*. The rocks of the Michigan Basin form the most important Paleozoic fossil-bearing strata that will be discussed here. The Michigan Basin is remarkably circular and symmetrical. In its deepest part it holds about 14,000 feet of sedimentary rocks. The rocks of the basin can be divided into four basic units: (1) the sandstone formations of the Cambrian, (2) the carbonate and evaporite sedimentary sequence of the Ordovician, Silurian, and early and middle Devonian, (3) the shales and the sandstones of the late Devonian and Mississippian, and (4) the coal-bearing strata of the Pennsylvanian.

Cambrian period. The Cambrian is the first period of the Paleozoic era and lasted for about 50 million years, from about 550 million to about 500 million years ago. Fossils become abundant for the first time in the Cambrian, but in the Great Lakes region Cambrian rocks are rather restricted, and fossils are not abundant.

In the Great Lakes region the Cambrian period is mainly represented by (1) sandstones deposited by stream erosion of the ancient Precambrian rocks and (2) later sandstones that were deposited by the action of ancient invading seas. These rocks occur in a thin belt that starts at the eastern part of the Upper Peninsula of Michigan on the south shore of Lake Superior, extends westward along this shoreline for about 160 miles, and then turns southward as a thin belt down into Wisconsin.

Rocks of early and middle Cambrian age form the Jacobsville Sandstone, which accumulated as a result of stream action on an irregular Precambrian rock surface. Lovely exposures of the Jacobsville Sandstone may be seen along road-cut exposures or in bluffs along the southern shore of Lake Superior between Baraga and L'Anse in the Upper Peninsula of Michigan. Jacobsville Sandstone is reddish brown in color and has been used locally as a building stone.

By middle Cambrian times seas began to invade the Great Lakes region from the west, northwest, and south. Sedimentary rocks, mainly sandstones, were deposited in the region by wave action and other processes of these inland seas. The Munising Formation in the Upper Peninsula of Michigan is a well-known example of late Cambrian rocks. The erosion of the sandstone members of this formation has produced some of the exquisite scenery of northern Michigan. This includes the Pictured Rocks along the south shore of Lake Michigan near Munising and the Upper and Lower Tahquamenon Falls, where streams churn through the sandstones of the Munising Formation.

Ordovician period. The Ordovician period was a rather long one that occurred from about 500 million to about 440 million years ago. Many more Ordovician rocks occur in the Great Lakes Basin than Cambrian ones, and fossils are much more abundant. The Ordovician was the time that Paleozoic seas became completely established in the Michigan Basin.

Ordovician bedrock in the region occurs from New York around the eastern part of Lake Ontario; in a wide band across Ontario north of Lake Ontario; in an isolated area north of Georgian Bay; in the northern part of St. Joseph Island, Ontario; across the Upper Peninsula of Michigan for about 160 miles in a band south of the Cambrian bedrock area; and thence into Wisconsin in a band east of the Cambrian bedrock area.

During a good part of the Ordovician the Michigan Basin was covered by seas. Since the position of the shorelines of these seas fluctuated during the period, sediments were sometimes deposited in shallow water near the shore and other times in the deeper, offshore waters. Sediments deposited by these Ordovician seas mainly include marine dolomites, sandstones, and shales.

Good outcrops of Ordovician rocks occur in the southern part of the Upper Peninsula of Michigan in the Escanaba River valley, and several kinds of marine fossils may be found in these exposures. Ordovician rocks are mainly unexposed in southern areas of the Great Lakes Basin, but rocks representing most of Ordovician time have been found in the cores from oil and gas well drillings in the Lower Peninsula of Michigan.

Of special significance is the Queenston Shale that thickens as it extends east from Michigan into Ontario and New York State and is an important part of the Ordovician bedrock in the latter two places. This shale is part of a huge amount of deltaic sediments that were carried into the sea by rivers and streams that flowed westward from mountainous areas to the east.

Silurian period. The Silurian period is a short one in the geological scale of time, occurring from about 440 million to about 410 million years ago. But the Silurian was an extremely important period in the Great Lakes region (fig. 10), where it is known for its shallow, landlocked seas, its great reef formations, and its deposits of salt and gypsum. Fossils are abundant in some areas.

The distribution of Silurian rocks near the surface is somewhat complex in the region. Rocks of early Silurian age are found in a narrow

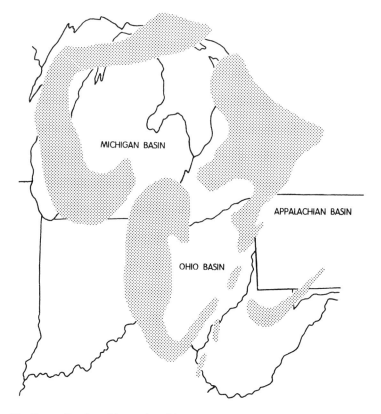

Fig. 10. Generalized positions of reef formations (stippled) in the Silurian relative to interior Paleozoic basins

band in New York State south of Lake Ontario and then swinging up into Ontario east of the lake; and in a very narrow band extending westward in the eastern part of the Upper Peninsula of Michigan.

Middle *Silurian* rocks are abundant in the region. They occur in Ontario in the middle of the land mass between Lake Ontario and Lake Huron in a wide band that narrows as it extends northward to the tip of Bruce Peninsula. They occur in the southern part of St. Joseph Island, Ontario; around the northern shores of Lake Huron and Lake Michigan in the Upper Peninsula of Michigan and down and around the eastern shore of Lake Michigan in Wisconsin; and into northeastern Illinois and across Indiana and Ohio. Many important Silurian salt-bearing rocks in Michigan are buried under Mississippian and Pennsylvanian rocks in the central and southeastern part of the state; but some salt-bearing rocks of the Salina Group of rocks are relatively near the surface in central Ontario between the lakes and in the St. Ignace area of the Upper Peninsula of Michigan. Finally, rocks representing the late Silurian age occur in a narrow band south of Lake Ontario and then bending upward toward Bruce Peninsula in New York and Ontario.

In the Silurian period the positive and negative areas previously discussed were very pronounced, producing significant arches and basins. Important reef formations existed in areas around the Michigan Basin (see fig. 10). Fossil reefs are structures formed not only of the skeletons of coral animals, but of many other kinds of animal and other organic remains. Later, these reefs were buried under younger formations, but the reefs were so resistant to erosion that some of them are topographic features today. In fact, some of the shoals along the western edge of Lake Michigan from Chicago, Illinois, to Racine, Wisconsin, are significant remnants of Silurian reefs. Several important fossil localities are associated with these reefs.

In later Silurian times the seas became shallower, and the waters of the Michigan Basin and part of the Appalachian trough became a sea that was mainly isolated from the ocean. In this area, important deposits of evaporites accumulated, including gypsum and salt. In Michigan these deposits of salt are very important commercially both in the chemical industry and for table salt. Toward the end of the Silurian period, the seas became extensive again, and more usual marine sediments consisting mainly of dolomites were laid down.

Devonian period. The Devonian period was a long one that lasted from about 410 million to about 360 million years. This period is often referred to as "the age of fishes," as during this time span, fishes of many groups became abundant in the fossil record. The Devonian was a time of widespread seas, although these fluctuated quite a bit. Limestones, dolomites, shales, and commercially important evaporites were deposited during the Devonian, and fossils were abundant in several areas of the Great Lakes Basin.

Rocks representing the middle Devonian age occur in a belt from eastern New York extending across the upper part of Lake Ontario and swing upward in Ontario as a fingerlike projection and finally contact the southeastern shore of Lake Huron. Blocked by upper Devonian rocks in western Ontario and eastern Michigan, the middle Devonian rocks pick up again south of Lake Sinclair and extend around northern Indiana as a very narrow band that finally swings upward to contact the southern tip of Lake Michigan. Middle Devonian rocks also occur in an isolated arc in the tip of the Lower Peninsula of Michigan.

Upper Devonian rocks, mainly shales, extend across New York, Ontario, and northern Ohio and Indiana to the south shore of Lake Michigan. Finally, an isolated belt of Upper Devonian shales swings as a northward-bending arc across the northern part of the Lower Peninsula of Michigan roughly from Alpena on Lake Huron to Frankfort on Lake Michigan.

By the middle part of the Devonian the Michigan Basin was totally covered by seas, and these seas remained in the area until the close of the period. The upper Devonian is dominated by black shales. These rocks were derived from anaerobic black muds and were transported into Michigan from uplifted areas in the Appalachian region.

Mississippian period. The Mississippian period represents about the lower one-half of the Carboniferous period that is recognized in Europe. The Mississippian lasted about 40 million years, from about 360 million to about 320 million years ago. The Mississippian is known in North America for its extensive limestone deposits, but these are found mainly south of the Great Lakes region. Mississippian rocks occur extensively in New York and Ontario, mainly south of Lake Ontario, but their primary occurrence is in the Michigan Basin.

In the Michigan Basin the Mississippian rocks lie peripherally to the Pennsylvanian rocks that lie nearest the surface in the center of the basin. During the Mississippian period, shales, siltstones, and sandstones were the most common sedimentary rocks deposited in the Great Lakes Basin, with the great characteristic limestone formations being deposited south of the region.

In very late Mississippian time the Michigan Basin was uplifted, the seas retreated, and parts of the earlier marine-deposited sediments were eroded away. The unconformity between the Mississippian and the following Pennsylvanian rocks may have been the most extensive time of uplift and folding in the Michigan Basin since early Ordovician times. Mississippian rocks in the Great Lakes Basin, mainly sandstones and shales, have yielded some excellent collecting localities, especially in the Michigan Basin.

Pennsylvanian period. The Pennsylvanian period is the last period before the great Lost Interval in the Great Lakes region. The Pennsylvanian corresponds with about the upper half of the Carboniferous period recognized in Europe and lasted about 30 million years, from about 320 million to about 290 million years ago. The Pennsylvanian is known for its extensive coal-bearing strata; and although coal is found in the Great Lakes region, it has never had the commercial importance it has in more southern areas.

The Pennsylvanian rocks in the Great Lakes region occur nearest the surface in the middle of the Michigan Basin and are surrounded by Mississippian rocks. Pennsylvanian outcrops are rare in the region; thus fossil collecting from this period is quite localized. In the Pennsylvanian period the Appalachian low area filled with sediments, and almost all of the northeastern United States became a region of cyclic sedimentation of marine and terrestrial environments. In other words, the seas came in and then went out again in a cyclical pattern. During a portion of each cycle there was usually a time when great swamps existed. The plant remains from these swamps became altered into coal formations. It has been said that the Pennsylvanian commercial coal beds (mainly south of the region) and the Precambrian iron ores of the Great Lakes region formed the main raw materials for the industrial development of the Great Lakes area.

The Lost Interval

A long Lost Interval that lasted from the end of the Pennsylvanian period to the latter part of the Quaternary period—spanning almost 290 million years—occurred in the Great Lakes region. The only record of rocks in the region from this great time span consist of some Jurassic red beds found in oil well cores in Michigan. These rocks have yielded microscopic pollen grains but no larger fossils.

The interval was lost because at the end of the Pennsylvanian, a great general uplift occurred in the eastern part of North America, including the building of the huge Appalachian chain of mountains. As a part of this process, the Michigan Basin, as well as the entire Great Lakes region, was warped upward. The region then was transformed from a major low area of sedimentation to an upland area where the major process was erosion for about the next 290 million years. One must think back to Precambrian times to imagine such a lost time interval in the region.

Why No Dinosaurs Have Been Found in the Great Lakes Basin

People are eminently curious about why dinosaur remains have never been found in the Great Lakes region. The answer is simple. Dinosaurs occurred only in the Triassic, Jurassic, and Cretaceous. They arose in the late Triassic and became extinct at about the Cretaceous and Tertiary boundary. Since Triassic, Jurassic, and Cretaceous rocks (with the exception of the wee sample of Jurassic rocks from Michigan) have been eroded away in the region, the dinosaurs that they might have borne have not been found. Thus, one could say that searching for dinosaurs in the Great Lakes region would be about as productive as digging for buried treasure in a sandbox.

Uplift in the Michigan Basin: The Key to Understanding the Distribution of Great Lakes Region Rocks and Fossils

At the end of the Pennsylvanian period, as we have seen, there was an upwarping of the Great Lakes region that resulted in an erosional interval for the next 290 million years. As the gently downward-curving layers of sedimentary rocks in the Michigan Basin were slowly pushed upward, they were eroded away to form a pattern in which the youngest Paleozoic rocks were closest to the surface at the center of the basin, with successively older rocks closest to the surface away from the center of the basin.

These exposures do not occur as completely symmetrical rings because of certain local geological processes that have occurred (such as the formation of Lake Michigan and Lake Huron!). But if one looks carefully at figure 5, one will note that the Pennsylvanian rocks occur at the center of the basin, the Mississippian rocks are peripheral to the Pennsylvanian rocks, and the Devonian rocks are mainly peripheral to the Mississippian ones.

Therefore, if you are interested in locating Pennsylvanian sedimentary rocks and coal-swamp forest fossils, you should look in the central part of the Lower Peninsula of Michigan. And, indeed some of the best Pennsylvanian collecting localities are near Lansing, Michigan, where the Grand River has eroded its way down into Pennsylvanian strata.

On the other hand, if one is looking for Devonian rocks and fossils, one would look for limestone quarries in the northern tip of the Lower Peninsula of Michigan or in northwestern Indiana.

The Great Ice Age (Pleistocene)

Erosional cycles during the lost interval shaped an ancient topography that occurs in the bedrock under the superficial glacial sediments of the Great Lakes region. This topography has a profile of ancient hills, ridges, and valleys that has recently been generated in three dimensions by computerized studies from hundreds of well cores. But the surface topography that we see about us today is mainly the result of processes associated with the movements and melting of the great glaciers of the Ice Age.

During the Ice Age several great ice sheets advanced and retreated in North America. These glacial advances are associated with time intervals that are called glacial ages, and they have been given names in North America and elsewhere. Glacial retreats are associated with time intervals called interglacial ages, and they also have been named (table 2). There were also lesser advances and retreats within some glacial ages. Best documented in the Great Lakes region is the Wisconsinan glacial age.

Impact and features of glacial ice. Figure 11 is a drawing made from a photograph of the leading edge of the modern Greenland ice sheet. The edge of this ice sheet is a sheer cliff. Ahead of this ice cliff is a glacial outwash area with braided streams. Adjacent to the streams are

TABLE 2. North American Glacial and Interglacial Ages and the Holocene

Recent	
Holocene	(The last 10,000 years)
Pleistocene	
Wisconsinan glacial	(110,000 yrs. duration)
Sangamonian interglacial	(10,000 yrs. duration)
Illinoian glacial	
Yarmouthian interglacial	
Kansan glacial	
Aftonian interglacial	
Nebraskan glacial	

Fig. 11. The edge of the Greenland ice sheet in Christians Land. The edge of the ice sheet is in the form of a sheer cliff. In front of the cliff is a glacial outwash area with braided streams and other glacial features. Similar conditions existed for thousands of years during the Pleistocene of the Great Lakes Basin. (Redrawn from a photograph courtesy of the National Survey and Cadastre, Denmark.)

other glacial features. One must realize that similar conditions existed for countless thousands of years in the Great Lakes region in the Pleistocene.

Glacial ice impacts the environment in several ways. Mainly it (1) erodes away the land that it moves over and transports rock debris and soil that it has plucked from the surface of the land and (2) deposits this material either directly by melting in place or by its meltwater that spreads out over the countryside.

Almost all of the material carried by the ice is held in suspension within it, but most of the material is found near the bottom of the ice sheet. There appears to be practically no limit to the size of particles that can be transported by glacial ice. *Megablocks*—massive sections of sedimentary rock—transported for up to 200 miles by glacial ice in western Canada are large pieces of real estate over a mile in diameter and hundreds of feet deep!

The matter transported by the ice may be laid down at any point where the glacial ice melts. These deposits are classified either as *till* or *outwash* deposits. Till comes directly from the ice and consists of particles of all sizes and shapes mixed together. Till forms structures called *moraines.* Common moraines are called *end* moraines, *lateral* moraines, or *ground* moraines. End moraines form at the end of the ice lobe, lateral moraines form at the side of the ice lobe, and ground moraines form when the ice moves across the land at a relatively rapid rate. Most of the big hills in northern Michigan south of the straits area (some looking like small mountain ranges from a distance) are portions of end moraines. *Terminal* moraines mark the very end points of major glacial advances, and *recessional* moraines mark the various lines of temporary stops during a glacial retreat.

In many areas of the Great Lakes region there are typical glacial features called *drumlins, eskers, kames,* and *kettle holes* (fig. 12). Drumlins are graceful looking elliptical hills composed of glacial till that was left over when the glacier retreated. The long axes of drumlins are oriented in the direction of the ice flow. Eskers are narrow, snakelike ridges that come from deposits laid down in tunnels in or under the ice, left over when the ice retreated. Kames are isolated rounded hills of glacial outwash sand and gravel, and kettle holes arise from rounded ice blocks that melted after the glacial retreat. *Outwash plains* are deposited in the form of glacial lobes as aprons of sediments. They typically develop in front of moraines and are well developed in Michigan in these situations.

Ice flow and the Great Lakes basins. The basins that contain the present Great Lakes were mainly developed in the relatively soft limestones and shales of Paleozoic age discussed previously. These basins were repeatedly eroded out of preglacial valleys that at one time drained the midcontinental area of America. This erosion was the product of the several glacial episodes of the Pleistocene. As we shall see, each glaciation tended to remove the sedimentary and fossil evidence of the previous one in the Great Lakes region; so that our main record is derived from the last glacial event, the Wisconsinan.

The actual amount of erosion in these preglacial valleys is hard to

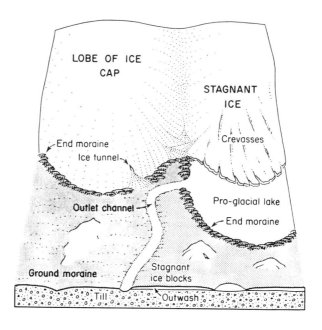

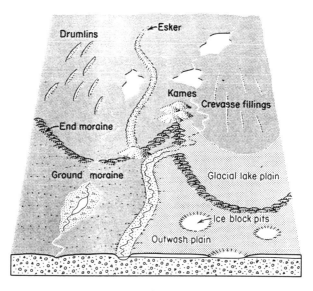

Fig. 12. Generalized diagram to show relationships between glacial ice and glacial topographic features before (above) and after (below) the retreat of the ice. (From J. A. Dorr, Jr., and D. F. Eschman, *Geology of Michigan* [Ann Arbor: University of Michigan Press, 1970].)

estimate, but the glacial scouring must have been great, as indicated by the fact that the present floors of Lake Huron and Lake Michigan are well below present sea level. The effect of the Paleozoic bedrock topography on the flow of glacial ice in the southern part of the Great Lakes region is shown by the looping position of the end moraines (fig. 13).

These moraines show that the margin of the ice during the last glaciation (Wisconsinan) consisted of separate ice lobes that projected into these southern areas from the lake basins. It has been estimated that the depth of these ice lobes ranged from between one-half mile to one and one-half miles in thickness. Thus one may imagine the power that must have been generated by the movements and periodic meltwaters of this mountain of ice.

The Pleistocene ages. The Pleistocene ages are listed in table 2. The Nebraskan glacial age is presently recognized as the earliest glacial age of the Pleistocene, although some individuals believe that pre-Nebraskan sediments may exist. The outer limits of the Nebraskan sediments have been mapped in eastern Nebraska, northeastern Kansas, and northern Missouri.

The Nebraskan glaciation is thought to have extended throughout the Great Lakes region, but there is no evidence for it. It is believed that erosional processes caused by later ice advances have removed evidences of the Nebraskan glaciation in the region. Where there is evidence of Nebraskan glaciation, the upper part of its till is highly weathered. This long period of weathering represents the Aftonian interglacial age that followed. There is also no record of Aftonian times in the Great Lakes region.

The Kansan glacial age is known from approximately the same areas as the Nebraskan. Kansan sediments have also never been defined in the Great Lakes Basin, although in parts of Pennsylvania and New Jersey glacial drift sediments are believed to represent the Kansan, as are cave sediments with associated vertebrate faunas in western Maryland and in West Virginia. In places, the Kansan till is as much as 12 feet thick. In addition to till, the Kansan also has deposits of *loess* (wind-blown silt) and peat. Weathering of the top of the Kansan till also occurred during the following Yarmouthian interglacial age, which is thought to have been the warmest and the longest of all the interglacial stages in North America. No evidence of the Yarmouthian exists in the Great Lakes Basin.

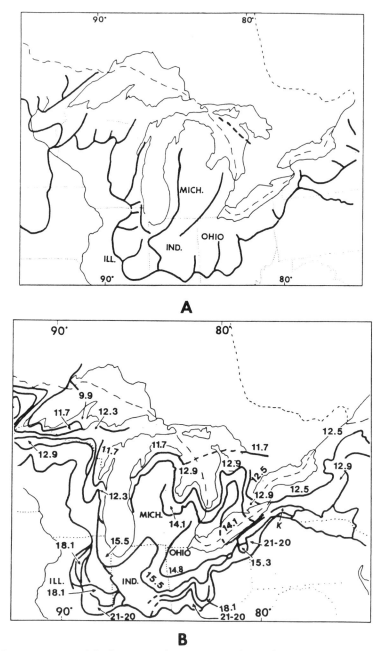

Fig. 13. Position of the looping end moraines (A) during the maximum Wisconsinan ice sheet advance about 20,000 years ago, and positions of the ice margin withdrawal (B) in thousands of years ago at the end of the Pleistocene. (Reprinted from *Quaternary Science Reviews* 11, J. A. Holman, Late Quaternary Herpetofauna of the Central Great Lakes Region, U.S.A.: Zoogeographical and Paleoecological Implications, 345–51, Copyright 1992, with kind permission from Elsevier Science Ltd, The Boulevard, Langford Lane, Kidlington 0X5 1GB, UK.)

The third ice sheet, the Illinoian, extended over much of Illinois, Indiana, and Ohio, where it laid down a large sheet of till. But these sediments have yet to be identified in the Great Lakes Basin except for cave sediments in southwestern Ontario that have yielded a vertebrate fauna possibly of Illinoian age. Again, this lack of sediments in the region is thought to be the erosional effect of a later glaciation, in this case the Wisconsinan. During the Sangamonian interglacial age, which followed the Illinoian and was the last interglacial age of the Pleistocene, much of the Illinoian till was weathered. Sangamonian deposits have been identified in Ontario, where they yielded Pleistocene fauna.

The Wisconsinan glacial age is the last age of the Pleistocene. It is responsible for almost all of the surficial topography in the Great Lakes Basin. Since it is the last glacial age, it has only been slightly weathered, so that its surface reveals an almost unchanged glacial topography. Because of its fine state of preservation, it has yielded much more information than any of the other Pleistocene ages anywhere.

Pleistocene record in the Great Lakes Basin. Most ancient life that has been recorded in the Pleistocene of the Great Lakes Basin has been found in sediments of the Wisconsinan glacial age, especially from the postglacial interval from about 14,000 to about 10,000 years ago. The pre-Wisconsinan sediments that do exist include material from Kelso Cave, southwestern Ontario, which has yielded a vertebrate fauna of possible Illinoian age. In addition, in the Toronto area of Ontario, Sangamonian sediments of the Don Formation and Scarborough Formation were deposited during an important rise of lake level in the basin that presently contains Lake Ontario.

No pre-Wisconsinan deposits have been recorded in Michigan, but it is thought that they possibly occur in the subsurface somewhere where the glacial drift is very thick. Evidence of Sangamonian deposits does occur, however, somewhat south of the Great Lakes region. In southeastern Indiana, deposits of peaty silt and sand are associated with a Sangamonian soil horizon; and Sangamonian lake sediments that accumulated in kettles may be found within the Illinoian drift in south central Illinois.

The Wisconsinan glacial age is thought to be roughly the same length as the Devensian glacial age in Britain. Both ages are thought to have lasted about 100,000 years, from about 110,000 to about 10,000 years ago. The Wisconsinan is known to have had small retreats and advances that have been given substage names. The end of the Ice

Age (Pleistocene) corresponds with the end of the Wisconsinan about 10,000 years ago.

Early Wisconsinan tills occurred in the Great Lakes Basin from about 75,000 to 64,000 years ago. Probable early Wisconsinan glacial tills occur in southwestern Ontario that overlie the Sangamonian Scarborough Formation previously discussed. Further east in Ontario, along the north side of Lake Erie, other deposits of till that must represent early Wisconsinan times lie beneath (dated) middle Wisconsinan lake sediments.

Moreover, in northeastern Ohio, tills from several localities have been assigned to an early Wisconsinan age. Although early Wisconsinan glacial deposits have not been definitely identified in southern Michigan, there are a few places where these early tills might exist; although it has been said that they might also be of Illinoian age. There are also early Wisconsinan tills in place in northern Illinois and southern Wisconsin and south of the Great Lakes region in southwestern Ohio and southeastern Indiana.

Middle Wisconsinan sediments were deposited from about 64,000 to about 23,000 years ago. The Middle Wisconsin has been divided into three substages that have been named (from oldest to youngest) the Port Talbot, the Cherry Tree, and the Plum Point. In southwestern Ontario, several dates obtained from peat and other organic remains within the middle Wisconsinan average about 44,000 years old and thus represent the Port Talbot substage of the middle Wisconsinan. These beds are underlain by a green clay that must be of an even older Port Talbot age, estimated to be between 50,000 and 65,000 years.

In Michigan the oldest dated (about 48,000 years old) Port Talbot sediments occur near the base of a stream along Mill Creek in St. Clair County. This deposit contains various organic remains and a very important vertebrate fauna that will be discussed later. Another Port Talbot organic deposit occurs along the Pine River in Manistee County, Michigan. This deposit contains peat, logs, and twigs.

Deposits of Cherry Tree age (about 35,000 years old) have been found in Michigan in water wells in Kalkaska County. Several other buried organic deposits in Michigan ranging from about 24,000 to about 48,000 years old have been reported from sediments from water well drillings, but these have not yielded important faunas. Plum Point age sediments have been identified in Michigan on the basis of radiocarbon-dated wood from two sites in the central part of the Lower

Peninsula; one a water well site and the other from a stream-deposited site. Both of these sites have yielded important vertebrate fossils that will be detailed later.

The late Wisconsinan represents an interval that lasted from about 23,000 to about 10,000 years ago and is by far the best documented part of the Wisconsinan glacial age in the Great Lakes region and elsewhere in North America. The Pleistocene ice sheet that impacted the Great Lakes region is called the Laurentide ice sheet. This ice giant stretched from Alberta in Canada to Maine in the United States, and as we know, made several advances and retreats in the Pleistocene.

The greatest advance of the Laurentide ice sheet in the Wisconsinan occurred about 20,000 years ago, when it probed southward to almost identical latitudes in Illinois, Indiana, and Ohio (fig. 13). All of Ontario and Michigan as well as the northern portion and eastern half of Wisconsin were blanketed by this mountain of ice.

After the 20,000-year-old advance at least 10 other advances and retreats occurred before the final retreat of the ice began about 14,000 years ago. It is not possible to trace the exact ice margins everywhere in the Great Lakes region, but in Michigan, by about 12,900 years ago the ice margin was in the upper part of the Lower Peninsula in the east and the lower part of the Upper Peninsula in the west. Since most of lower Michigan was deglaciated by this time, it was possible for biological communities to begin to develop on the sterile gravels, muds, and sands left behind by the Laurentide ice sheet.

Building the Great Lakes. The Great Lakes we know today are products of the bedrock topography produced during the Paleozoic era, the subsequent vast erosion of these rocks, and finally the recent glacial processes of the Pleistocene. Geologically they are infant lakes but eventually, like all lakes, will fill in with sediments and disappear. But right now they are immensely important in the economy of the earth, as they hold one-sixth of the planet's freshwater supply!

Before the Pleistocene, the basins that hold the present Great Lakes were stream valleys in the bedrock and products eroded from the bedrock during the Lost Interval. When the ice sheets came, they tended to move along these valleys following the path of the least resistant rocks. Finally, water from the melting ice filled the gouged-out basins.

The glacial basins producing the Great Lakes are such a large feature on the earth that they are plainly visible from the moon. In fact, it has been said that they are the only glacially produced structure that can be seen from the moon. The lakes occupy 95,000 square miles of the earth's surface and have over 8,000 miles of shoreline.

The modern lakes all drain in an easterly direction. Superior drains into Huron at Sault Ste. Marie, Michigan into Huron through the Straits of Mackinac; Huron drains south along the St. Clair River into Erie, and Erie into Ontario. Finally, Ontario drains into the Atlantic Ocean down the St. Lawrence River.

Lake Superior is the coldest and deepest of the Great Lakes, Lake Erie the shallowest and warmest. Glacial erosion ensured that the deepest parts of all of the lakes, except for Lakes Huron and Erie, are more than 300 feet below sea level. The deep hole in Lake Huron is 170 feet below sea level, but Lake Erie has its deepest hole 362 feet above sea level because of differences in patterns of crustal uplift.

The geological processes that formed the Great Lakes are complex and somewhat controversial, so that a full discussion would be too long and detailed for the present book. The lakes began to fill up in earnest in the late Wisconsinan, somewhat before 13,300 years ago, and different lake stages have been given different names even though they are all part of the same general process. Glacial Lake Chicago, which filled in the lower part of the present Lake Michigan Basin, and Glacial Lake Maumee, which filled in the lower part of the present Lake Erie Basin, were the earliest of these named glacial lakes and existed somewhat before 13,300 years ago. The Great Lakes were nearly in their present stage of development by the so-called Nipissing stage, which occurred about 4,000 years ago. Between these times, the lakes had various shapes caused by fluctuating shorelines, as the various glacial comings and goings occurred.

The Great Lakes have been supremely important bodies of water for all of the ancient life that existed in the area. They have provided habitats for aquatic life and a water supply for terrestrial life and have had a great effect on the climate of the entire region.

Summary

During the billions of years of the Precambrian era countless major geological cycles repeated themselves, and much of the original structure of the rocks that formed during that time was changed by metamorphic processes and eons of erosion. It is known, however, that mountains were built, seas encroached the land, and even periods of glaciation occurred. Life-forms were first recorded in the Precambrian about 3.5 billion years ago, and life stayed relatively simple in form for the next 2 billion years. Evidence of Precambrian life in the Great Lakes region consists of algal plants and microscopic organisms.

During the Paleozoic era the history of the Great Lakes region was ruled by high areas that eroded and supplied sediments to low, sinking basins. These basins often became great inland seas where sediments and fossils accumulated along with evaporites such as salt and gypsum. The central basin where these sediments accumulated is called the Michigan Basin. Fossil-bearing rocks accumulated in the Michigan Basin during the Cambrian, Ordovician, Silurian, Devonian, Mississippian, and Pennsylvanian periods, before a general uplift of the area led to the Lost Interval of geological time.

The Lost Interval resulted from countless millions of years of erosion of the ancient Paleozoic bedrock, and it included the Permian, Triassic, most of the Jurassic, Cretaceous, Tertiary, and most of the Quaternary periods. Thus, no dinosaur fossils have been found in the Great Lakes region because the rocks that contained their remains have been eroded away. Finally, the ice sheets of the Pleistocene epoch (Ice Age) put the finishing touches on this already eroded topography.

The key to understanding the distribution of rocks and fossils in the Great Lakes region is the realization that during the Lost Interval the gently down-curving Paleozoic beds of the area were eroded away to form a pattern in which the youngest rocks are presently closest to the surface at the center of the basin, with successively older rocks exposed away from the center of the basin. Thus, one searches for Pennsylvanian rocks and fossils near the center of the Lower Peninsula of Michigan and for Devonian rocks and fossils near the periphery of the lower part of this state.

During the Pleistocene, at least four great ice sheets are thought to have impacted the Great Lakes region. These glaciers occurred during the Nebraskan, Kansan, Illinoian, and Wisconsinan glacial ages. However, the only good record of glacial processes and products in the area is from the Wisconsinan.

The ice sheets of the Pleistocene followed the eroded valleys of the ancient Paleozoic rocks and gouged out these valleys into basins that were to become the modern Great Lakes. It is believed that each of the major ice sheets had small retreats and advances, and it is known that the Wisconsinan had at least 10 of these episodes. Finally, about 14,000 years ago the last great glacier began its final retreat, and the meltwater from glacial retreats filled up the basins of the individual Great Lakes.

Other processes that went on within the ice sheets and in front of the ice sheets due to glacial meltwaters buried the ancient bedrock under a blanket of silt, sand, and gravel. These glacial processes also created the terrestrial topography of lakes, kettle bogs, and hills (variously described as moraines, drumlins, eskers, and kames) that form the landscape of the area today.

Chapter 3
The Five Biological Kingdoms

We have already stated that fossils are recognizable evidence of living things preserved from prehistoric times. Biology is concerned with the study of life. Thus it is well to review some basic biology before we launch into the sections on fossils. This will include a basic review of the diversity of life and of classification, as living things (organisms) are put in the same classification system as fossils.

The basic unit of all living things is the cell (fig. 14). Cells by themselves are able to carry out all of the necessary processes of life, such as respiration, metabolism, and reproduction. Cells may or may not have a *cell wall,* but all cells have a *cell membrane* that encloses the living material (*cytoplasm*) of the cell. The cell membrane is semipermeable; that is, it allows some things into and out of the cell and restricts the passage of other substances. The *nucleus* contains the major part of the genetic material (DNA) of the cell. Because they are not capable of generating and regulating their own life processes and cannot reproduce by themselves, some large and complex organic molecules below the level of cells are not considered to be living things by most biologists.

It may surprise the reader to realize that modern biologists recognize three kingdoms of living things other than plants and animals. The presently recognized kingdoms of living things are as follows.

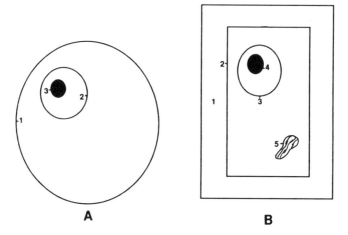

Fig. 14. Schematic representations of eukaryotic (nucleated) cells. *A*, a typical animal cell with cell membrane (1) surrounding the cell contents; nuclear membrane (2) surrounding the contents of the nucleus; and genetic material (3) inside the nucleus. *B*, typical plant cell with thick cell wall (1) surrounding the cell contents; cell membrane (2) surrounding the rest of the cell; nuclear membrane (3) surrounding the contents of the nucleus; genetic material (4) inside the nucleus; and chloroplasts (5) free in the cytoplasm within the cell membrane.

Monerans
Protistans
Fungi
Plants
Animals

Monera

The kingdom *Monera* contains the gigantic group of organisms called *bacteria* as well as the bacterialike *cyanobacteria* ("blue-green algae"). Bacteria (fig. 15a) are at once the simplest and the most abundant organisms, normally about 10 times smaller than most other cells. We find bacteria troublesome because some of them make us sick. Yet if it were not for bacteria, the world would be smothered with the dead bodies of plants and animals, as bacteria (along with fungi) are the great agents of decay in the world. Bacteria secrete digestive materials (*en-*

zymes) that separate complex organic material into simpler ones that can be recycled back into nature.

Bacteria are called *prokaryotic* cells because they lack the membrane-bound *nucleus* that is found in the cells of all of the other kingdoms of living things. In bacteria the genetic material (DNA) is loosely concentrated as "naked" chromosomes (without any associated proteins). Moreover, the protein-building materials called *ribosomes* are scattered in the sparse cytoplasm of the bacterial cell.

Bacteria have three general shapes: spherical, cylindrical, and spiral (fig. 15b–d), and many of them live either inside or on the surface of other organisms. As previously stated, bacteria can break down complex organic materials into simpler ones. For instance, some bacteria break down muscle tissue into simpler *amino acids* that are used as food by the bacteria as well as by other units in nature. Other bacteria can, like other plants, provide their own nutriment by the process of *photosynthesis;* and still others are able to use inorganic compounds such as iron, hydrogen sulfide, hydrogen gas, and carbon monoxide as a source for their energy. The earliest forms of cellular life, bacteria have lived on earth for more than 3.5 billion years!

What are viruses then? Viruses can make us very uncomfortable and sick or even kill us sometimes. It's hard to say anything good about them. They are nasty little bits of reproductive material that parasitize living things and utilize the reproductive mechanisms of real cells to duplicate themselves. Since they are incapable of generating and regulating their own life processes and cannot reproduce themselves by themselves, viruses are not considered to be living things by most biologists. Viruses are even smaller and simpler than bacteria.

Protista

The kingdom *Protista* comprises organisms with nuclei in their cells (*eukaryotes*) that are composed of a single cell. Sometimes these single cells occur as colonies that represent rather complex organisms. Some protists can produce their own food by the process of photosynthesis, while others must feed on other organisms or organic compounds. Still others do both. Protistan groups are as follows.

Autotrophs (those able to produce their own food)
  Euglenoids

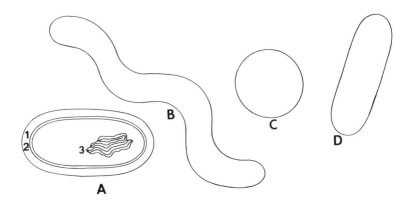

Fig. 15. Monerans. *A*, schematic representation of a prokaryotic (nonnucleated) bacterial cell showing cell wall (1), cell membrane (2), and genetic material (3) free in the cytoplasm. *B*, spiral; *C*, spherical; and *D*, rod-shaped bacterial forms.

Chrysophytes
Dinoflagellates
Red algae
Brown algae
Green algae
Heterotrophs (those utilizing other sources of food)
Protozoans
Slime molds

Autotrophic Protists

Euglenoids (fig. 16a) are simple organisms that have features of both plants and animals. They move around in fresh water by means of a whiplike flagellum and have an eyespot that enables them to find places where the light is best for photosynthesis. Yet, when the light goes out, some kinds of euglenoids can get along quite well by absorbing organic nutrients; and some can live in the dark much of the time.

Chrysophytes are also photosynthetic protists, but they occur both in freshwater and in saltwater habitats. They are commonly called *golden algae*, as they have a color pigment that masks their green photosynthetic elements (*chlorophylls*). Most of these organisms have flagella, and many of them have shells of the hard material *silica*. A

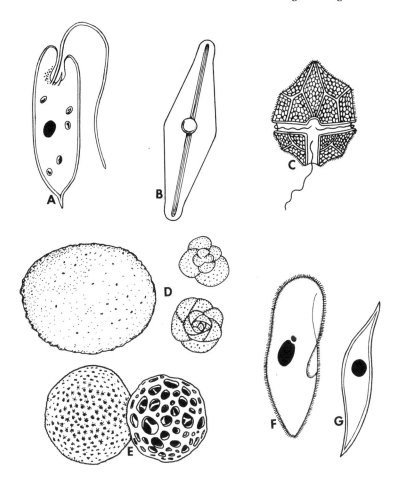

Fig. 16. Microscopic protists. *A*, a euglenoid (*Euglena*); *B*, a diatom (*Navicula*); *C*, a dinoflagellate (*Peridinium*); *D*, three foraminifera; *E*, radiolarian tests (shells); *F*, a ciliate protozoan (*Paramecium*); and *G*, a sporozoan protozoan (*Plasmodium*).

very important group of the chrysophytes are the diatoms (fig. 16b). The silica shells of diatoms are perforated with an abundance of holes that occur in very orderly patterns. These diatom shells began to accumulate as fossils over 100 million years ago; thus huge deposits of diatomaceous earth are found in many parts of the world.

Dinoflagellates spend their lives endlessly spinning around. They are enclosed by stiffened plates of *cellulose*, a semihard, but tough, material (fig. 16c), and have two whiplike flagella that cause the spinning motion. Some of them are photosynthetic, while others feed upon organic material. Because dinoflagellates have several kinds of pigment in their bodies, they may look yellow, green, brown, or red. These organisms occur in both freshwater and marine situations and are so abundant in some cases that they can color the seas brown or red. Some of the red dinoflagellates produce poisons that produce the so-called red tides that periodically kill millions of fish. Dinoflagellates may occur as microscopic fossils because of the resistant nature of their cellulose plates.

Brown algae (fig. 17a) are either dark brown, olive green, or a pleasant golden color. Many of them are large "seaweeds" that are a very critical part of the marine ecosystem. The oarweed forests of the North Sea and the massive kelp beds of the Pacific are examples. Most brown algae are anchored to the bottom by *holdfasts,* which are rootlike structures. Many brown algae have bubblelike *floats* on them that hold them in an upright position. But *Sargassum* is a floating brown alga that is a legendary and very important part of the ecosystem in warm seas.

Green algae are green. They live mainly in freshwater but can live on bare ground, tree trunks, the sides of flower pots, and even on snow. Some kinds, such as the brilliantly green sea lettuce (fig. 17b), live in the ocean. Green algae are the algal group that is most similar to complex land plants in the type of photosynthetic elements they have and in their ability to store starch.

Red algae (fig. 17c) are mainly marine, plantlike organisms that are not always red but may be greenish, purplish, or a rather sickening greenish black color. Most of them are attached to rocks and other objects on the seafloor. Material from red algae is used in making ice cream, chocolate milk, and agar to grow bacterial cultures on.

Heterotrophic Protists

Protozoans capture the minds of most of us who have seen a group of them oozing, darting, and whipping around in a drop of water on a microscope slide. Protozoans are single-celled organisms that exist in a myriad of forms. Although thousands of species of protozoans exist, only a few cause disease, and fewer still cause deadly ailments. Four major groups of protozoans exist, and they are characterized by their movement: flagellated, amoeboid, ciliated, and gliding or immobile.

Flagellate protozoans are mainly animal parasites and include the

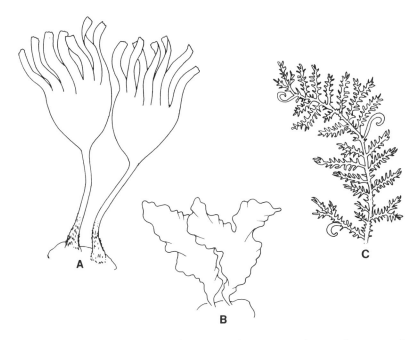

Fig. 17. Large protists. *A*, brown alga (oarweeds); *B*, green alga (sea lettuce); and *C*, red alga (sea lace).

trypanosomes, which cause sleeping sickness, and others that cause problems in the urinary and reproductive tracts of humans.

Amoeboid protozoans move and capture food with extensions of their own unicellular bodies called *pseudopods*. Pseudopods have the ability to surround and engulf organic bits or other organisms, which are then digested inside the protozoan. Some amoeboid protozoans constantly change their shape, and several of these types cause amoebic dysentaries, very serious diseases in humans.

Other amoeboids have shells and are very important in the fossil record. The *foraminifera* ("forams") occur from Cambrian to modern times. Forams have been very important as indicators of oil-bearing strata of rocks. Most forams (fig. 16d) have limy shells formed of calcium carbonate. These shells have a plethora of tiny openings called foramina through which filamentous pseudopods are thrust out.

Almost every kind of shell that one can imagine has been perfected by the foraminifera. Some giant forams are as big as a fifty-cent piece, but most of them are tiny and must be viewed through a microscope.

Limy forams are abundant in the fossil record. In fact, the so-called Florida carbonate platform, which is hundreds of feet thick in some places and presently supports the whole state of Florida, is composed largely of trillions of limy forams, including some of the giant ones. Other kinds of forams secrete a binding substance called *chitin* and form a shell by gluing sand grains together. Forams are probably the most important group studied by micropaleontologists, especially those who are employed by oil companies.

The *radiolarians* (fig. 16e) are another amoeboid group with a very important fossil record. Radiolarians occur from the Cambrian to modern times; they usually have a perforated, nonchambered shell composed of the very hard material called *silica*. Very fine pseudopods are extruded from these perforations. Radiolarian ooze has accumulated in vast amounts on the ocean floor.

The *ciliate* protozoans move around by the means of the synchronized beating of hundreds or sometimes thousands of cilia. They are the sprinters of the microscopic world, and one form, *Paramecium* (fig. 16f) can dash through its drop of water at the amazing speed of 1,000 micrometers per second! The gliding *sporozoans* (fig. 16g) are not important in the fossil record, but species of *Plasmodium* cause malaria in humans.

Slime molds consist of a mass of cells that moves around in an amoebalike way. This mass absorbs dead organic matter as well as bacteria and spores. The classification of this group is difficult and controversial. Although slime molds must have had an ancient origin, they have not been identified in the fossil record.

Fungi

The fungi kingdom was included among the plants for many years, but they now are considered to be as different from plants as they are from animals, protists, and bacteria. The few fossil evidences of fungi indicate that they have been on earth since Precambrian times!

Fungi cannot manufacture their own food; and this is the most significant way that they are distinguished from plants, the vast majority of which can make their own food. Fungi are able to decompose almost anything organic. Humans are generally good-natured about this aspect of fungal life if it deals with ridding the environment of unwanted dead bodies. But some fungi cause irritating itchy diseases such as athlete's foot and other complaints that may be difficult to cure. Still other fungi cause terrible damage to living plants, including crops valued by humans.

Unlike the first two kingdoms we have discussed, the fungal body is multicellular. The *mycelium* (fig. 18a) is the main structure that forms the body of a fungus. The mycelium is a composed of a meshwork of tiny tubelike filaments called *hyphae* that spread over, around, or inside the material or body of material upon which the fungus feeds. Mycelia may form rather indiscrete-looking structures such as yeasts, molds, mildews, and rusts; or discrete-looking bodies such as mushrooms, brackens, club fungi, and lichens. Lichens are fascinating organisms consisting of a partnership between fungal mycelia and green algae or energy-producing bacteria.

Some discrete structures produced by fungi such as mushrooms (fig. 18a) are very short-lived and produce asexually by spores. Fungal cells secrete digestive enzymes that break down the substrates upon which they feed into simpler substances that the fungi absorb.

Plants

The plant kingdom is generally composed of multicellular organisms that differ from fungi in that they can manufacture their own food by the process of *photosynthesis*. In the process of photosynthesis, energy from the sun is trapped by *chloroplasts* in the plant cells that convert carbon dioxide and water into sugars and other food molecules. Plants are divided into two basic groups; *nonvascular* plants that lack transport tissues; and *vascular* plants that have transport tissues called *xylem* and *phloem*. Xylem carries water and minerals throughout the plant, and phloem transports sugars and other foods produced by photosynthesis. Plants are further divisible into categories called *divisions* that are equivalent to the *phyla* of the animal kingdom.

Nonvascular Plants (Bryophytes)

Bryophytes are the elfin mosses (fig. 19a), hornworts, and liverworts (fig. 19b). Bryophytes lack vascular tissues, so that their leaflike, stemlike, and rootlike structures are not considered to be true leaves, stems,

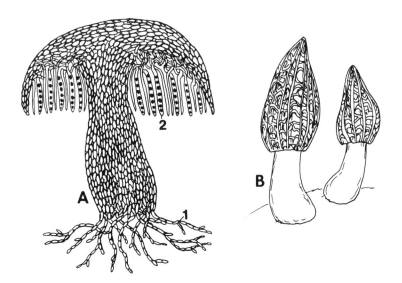

Fig. 18. Mushrooms. *A,* generalized mushroom composed of a meshwork of hyphae (1) that forms a mycelium that is a discrete asexual fruiting body bearing gills with spores (2). *B,* a morel mushroom, a type found in the Great Lakes region today.

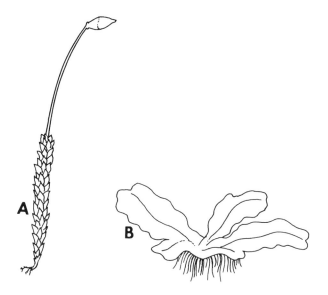

Fig. 19. Bryophytes. *A,* moss; *B,* liverwort. The leaflike, stemlike, and rootlike structures of these little plants are not true leaves, stems, and roots.

and roots. These lovely little plants mainly live in moist areas, and some are very resistant to drying out or to freezing conditions.

Vascular Plants

We are now ready to climb the scale in plant evolution and take a look at the *vascular* plants. There are three major groups of vascular plants, each of which has a division or divisions under it. The three main groups of vascular plants are

Ferns and fern relatives (seedless)
Gymnosperms (nonflowering plants)
Angiosperms (flowering plants)

Ferns and Relatives

Ferns and their kin do not bear seeds, and they depend on water for fertilization to take place. Thus they are said to be the "amphibians" of the plant world because they depend on water to complete their life cycle. Both ferns and their relatives the horsetails are important parts of the understory vegetation in the Great Lakes Basin. The three divisions of this group are lycopods (club mosses), the sphenopsids (horsetails), and the ferns.

The *lycopods* were a very diverse group over 350 million years ago. Some of these ancient fossil lycopods were the size of trees and will be discussed in detail later in this book. Modern ones called club mosses or ground pines are small and typically grow in moist forest floors in warm regions of the world. They can be recognized by the conelike *strobili* (fig. 20a) that grow on their stems.

The *sphenopsids* or horsetails consist of only one living genus, *Equisetum* (fig. 20b), and many ancient relatives of the horsetails, some of which were as large as trees. Most of us in the Great Lakes Basin have had fun pulling horsetails apart at the joints and then sticking them back together again.

Ferns, unlike club mosses and horsetails, have conspicuous leaves (fig. 20c). Ferns are also important in the fossil record. All ferns, except for the tree ferns that grow in the tropics, have underground stems. Ferns are found in many more habitats and in more places in the world

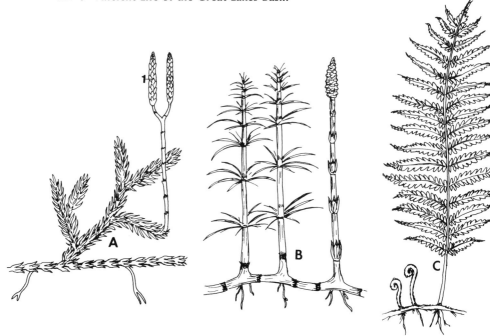

Fig. 20. Lycopods, sphenopsids, and ferns. *A*, a common lycopod (club moss or ground pine, *Lycopodium*) bearing a conelike strobilus (1); *B*, a sphenopsid (horsetail, *Equisetum*) with jointed stems; *C*, the compound leaf of a fern plant (*Onoclea*).

than club mosses and horsetails. Some are *epiphytes*—attached to trees, other plants, or even roofs of buildings.

Gymnosperms

The gymnosperms are nonflowering plants, unlike the angiosperm group that follows. But both the gymnosperms and the angiosperms are seed plants. A plant seed is a complicated structure and contains the plant embryo and other structures that form the seed coat. The seeds of the gymnosperms occur on the surfaces of the reproductive structures and are not surrounded by a protective layer of tissue as they are in angiosperms. The divisions of the gymnosperms are as follows: cycads, ginkgos, gnetophytes, and conifers.

Cycads are tropical and subtropical plants that resemble squatty palm trees with bulbous trunks (fig. 21a). But despite the fact that

Fig. 21. Gymnosperms. *A,* cycad plant; *B,* ginkgo stem and leaves; *C, Welwitschia,* a living gnetophyte; *D,* a conifer (pine tree, *Pinus*).

cycads have superficially similar leaves and stems, they are not close kin to the palms. Cycads have huge cones, and palms are flowering plants. Cycads were important plants of the Mesozoic period and formed an important part of the vegetational landscape during the days of the dinosaurs.

Ginkgos are familiar to us because of their pretty fan-shaped leaves (fig. 21b) and sometimes because of the smelly by-products of the female trees. The ginkgos were a very diverse group during the Mesozoic but survive as only a single cultivated species that was domesticated thousands of years ago from a now extinct native population in southeast Asia.

Gnetophytes are land plants of warm regions and occur on sandy or rocky soil. The oddest gnetophyte is *Welwitschia* of southwestern Africa, which consists mainly of a very deep-thrusting taproot. Above ground the plant consists of a disklike stem that bears a bunch of cones and two large, floppy leaves (fig. 21c).

Conifers occur mainly in the form of woody trees or shrubs and have needlelike or scalelike leaves. Most conifers are green throughout the year, although old leaves are lost from time to time. Conifers (fig. 21d) were the dominant plants of the Mesozoic and are still dominant parts of the vegetation in many parts of the world, including parts of the northern Great Lakes region today. Conifers are also an important part of the landscape in the region today in tree farms, where they are grown as sources of paper, lumber, Christmas decorations, and many other commercial products.

Angiosperms

The angiosperms are the flowering plants, and they are the most highly evolved of all of the plant groups. Angiosperms all house their seeds in a container. There are more than a quarter of a million species of angiosperms, and new species are continually being discovered, especially in remote tropical and semidesert areas. Although it is possible that the ancestor of flowering plants occurred in late Permian or Triassic times, angiosperms did not become abundant until the late Mesozoic.

In fact, it has been suggested more than once that one of the reasons for the extinction of the dinosaurs at the end of the Mesozoic was because the digestive tracts of the herbivorous dinosaurs could not accommodate the newly abundant angiosperms. It follows that if the herbivorous dinosaurs became extinct that the carnivorous ones would soon follow them into oblivion. Flowering plants range from the tiny duckweeds that often clog the surface of small ponds in the summer to giant tropical trees that grow to heights of 200 feet or more. Angiosperms are abundant on land and in freshwater, but rarely occur in marine environments.

Angiosperms consist of a single division, the *Anthophyta,* that has two distinct subdivisions (classes): monocots and dicots. *Monocots* have a single embryonic leaf within the seed, their flower parts usually occur in threes or multiples of threes, and they commonly have parallel main veins in their leaves (fig. 22a). Common monocots include bamboos, grasses (including barley, corn, oats, rice, and wheat), lilies, or-

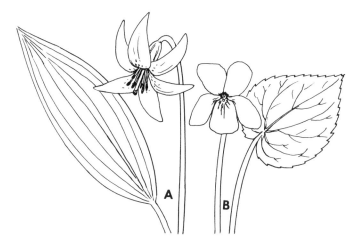

Fig. 22. Angiosperms. *A*, a monocot plant with flower parts in two groups of threes and parallel veins in its leaves. *B*, a dicot plant with five flower parts and with a network of veins in its leaves.

chids, onions, palms, and pineapples. A great expansion of grasslands occurred in the Miocene epoch of the Tertiary that led to great evolutionary events that will be discussed later.

Dicots have two embryonic leaves within the seed; the flower parts usually occur in fours or fives or multiples of fours and fives, and they commonly have a network of veins in the leaves (fig. 22b). Dicots include the plethora of modern fruit-bearing trees including those that provide us with apples, cherries, plums, pears, and many other delicious products. They also include an enormous variety of shrubs, vines, prostrate plants, and cacti, including domestic varieties that provide us with food. And finally, they include thousands of pesky plants that we refer to collectively as "weeds."

Animals

If you have the idea that the term *animal* refers only to those warm furry creatures called mammals, you have nothing to be embarrassed about. A museum at a very large university once had a hall of mammals labeled Hall of Animals for years, and very few people complained. Actually, mammal species compose only a small fraction of the almost countless numbers of animal species.

Animals may be divided into two groups. Invertebrate animals lack a backbone and occur in about thirty phyla. Phyla are roughly equivalent to the divisions of the plant kingdom. Vertebrate animals have a backbone and occur in only one phylum. Animals usually have the following characteristics.

1. They are multicellular with the cells organized into tissues and the tissues organized into organs and organ systems.
2. They either eat other organisms, or, if they are parasites, they absorb nutrients from the organism that they parasitize.
3. Most of them reproduce sexually, but many of them, including vertebrates, can reproduce asexually.
4. They move around during at least a part of their life cycle.
5. They have embryos that undergo a sequential stages of growth and differentiation of parts.

Characteristics that are important in classifying animals into major groups include the type of body form (*symmetry*); the type of internal food tube (*gut*); the presence or absence of body segments (*segmentation*); and whether they have a head or not (*cephalization*).

The phyla discussed here are only about one-third of the phyla that are currently recognized. They have been chosen either because they are generally important phyla or because they are important in the fossil record of the Great Lakes region or both. These phyla include the following: poriferans, cnidarians, bryozoans, brachiopods, platyhelminths, nematodes, annelids, mollusks, arthropods, echinoderms, and the chordates.

The *poriferans* or *sponges* (fig. 23a) are barely at the tissue level of organization. In fact, it is questionable whether sponges are individuals or merely a colony of cooperating cells. Most of the upwards of 8,000-odd species of sponges live in the marine environment, but a few freshwater species exist. Some sponges are rather shapeless, but others are in the form of vases or cups.

They range from the size of a dime to forms that one would need a truck to carry around. The cells of sponges are arranged around either an uncomplicated or complicated system of canals, chambers, and pores (hence the name Porifera). Water moves into the sponge through uncountable numbers of these pores and then out of the sponge by one or more excurrent openings.

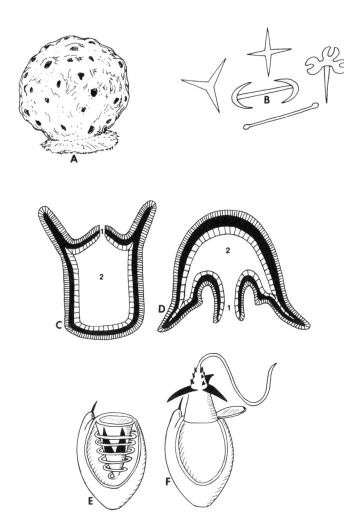

Fig. 23. Sponges and cnidarians. *A*, a typical marine sponge (demosponge). *B*, sponge spicules. *C*, cnidarian polyp (hydra) form. *D*, cnidarian medusa (jellyfish) form. The three layers in *C* and *D* are an outer epidermis, a middle mesoglea (black) and an inner gastrodermis; food enters the mouth (1) and is digested in the gut (2). *E*, closed stinging cell (nematocyst) of cnidarians. *F*, activated stinging cell of cnidarians.

Flagellated cells within the various sponge cavities keep water circulating through the sponge. These flagellated cells either digest the bacteria and other food particles that come into the sponge or they transfer them to amoeboid cells that may further digest the material or pass it on to the other cells that make up the sponge. These amoeboid cells secrete substances that build up the skeletal structure of the sponge. The skeleton of a sponge may be made up of needlelike hard *spicules* (fig. 23b) composed of silica or calcium carbonate, or they may be composed of a meshwork of flexible protein structures, as in the bath sponges. Sponges are known in the fossil record from as early as the Cambrian, and the fossils may be individual spicules or parts of the entire body.

Cnidarians are the first animal group that have two true body layers, an outside *epidermis* and an inside *gastrodermis* (fig. 23c–d) that lines the gut cavity. In between the epidermis and the gastrodermis is a jellylike *mesoglea*. Some of the cells in the epidermis can contract and are involved in changes of shape that occur in the cnidarians in the process of movements and feeding. These animals sense their environments through a network of nerve cells in the epidermis and gastrodermis, and the jellyfishes have special sensory structures that can detect differences in light and changes in the position of the animal.

The cnidarians have *radial symmetry* in that the parts of the body are arranged around the center of the animal like the spokes of a bicycle. Cnidarians include the hydras, sea anemones, jellyfishes, corals, and an extinct group of colonial organisms called *stromatoporoids*. The mouth of the cnidarians is surrounded by tentacles, and it opens into a single internal gut cavity. All of these animals are carnivores.

One of the unpleasant features of cnidarians, as far as humans are concerned, is their stinging cells, called *nematocysts* (fig. 23e–f). The epidermis of a jellyfish tentacle may have thousands of these nasty cells. Each stinging cell is composed of a tiny capsule with a thread inside. In turn, each thread has a triggering mechanism, so that when its prey, a predator, or even an errant human swimmer touches the tentacle, the thread is ejected and releases a toxin on contact. These jellyfish threads often get tangled around the hairs of swimmers, making the burning-itching sensation even worse. The cnidarians have been around since the Cambrian; corals have been very important fossils since the Ordovician.

The *bryozoans* (fig. 24a), or "moss animals," are tiny animals that

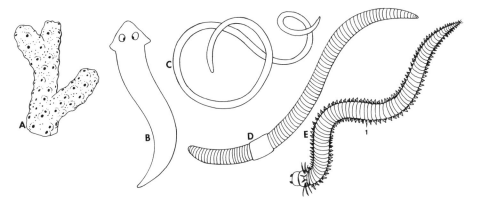

Fig. 24. Bryozoans, flatworms, roundworms, and annelid worms. *A*, branching bryozoan colony. *B*, a flatworm (*Dugesia*). *C*, a roundworm (soil nematode). *D*, an annelid (the earthworm, *Lumbricus*). *E*, an annelid (the marine worm *Nereis*) with prominent setae (1).

have not only a mouth into which food enters but an anus by which digestive and other wastes exit the body. This mouth-anus arrangement occurs within a curved structure called a *lophophore* that bears tentacles around the mouth region. These soft animals are called *polyps;* they are able to form exoskeletons of calcium carbonate and sometimes of chitin. Very large numbers of polyps occur together in bryozoan colonies, which may appear as netlike, lacy, mosslike, branching (fig. 24a) or as stacks of hemispheres. Colonies of bryozoans are part of the coral reef complex. These animals are very important in the fossil record and have existed since Ordovician times.

The *brachiopods* are also very important in the fossil record and have been around since the early Cambrian. Brachiopods are *bilaterally symmetrical* animals, meaning that each side of the animal is the mirror image of the other. Brachiopods have an unsegmented soft body with a circulatory and an excretory system but no discrete respiratory system. The main part of the brachiopod body is enclosed by a thin layer of tissue called the *mantle*. The mantle secretes the brachiopod shell.

The shell is composed of two parts called *valves*, which close along a hinge line. A stalk or *pedicle* extends through a hole in one of the valves and attaches the animal to the bottom of the sea or to some solid object. Brachiopods feed on minute animals by means of a ciliated lophophore. It should be pointed out that the axis of symmetry in these bilaterally symmetrical animals passes through the middle of each valve, not between the two parts of the shell. Brachiopod shells are usually composed of calcium carbonate, but they occasionally are composed of chitin.

The *platyhelminths,* or flatworms (fig. 24b), are soft-bodied flattened animals that do not secrete a skeleton like the previous two groups, the bryozoans and brachiopods. The flatworms are very simple animals, but they differ from the cnidarians (jellyfishes and their kin) in two important ways. They are bilaterally symmetrical, and they have a layer between the epidermis and the gastrodermis called the *mesoderm* that gives rise to a more complex muscular and reproductive system. Nevertheless, the flatworms lack the important body cavities that are found in more advanced groups.

Flatworms include free-living forms that are predators and scavengers, as well as the parasitic *flukes* and *tapeworms.* Some flukes and tapeworms live in the organs or intestines of humans as annoying or dangerous parasites. A schistosome fluke causes swimmer's itch, an extremely bothersome condition that occurs in humans who bathe or swim in some lakes of the Great Lakes Basin.

The roundworms (fig. 24c) have cylindrical bodies covered by a tough, resilient *cuticle.* Roundworms are more advanced than flatworms in that they have a cavity between the gut and the body wall called a *pseudocoel.* Fluid in the pseudocoel oozes around between the organs housed there and creates a sort of primitive circulatory system. Nematodes are quite important as parasites and as consumers of vast amounts of organic materials. They live almost everywhere and a handful of good soil will contain thousands. Other types of roundworms are harmful parasites on plants and animals, including humans, livestock, and crops.

Protostomes and Deuterostomes

The remaining animals that will be discussed here fit into two evolutionary groups called the protostomes and the deuterostomes. All of these animals have a true *coelom,* a lined body cavity into which major organs are suspended and that separates the gut from the muscular body wall. In the *protostomes* a single opening in the early embryo called the *blastopore* becomes the mouth. In the deuterostomes the blastopore becomes the anus. Protostomes include the annelids, mollusks, and arthropods, while the deuterostomes include the echinoderms, hemichordates, and the chordates.

Annelids, Mollusks, Arthropods

The *annelids* are thought to have evolved from flatworm ancestors, but they are much more complex. Annelids have a *segmented* body that has a well-developed coelom with organ systems that are much more complex than those in the flatworms. Many of the annelids have external bristles (fig. 24e) called *setae* that provide the traction required in crawling around and in burrowing. One group of annelids has relatively few or no bristles, the other group lots of them. The first group (fig. 24d) includes such forms as earthworms, with few bristles, and leeches, with none. The second group (fig. 24e), which includes the free-swimming or burrowing marine worms, have many setae.

Earthworms are valuable animals that help all ecosystems by eating their way through the soil. This not only aerates the soil, but it carries the subsoil to the surface. Leeches are predators that swallow small invertebrates whole or that suck juices out of larger animals such as humans.

Many marine worms burrow, and some construct tubes in the soft sediments of the seafloor. Some tubelike structures found in the fossil record have been interpreted as those from worm tubes. Annelids have been around since the Cambrian, but since their only hard parts are certain chitinous structures associated with feeding, fossils of these animals are few.

Mollusks play a very important part in the fossil record and have been around since the early Cambrian. This phylum includes animals with shells as well as soft-bodied forms, some of them extremely advanced. Obviously the shelled animals are the ones most often preserved as fossils. It is believed that mollusks may have evolved from flatworms.

All mollusks (fig. 25) have a head, a foot, and internal organs that comprise a *visceral mass*. When a shell is present, it is composed of chitin and calcium carbonate. A fold of tissue called the *mantle* hangs down from the shell around part or all of the animal's body. Mollusks that have a discrete head have well-developed sense organs, such as eyes and tentacles. In fact, the eyes of squid are as highly developed

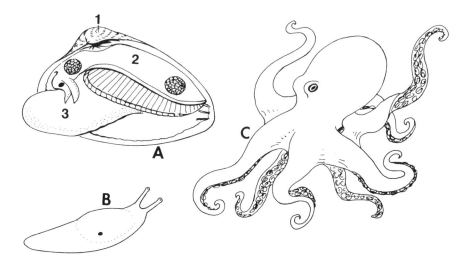

Fig. 25. Mollusks. *A*, clam (with half of its two-piece shell removed) showing the shell (1), mantle (2), and foot (3). *B*, a garden slug, a mollusk without a shell. *C*, an octopus, a mollusk with highly developed eyes.

in their own way as the eyes of vertebrates. The shells of mollusks are highly variable. Some consist of a single part, others have two parts, and others, rather shapeless.

It appears that mollusks were common first in shallow seas, later invaded deeper marine waters, then moved into brackish and fresh water, and finally conquered the land. Familiar types of mollusks include clams (fig. 25a), mussels, scallops, slugs (fig. 25b), snails, octopuses and squids, as well as extinct nautiloids and ammonoids that will be discussed later in the fossil section of this book. The octopuses (fig 25c) and squids are highly evolved soft-bodied predators that have brains and eyes that are more highly developed than those of any other invertebrates.

The *arthropods* have a flexible, lightweight *exoskeleton* that is mainly composed of a mixture of protein and chitin. But in some arthropods the skeleton is secondarily hardened by the deposition of calcium salts that make a system of hard plates, such as occur in crabs. The arthropods are such a large and diverse group that we need to divide them into subphyla in order to put them into proper perspective. The subphyla of the arthropods are the trilobites, the chelicerates, the crustaceans, and the uniramians (includes insects).

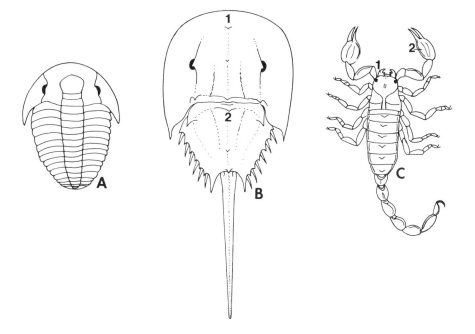

Fig. 26. Trilobites and chelicerates. *A,* a generalized trilobite; the exoskeleton (carapace) shown is divided into three long sections (lobes). *B,* horseshoe or king crab, (a chelicerate) with forebody (1) and hindbody (2) indicated. *C,* scorpion (a chelicerate) with chelicerae (1) and pedipalps (2) indicated.

Trilobites (fig. 26a) exist only as fossils. These animals lived from the Cambrian through the Permian and will be discussed in detail later. The trilobite exoskeleton is called a *carapace* and is divided into three transverse lobes, hence the origin of the name trilobite. The trilobites were marine animals and bottom crawlers that researchers suggest had habits somewhat similar to the living horseshoe or king crabs.

Chelicerates are a very diverse group of arthropods that contain the horseshoe or king crabs (fig. 26b), the spiders, the scorpions (fig. 26c), and the worrisome ticks and mites. The chelicerates are first known from the Cambrian and were abundant in the early Paleozoic seas. But the only living marine chelicerates are the horseshoe crabs and the sea spiders. The most spectacular chelicerates that ever existed are the giant eurypterids or "water scorpions" of the Paleozoic seas. Eurypterids were top predators in this early marine environment, and their predatory habits may have been responsible for the fact that most of the earliest known vertebrates were heavily armored.

The chelicerate body is composed of two units called the forebody and the hindbody (fig. 26b), but in the mites and the ticks the forebody and hindbody are indistinctly separated. The forebody has six pairs of jointed appendages, including four pairs of walking legs and *chelicerae* and *pedipalps* (fig. 26c) that are mainly used to capture prey and handle particles of food. The male scorpions have pincerlike pedipalps used to grab females for the mating process. When appendages occur on the hindbody, they are highly modified for specialized tasks, such as web spinning by spiders.

Crustaceans differ from the former two arthropod groups in being highly segmented, some having more than thirty. The head portion of crustaceans normally consist of two pairs of sensory antennae, a pair of *mandibles* and two pairs of *maxillae*. Mandibles are appendages that are used as jaws, and maxillae are used for sorting out and handling particles of food. Crustaceans are mainly aquatic animals and include such creatures as barnacles, crabs, crayfish (fig. 27a), copepods, ostracods, shrimp, and water fleas. Some forms, such as the pill bugs (commonly called rollybugs) that occur under the rocks in our backyards or sometimes get into the basement, are mainly terrestrial. These animals may be herbivores, parasites, or scavengers. Crustaceans have been around since the Cambrian, and the tiny shelled ostracods are important fossils that have been studied for years by micropaleontologists.

The *uniramians* include the millipedes, centipedes, and insects (fig. 27b). These animals are included together because the trunk region of the millipedes and centipedes appears to be equivalent to the thoracic-abdominal unit of the insects. In centipedes the body segments are clearly separate, and each segment has a pair of legs. In the millipedes the body segments are fused together in groups of twos, so that it looks like each unit has two pairs of legs.

The body of insects (fig. 27b) is composed of three parts: head, *thorax*, and *abdomen*. The thorax has three pairs of legs and a pair of wings that fold together at the top of the body. Insects are the most numerous and successful of all of the land invertebrates and exist in an overwhelming myriad of body styles. Insect mouth parts are specialized for many different kinds of diets. Insects began to become quite diverse in the Pennsylvanian period, and their prominence as a part of the food supply on land is thought to have been very important in the

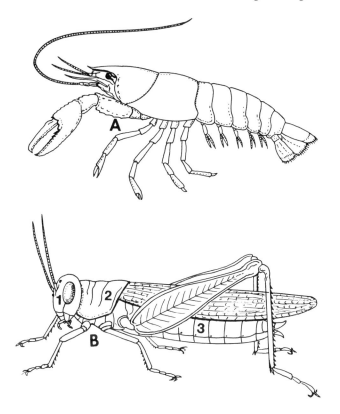

Fig. 27. Crustaceans and insects. *A,* crayfish (a crustacean). *B,* grasshopper (an insect) with head (1), thorax (2), and abdomen (3) indicated.

origin of the reptiles in the early part of the middle Pennsylvanian. Hard parts of insects, especially those of beetles, occur as fossils frequently, particularly in the Tertiary period. Beetle fossils are very important in interpreting the varying climates of the Ice Age in both Europe and North America.

Echinoderms, Hemichordates, Chordates

The echinoderm, hemichordate, and chordate phyla are thought to be evolutionarily related to one another and comprise that group of animals called the deuterostomes. It is believed that they had a common ancestor somewhere in the remote geological past. But such an ancestor has not been found, probably because it was soft bodied.

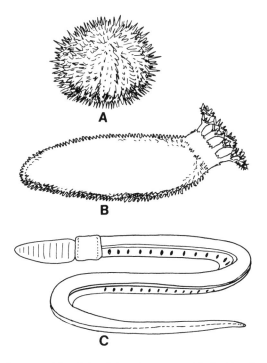

Fig. 28. Echinoderms and hemichordates. *A,* a sea urchin (echinoderm); *B,* a sea cucumber (echinoderm); *C,* a tongue worm (hemichordate).

Echinoderms (fig. 28a–b) comprise another ancient group that traces its fossil history back to the Cambrian. These animals have either spines or plates composed of calcium carbonate in their body walls. They tend to have their body parts arranged in a radial symmetry composed of five parts. Echinoderms are unique in the animal kingdom in having a water vascular system, in which internal canals filled with water connect to hundreds of tiny projections called *tube feet.* Tube feet are wonderful little devises that allow the animals to slowly crawl around, procure food, and breathe. Echinoderms have little personality; in fact they are little more than living machines, as they have no brain tissue at all. Animals in this phylum include brittle stars, crinoids, sand dollars, sea urchins (fig. 28a), sea cucumbers (fig. 28b), starfish, and the extinct cystoids and blastoids that will be discussed later.

Hemichordates are a group of deuterostomes that include the living *tongue worms* (fig. 28c) and the fossil *graptolites.* Tongue worms live in U-shaped burrows in the sea and make their living by filter feeding.

It was once believed that tongue worms were chordates because a structure in the anterior part of the body was considered to be a short notochord. Detailed studies showed, however, that it was not a notochord at all, and tongue worms were kicked unceremoniously out of the phylum Chordata. Possibly the hemichordates were a sister group of the animals that gave rise to the chordates.

Chordates

Finally we arrive at the phylum that contains ourselves and our important relatives, the vertebrates. Figure 29a depicts what a generalized chordate might look like. The phylum Chordata is characterized by the presence of a very basic structure, the *notochord*. The notochord is a rodlike structure that supports the body of primitive chordates and that later in evolutionary history becomes surrounded by the vertebral column in vertebrates. The structure of the notochord may be likened to that of a very long, slim hot dog. The soft tissue inside the notochord may be compared with the meaty part, and the tough *notochordal sheath* on the outside may be compared with the skin of the hot dog. Thus, the notochord is both tough and flexible.

Above the notochord lies a tubular *dorsal nerve cord,* which may or may not have a swelling at the end that becomes the brain. Alongside the notochord and nerve cord are V-shaped *segmental muscles.* The three structures function together to allow the chordate to swim actively. The notochord firms up the body so that it does not writhe around aimlessly when swimming is attempted. The muscles move the body (especially the tail portion) from side to side, so that swimming occurs by lateral side-to-side movements of the body. The nerve cord coordinates this activity.

It is easy to see that, by the addition of a brain and sense organs at the front end, this bilaterally symmetrical animal can actively look for food, seek shelter, and more effectively run away and hide from predators. What a difference from foot-crawling, shelled animals; blindly crawling starfish oozing slowly along on their tube feet; stalked brachiopods and crinoids anchored to the bottom; and all of the aimlessly squirming wormlike forms that occur in the invertebrate phyla. Now, all that is needed is a skeletal structure to further support the body, and we have a primitive vertebrate! Modern chordates are divided into three subphyla: the cephalochordates, the urochordates, and the vertebrates.

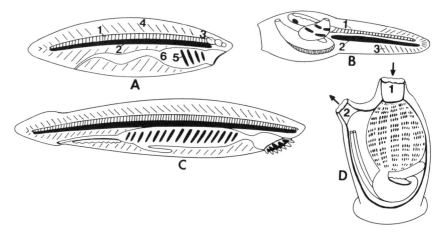

Fig. 29. Nonvertebrate chordates. *A,* hypothetical generalized chordate with nerve cord (1), notochord (2), brain (3), segmental muscles (4), gill slits (5), and digestive tract (6). *B,* tunicate larva with nerve cord (1), notochord (2), and segmental muscles (3) in the tail. *C, Amphioxus,* a living nonvertebrate chordate. *D,* adult tunicate, a simple attached form, that has lost the tail and siphons water into (1) and out of (2) the body.

Living *cephalochordates* are tiny fishlike animals called *lancelets* (formerly included in a single genus, *Amphioxus*) that can rapidly bury themselves in the mud or sand of the seafloor by wriggling their muscular little body. *Amphioxus* (fig. 29c) is always the first chordate animal that students look at in vertebrate zoology classes because it compares so well with our idea of what the ancestor of the vertebrates must have looked like. Actually *Amphioxus* has several characteristics that do not occur in vertebrates, indicating that it came from a side branch or sister group of the actual vertebrate ancestors. Lancelets are *filter feeders* that draw water and tiny particles into their throat (*pharynx*) where the food particles are retained and water and unwanted particles are expelled. We shall see that the first vertebrates were also filter feeders.

The *urochordates* (fig. 29b and d) are commonly called *tunicates.* Tunicates are an ancient group of sea animals that secrete a gelatinous or leathery tunic around themselves. Some of these tunicates spend their adult lives attached to the sea bottom, pilings, or other objects, mindlessly filter feeding on particles from the seawater. Occasionally, when something bothers them, they squirt out a jet of water by contracting their bodies. All of the structures that indicate that tunicates should be included in the chordate phylum are found in the tail of the larval form of the tunicate (fig. 29b), which looks something like a tiny tadpole.

A notochord, nerve cord, and muscles in this tail allow the larva to swim to a new home to settle on. When the larva finds such a place, it absorbs its tail and metamorphoses into the simple attached adult phase (fig. 29d). Some biologists have suggested that such a tadpole might have become the ancestral vertebrate simply by retaining the larval stage rather than by changing into the attached adult. In any case the protovertebrate has yet to be found in the fossil record; and undoubtedly this is related to the fact that the ancestral form was soft bodied.

Vertebrates are animals that are characterized by having a vertebral column (backbone) and a skeleton of cartilage or bone. The ancestral vertebrates were assuredly soft bodied; thus a good fossil record is lacking, and ideas about the origin of vertebrates are obscure. Vertebrates originated in shallow seas, later invaded freshwater habitats, and finally moved onto land—with a rather intermediate amphibious stage in between. The eight vertebrate *classes* that are recognized by virtually every biologist are the jawless fishes, the placoderms, the cartilaginous fishes, the bony fishes, the amphibians, the reptiles, the birds, and the mammals.

Bone and cartilage are the important elements of the skeleton in the vertebrate body. Bone is mainly composed of hard inorganic salts of calcium phosphate laced together by supple bands of proteins called *collagen fibers* that all set up in a matrix of mucoid gel. Although bone is a hard tissue, it is lighter and more resilient than the shells of invertebrates, which are composed of prismatic layers of calcium carbonate. When dropped, a fresh bone will bounce, but a clam shell of equal weight will usually shatter. Bone forms both the external and internal parts of the skeleton of vertebrates, including some small elements that become embedded in the skin of some animals. Moreover, teeth and scales are derivatives of primitive bony tissues. The most numerous vertebrate fossils consist of bones and teeth. Cartilage is a supple, translucent tissue composed of a mucoid gel (*chondromucsin*) impregnated by a network of collagen fibers. Cartilage and bone are found in both primitive and advanced vertebrates, including humans.

Vertebrates are active animals, so that a well-developed, closed circulatory system and an efficient muscular and nervous system are necessary. The brain and sense organs that developed early on in vertebrate evolution (to direct the animal in finding food, shelter, and sex, and to help the animal escape from predators) became increasingly important during the later evolution of many vertebrate groups, especially the mammals.

Fishes

Jawless fishes are first represented in the fossil record by phosphatic fragments in the upper Cambrian; these fragments have a microscopic structure that somewhat resembles that of the bony plates of later, more complete fossil fishes. In the Ordovician, more complex bone occurs in the fossil record, mainly in the form of scattered bits of dermal armor. But it is not until the late Silurian that good "whole fish" fossils are to be found.

These whole fishes are called *ostracoderms* (fig. 30a). Ostracoderm skeletons are composed mainly of external dermal shields and plates, some large, some small, and some pebblelike. If internal skeletons were present in ostracoderms, they probably were composed of cartilage. It has been suggested that the external armor of ostracoderms was developed to protect them from the *eurypterids,* or "water scorpions," that lived during the time. Ostracoderms were almost all filter feeders, although one might have been a fluid sucker and another might have had a large pumping mechanism for drawing in food. All ostracoderms lacked jaws; thus we picture them with permanently open, immovable mouths.

Modern jawless fishes include the lampreys and hagfishes that have lost the dermal armor and have only a cartilaginous skeleton left over. Lampreys (fig. 30b) are blood and fluid suckers, and the introduced sea lamprey practically destroyed the commercial lake trout industry in the Great Lakes region by its predaceous habits. Fortunately, a poison was developed that killed off most of the larval lampreys (*ammocetes*) in the small streams where spawning takes place. Lampreys have a round mouth that lacks tentacles and a rasping tongue that makes holes in other fishes. Hagfishes, on the other hand, have a mouth surrounded by tentacles and a pair of horny biting "false jaws" that enable them to consume dead and dying fishes.

Paleontologists have been able to study the minute structure of the brain and sense organs of some kinds of ostracoderms and have found

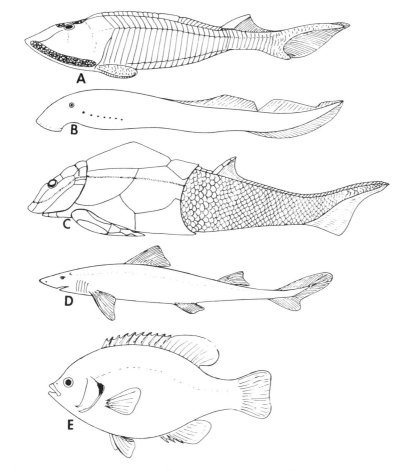

Fig. 30. Fishes. *A*, a bottom-dwelling osteostracan ostracoderm. *B*, a sea lamprey. *C*, a small, nibbling, antiarch placoderm. *D*, a dogfish shark. *E*, a rayfinned bony fish.

that these nervous system structures are very similar to those of modern lampreys, even down to the number of semicircular canals that are present in the inner ear.

Placoderms (fig. 30c) are the only entirely extinct class of vertebrates. Placoderms arose in the late Silurian and they may be grouped together because they are ancient armored fishes with jaws. Nevertheless, it is possible that they form a rather unnatural group whose subgroups are not related to one another. Generally, placoderms have bodies composed of a head shield and a thoracic shield.

In the evolution of the main group of placoderms, the *arthrodires,* the thoracic shield becomes reduced and the head becomes more mobile. During the Devonian the placoderms moved from freshwater into brackish water and finally into fully marine habitats. Some of them became huge predators with steel-trap jaws. One group of small placoderms, the *antiarchs,* was only a few inches long (fig. 30c) and had a peaky thoracic shield and little nibbling jaws. These little animals were the mice of the Devonian fish world, and they scraped around rocks for bits of algae and other kinds of organic matter.

Cartilaginous fishes are first known on the basis of fragmentary teeth from the late Silurian. These superb fishes lack dermal armor plates and have an internal skeleton composed of cartilage. Some of these cartilages may become impregnated and hardened by limy *calcite,* but true bone never forms internally. The body is typically covered by dermal denticles called *placoid scales* that look like tiny vertebrate teeth when viewed under the microscope. These scales make the body of a shark feel like sandpaper to the human hand.

Cartilaginous fishes include the ratfishes with whiplike tails; the more familiar sharks (fig. 30d) and rays; and some extinct sharklike fish. The fossil remains of these fishes mainly consist of teeth, as the cartilaginous skeletons do not fossilize very well; but sometimes some of the calcified cartilages are found as fossils. Many early sharklike forms had rather simple teeth for holding on to small prey or pavement teeth for crushing shellfish. But later sharks became highly adapted predators, some of which had cutting teeth with serrated edges like steak knives. In the Cretaceous some of these sharks became gigantic creatures that could have been from thirty to forty feet long. It has been suggested that these huge predators may have eaten so many of the large sea reptiles that they were forced into extinction. In the true sense of the term, modern sharks are not living fossils, as they are sometimes portrayed. They are actually highly evolved predators whose ancestors were much slower, simpler, and not nearly as efficient.

The final fish group considered here is the *bony* fishes (fig. 30e). These animals lack external armor and have a well-developed internal skeleton of bone. They are either covered by rectangular shiny scales with a good bit of bony material left in them; overlapping fibrous scales (like those of most of the fishes we eat); or by naked, slimy skins such as occur in eels and catfishes. There are two major groups of bony fishes; the *rayfinned* fishes, who have the visible portion of the fin supported by *fibrous* rays; and the *lobe-finned* fishes, who have the visible portion of the fin next to the body supported by bones in a lobe, and the portion of the fin away from the body supported by fibrous rays. It is believed that the tetrapods (four-legged animals) evolved from lobe-finned fishes.

Rayfinned fishes (fig. 30e) are the most abundant modern fishes both in freshwater and marine habitats and are represented by thousands of species. Rayfins began to diversify late in the Cretaceous and became dominant in the Tertiary period. This group developed their *air bladders* into structures that allow the fishes to adjust to changing pressures at various depths in the sea and in deep lakes. Some primitive living rayfins, such as the garpikes, have retained lunglike structures that allow them to gulp air at the surface of the water when the oxygen content is depleted.

Lobe-finned fishes were prominent in the Paleozoic, but the only living members of the group are the freshwater lungfishes of Africa, Australia, and South America; and one large living fossil named *Latimeria,* a predaceous big-mouthed form that lives in the seas near Madagascar. *Latimeria* comes from an ancient ancestral group of lobe-fins called the *crossopterygians,* which are thought to be the group that gave rise to the tetrapods.

Tetrapods

The remaining four classes of vertebrates are referred to as tetrapods because they have limbs rather than fins. The earliest tetrapods are placed in the class Amphibia. The general concensus among modern paleontologists is that tetrapods evolved from lobe-finned *crossopterygian* fishes (fig. 31a) in the late Devonian. Some paleontologists believe that tetrapod limbs evolved from lobe fins to allow the animals to scramble from ponds or swamps that dried up in times of drought to those that still contained water. But other scientists believe that limbs evolved in the water before the animals ventured out onto land, and there is some fossil evidence for this. A recently discovered very early tetrapod with "toes" on its back limb evidently had fins on its front limbs; and it is suggested that it used the toes to anchor itself to vegetation while peering around on the surface. Other early tetrapods have extra "fingers" and/or "toes," but soon the standard number of five digits at the end of each limb was established in most groups.

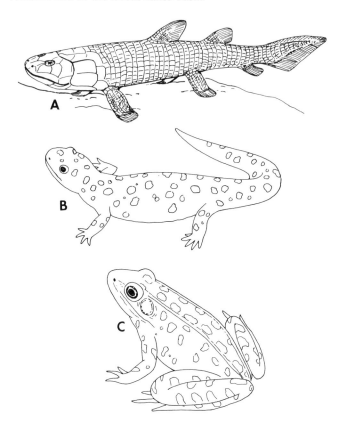

Fig. 31. Crossopterygian fish and amphibians. *A, Eusthenopteron,* a crossopterygian fish close to the ancestry of amphibians. *B, Ambystoma,* a modern salamander. *C, Rana,* a modern frog.

Amphibians (fig. 31b–c) were the first group of vertebrates to venture out on the land in earnest. This took place in the late Devonian. But amphibians were and still are tied to the water for part of their life cycle, because of their jellylike eggs that tend to dry out quickly. The ancient Paleozoic amphibians (some of which are very hard to distinguish from reptiles) have come and gone, leaving three very specialized modern groups, the salamanders (fig. 31b), the wormlike caecilians, and the anurans (frogs and toads) (fig. 31c). All of these animals differ from reptiles in their peculiar teeth, each composed of two parts; their weaker skeletons; and in their naked, slimy skins.

Reptiles (fig. 32a–b) are a gigantic assemblage of animals that have

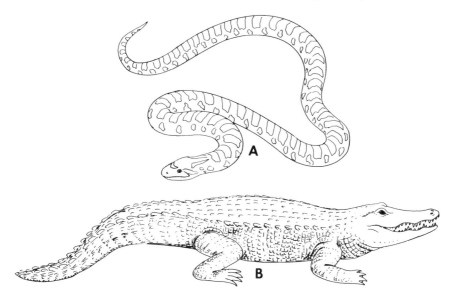

Fig. 32. Reptiles. *A, Lampropeltis,* a modern snake; *B, Alligator,* a modern crocodilian.

a shelled (*amniote*) egg but lack hair and feathers. According to modern ideas, reptiles do not form a natural evolutionary (*phyletic*) group because they gave rise to seperate lineages leading to birds and mammals. Nevertheless, we shall continue to use the term reptile for practical reasons. Reptiles were able to truly establish themselves on land because their shelled egg freed them from having to return to water to breed and because their study skeletons compensated them for the loss of the buoying effect of water. The first reptiles evolved in the Paleozoic in the early part of the Pennsylvanian period, diversified greatly during the rest of the Paleozoic, then absolutely dominated the entire Mesozoic era (Age of Reptiles).

The most important of all reptilian events may have been the origin of the dinosaurs in the late Triassic, for dinosaurs became the dominant land forms for about 145 million years. Dinosaurs were the rulers among a larger reptilian group called the archosaurs that contained animals such as the thecodonts, flying reptiles, and crocodilians. Modern reptile groups are diminished and include the turtles, lizards, worm lizards, snakes (fig. 32a), crocodilians (fig. 32b), and that living fossil, the tuatara of the New Zealand region. Snakes are the very latest reptile group to have evolved, with good fossils not appearing until the Creta-

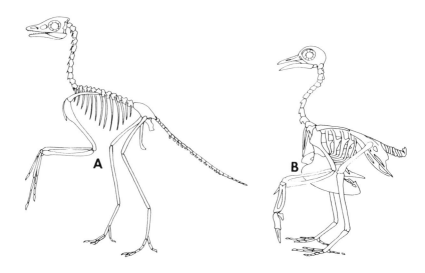

Fig. 33. A, *Archaeopteryx*, a Jurassic bird; B, a typical modern bird skeleton

ceous, and had a large diversification in the Miocene epoch of the Tertiary.

Birds sprang from a group of small bipedal dinosaurs that were in the process of evolving feathers. Some scientists have suggested that this event occurred as early as the Triassic. But the first complete fossil that is considered to be a bird by all vertebrate paleontologists represents essentially a small bipedal dinosaur with feathers and is called *Archaeopteryx* (fig. 33a). This very famous fossil is from the late Jurassic of Bavaria in southern Germany. Modern birds (fig. 33b) are much different than *Archaeopteryx*. They have lost the teeth, tail, and fingers of this protobird and have added a bill, a wingbone formed of fused fingers, a deeply keeled sternum, and hollow bones. Some modern classifiers argue that birds should merely be considered a subgroup of the dinosaurs.

Mammals sprang from a group of mammal-like reptiles called *cynodonts* in the late Triassic about the time that the first dinosaurs arose. But the dinosaurs ruled the planet for 145 million years, while the mammals bided their time mainly in the form of nervous, beady-eyed creatures of the night. When the dinosaurs became extinct at the end of the Cretaceous, the mammals took over early in the Tertiary. Their insulating hair and improved circulation and metabolism allowed them to cope well in the cooler parts of the globe. Like the dinosaurs before them, mammalian communities became organized around a system of large herbivores and carnivores, with scavengers feeding upon dead mammalian bodies. Most of these large herbivore-dominated mammalian communities collapsed at the end of the Pleistocene about 10,000 years ago.

We have now had an introduction to the major groups of living things and some of their biological structures and ways. The following chapter deals with how these ancient organisms related to each other and to their physical environment.

Chapter 4
Paleoecological Concepts

In the early days of paleontology, studies seemed to center on the evolution of single animal groups. In other words, studies on the evolution of the ammonoids or on the evolution of horses were common. Today, there is more emphasis on the evolution of *ancient communities*, an ecological approach to the study of paleontology. The term *ecology* was first proposed by the German scientist Haeckel in 1869. Ecology may be defined as the study of the relationship of organisms or groups of organisms to their environment. The environment may be broken down into two parts, the *biotic* environment and the *physical* or *abiotic* environment.

Perhaps a useful way to think of the biotic part of the environment is in terms of the concept of ascending levels of biological organization. Cells are composed of complex aggregations of organic molecules; tissues consist of specialized cells; organs are composed of related tissues; organ systems consist of groups of individual organs, higher organisms are composed of groups of organ systems; populations consist of individual organisms; communities are composed of populations; ecosystems consist of communities interacting with the abiotic environment; and the biosphere consists of interacting ecosystems. With this idea in mind it can be said that ecology mainly deals with the levels of organization beyond the organism.

Some definitions of these terms are in order at this point. A *population* may be defined as groups of individuals of one kind of organism.

In other words, all of the bluegills in a lake would be referred to as the *population* of bluegills in that respective lake.

A *community* may be defined as all of the populations of organisms living in a stated area. In other words, all of the organisms in the lake would interact as a community.

An *ecosystem* may be defined as the unit where the community and the abiotic (physical) environment interact, and the *biosphere* may be defined as that part of the earth where ecosystems function and interact.

The central unit for both modern and paleoecological studies is the community. All of the organisms that have ever existed have interacted with each other and with the nonliving environment. These interactions have produced powerful selective forces in evolution. Communities quite different from modern communities have existed in the past. However, enough similarities exist between ancient communities and modern ones that the principle of *uniformitarianism,* discussed previously, may be applied to our reasoning about fossil communities. A community has a definite structure relative to the energy that flows through it. There are several so-called *trophic levels* in this energy flow.

All of the original energy for any community ultimately comes from the sun as solar energy. A community without primary solar energy, such as a cave community or a community at the bottom of the sea, must depend upon "transformed" solar energy brought into the system. In a cave, a common major source of transformed energy comes from the bats that feed outside of the cave; these bats deposit a source of energy on the cave floor in the form of layers of feces. In the deep sea bottoms, the source of energy is the bodies of dead animals and plants that sink slowly downward.

Solar energy is necessary for the *producers* in a biological community. Producers are the photosynthetic *protists* and plants that capture the energy from the sun and use it to make organic compounds to nourish their own bodies. It has been shown that the microscopic protists of the sea, which occur by the countless trillions, are more important than terrestrial plants as sources of making organic sugars with the aid of solar energy.

Photosynthetic plants and protists are themselves consumed by primary consumers, which range in size from microscopic protists to elephants. There are secondary, tertiary, quaternary, and even higher levels of consumers. In other words, the photosynthetic protists in a Great Lakes Basin pond are eaten by larger protists; the larger protists are eaten by insect larvae; the insect larvae are eaten by bluegills; the bluegills are eaten by snapping turtles; and snapping turtles are eaten by humans and other predators. Finally, *decomposers* such as fungi and bacteria break down the dead bodies and waste material into nutrients that may be recycled by the community.

Energy flow through both fossil and modern communities may be depicted in various ways. A *pyramid of energy* (fig. 34a) illustrates the idea that energy is lost to the system as it flows through the trophic levels of the community. This energy is lost through various indigestible parts of plants and animals as well as inefficient use of organic material at each level. This has wide application in human populations. In general the poorer populations mainly consume producers (e.g., corn, rice, beans) and richer populations supplement their diets with portions of animal protein from the larger consumers (e.g., cow muscle in the form of burgers and steaks!). A *food chain* involves the simple concept of grass-cow-human energy flow or photosynthetic protist–larger protist– insect–bluegill–snapping turtle–human. A *food web* (fig. 34b) depicts the intricate interdependence between the organisms of a community. In tropical communities the food web may be enormously complex.

In most communities, both fossil and modern, it appears that some organisms—keystone organisms—are more important than others as far as the stability of the community is concerned. *Megaherbivores,* the very large plant-eating animals that occurred both in the dinosaur communities of the Mesozoic and the mammalian communities of the Tertiary, supposedly controlled the equilibrium of the energy flow through those communities. If megaherbivorous animals become extinct in modern communities, a domino effect ensues that can greatly disrupt the structure of the community and even lead to the virtual extinction of some kinds of communities. More will be said about this later.

The study of fossil communities is difficult. In order to get the most out of these studies several points should be kept in mind. First, one should find out as much as possible about the *sedimentary environment.* For instance, if the fossils come from sediments composed mainly of black mudstones, quiet anaerobic conditions might be indicated. Thus the fossils in such a community might represent aggregations of dead or dying animals.

It has often been assumed that red-bed sandstones indicate very dry or desertlike conditions. Recently, however, it has been shown that quite the opposite is true in some instances. Therefore, animals once

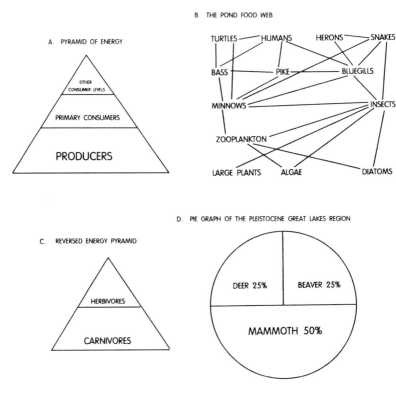

Fig. 34. Ecological diagrams. *A,* a normal pyramid of energy. *B,* a food web in a modern Great Lakes region pond. *C,* a reversed pyramid of energy (where carnivores are more abundant than herbivores) that sometimes may be indicated by fossil faunas where information has been lost. *D,* an oversimplified community (with no carnivores) that sometimes may be indicated by fossil faunas where information has been lost.

thought to be terrestrial desert creatures were probably semiaquatic predators. Course gravels usually indicate rapid deposition, but weakly cross-bedded sands indicate slow deposition in a small depression in a streambed. The former situation often selects for the larger members of the paleocommunity; the latter situation usually sorts out the smaller animals.

Limestones usually indicate a shallow seafloor environment on a continental shelf. Paleontologists often obtain a very good representation of at least the shelled animals of the time from such formations. The same may be said about fossil coral reefs, which not only depict many of the organisms that were present in the past, but indicate depths of less than 150 feet and a temperature range from about 65 to 95 degrees F. Radiolarian ooze, on the other hand, would indicate a deep seafloor away from the continental shelf. Some of the natural pitfalls of paleoecological studies are as follows.

A fossil assemblage is typically a death assemblage (*thanatocoenose*) that almost never comes close to adequately representing all of the organisms that were present. Imagine all of the different groups (taxa) that should be present in an ancient community: bacteria, protists, fungi, plants, and animals. When we imagine them, we realize that most paleontology is actually done in bits and pieces. Usually the decomposers (which consist mainly of bacteria, protists and fungi) are missing from the fossil site because they are so small and/or soft bodied.

Now, assume that we are lucky enough to find both plants and animals in the deposit. We will normally get only those species that have hard parts, unless we have exceedingly fine and soft sediments and perfect conditions of preservation. Thus the important, but smaller soft-bodied plants and animals are usually not preserved. Moreover, because of the randomness of preservation, the relative abundance of the various plants and animals that we do recover may be quite misleading relative to their abundance when they were alive. For example, a breeding pond that is drying up might trap only the frogs that were mating early in the year and miss other species of frogs that would have bred later.

Cave faunas may be especially misleading because the accumulated bones found in them tend to be from the discarded pellets of owls (e.g., from mice and shrews that the owl ate); from the remains of animals dragged in by large predators (e.g., chewed and broken bones of their prey); and finally from the skeletons of bats that roosted in the cave. Chimney caves that form natural traps for animals usually produce better samples of the community than walk-in caves, for obvious reasons. On the other hand, pitfall traps select for those species that were night-blind or nearsighted, or those that could not climb well or fly.

Quaking bog traps, such as those that occurred in the Great Lakes region during the postglacial Pleistocene, tended to trap large animals such as mastodonts that broke through the mats of vegetation. On the other hand, small mammals could run safely over the top of these mats; thus very few small mammals have been found in quaking bog Pleistocene traps in the Great Lakes Basin.

Because of these factors alone or in combination, fossil faunas may often depict paleoecological situations that are unreal. A topsy-turvy pyramid of energy such as is depicted in figure 34c with more carnivores than herbivores often occurs in the fossil record. This might be based either on chance (or on carnivore stupidity!). Sometimes only one trophic level is represented, and many times there are oversimplified food webs (fig. 34d) for the reasons discussed above.

The best way to study a fossil site, then, is to do it as thoroughly as possible with many experts in many related fields. These persons would include sedimentologists, geomorphologists, micropaleontologists, paleobotanists, invertebrate paleontologists, and vertebrate paleontologists. Even then what emerges will be a little like a picture puzzle with many missing pieces. Nevertheless, the more pieces that are added to the puzzle, the more the real picture will begin to emerge.

Chapter 5
Fossil Study

We have seen that fossils may be defined as any recognizable evidence of life preserved from prehistoric time. This chapter deals with the major kinds of fossils, how fossils are dated, and finally, how fossils are formed. Fossils may be somewhat arbitrarily divided into two groups: actual fossils and trace fossils. *Actual* fossils are preserved organisms, parts of organisms, or molds and casts of the actual organisms. *Trace* fossils are not parts of the original organism but offer identifiable evidence that the organism existed.

Actual Fossils

Some of the rarest kinds of fossils include the preserved soft parts of the organism. Most of these occur late in geological time. Some Ice Age mammals have been preserved in *tar pits* or *oil seeps,* especially if these sites have been intruded by salt seeps that tend to act as a natural preservative. A hairless, but muscular, wooly rhino was found in one of these tar-salt situations in eastern central Europe, and a spectacular cast of it was recently on display in the Natural History Museum in London.

The most spectacular "soft part" fossils have been found frozen in arctic soil. Several mammoths—complete with shaggy hair—have been found in Siberia. Many of these have had muscle tissue that, although "freezerburned," was readily eaten by sled dogs. A most exciting recent discovery was that of a frozen baby mammoth in Siberia. The baby had long reddish hair and small ears (unlike modern elephants) and was named Dima by the discoverers. A frozen bison carcass found near Fairbanks, Alaska, was determined to be about 31,000 years old. Other fossils with soft parts intact have been found in *mummified* form. These fossils are often covered by dry skin and hair. Most fossil "mummies" come from very dry areas, and mummified ground sloths and their dung have been found in caves in the southwestern United States.

Some relatively soft-bodied organisms have been preserved as somewhat ghostlike outlines of *black carbon residues* by a process called *distillation*. These carbon replicas mainly occur in very ancient shales. Other soft-bodied creatures have been preserved in ancient rocks that are composed of *extremely fine sediments*. One of the most famous fine-sediment sites in the world is at Solnhofen in Bavaria, southern Germany. Here, an amazing variety of fossils including the protobird *Archaeopteryx* (see fig. 33a) are preserved in *lithographic limestones* and *fine shales*. Marine annelid worms, shrimp, and other delicate invertebrates are found here also, along with many kinds of fishes and reptiles.

Sometimes whole organisms are trapped in soft material that later hardens. Fossil ants, bees, flies, and even frogs have been preserved in the resin of fossil trees, but these fossils in *amber* are rare. Certain soft cells and tissues have been preserved in *chert*, a derivative of limestone.

Most fossils, however, consist of the preserved *hard parts* of organisms (see fig. 1b). Fossil protists occur in the form of tiny shells of silica, calcium carbonate, or chitin. Large fossil plants usually are represented by the hard tissues found in cones, seeds, roots, and woody trunks and stems. Fossil invertebrate animals consist mainly of the exoskeletal shells or parts of these shells. Invertebrate shells are mainly composed of calcium carbonate, but occasionally there are chitinous shells. Vertebrate fossils mainly consist of bones and teeth; but other relatively hard parts such as scales and horns are preserved.

Molds, casts, and *imprints* are considered to be actual fossils because they duplicate the original structures of organisms. If a bone or shell becomes embedded in rock and that bone or shell dissolves away, the cavity left forms a *natural mold*. Sometimes the natural mold is filled in by other sediments that harden within the mold. The fossil formed in this manner is called a *natural cast* (see fig. 1d–e). Common invertebrate fossils are the *internal casts* that are formed by sediments that infill the chambers of buried shells (see fig. 1e). *Artificial molds* and *casts* (see fig. 1c) may be made by paleontologists by using various techniques. Molds of very thin, delicate animals are called *imprints*. Leaves (see fig. 1g), skins of dinosaurs and lizards, and even outlines of delicate invertebrate animals and plants have made imprints of themselves when they fell into the right kinds of ancient muds and clays.

Trace Fossils

Some trace fossils are structural by-products of the various life activities of organisms. *Stromatolites* (see fig. 1a) are a very ancient example of this type of fossil. Stromatolites look like mounds of sediments but are actually the result of the photosynthetic activity produced by masses of moneran cyanobacteria.

Footprints (see fig. 1f) and *trails* are very important trace fossils that help us to interpret the lives of the animals that left them. These tracks, trails, and footprints can range in size from worm trails to the huge footprints of dinosaurs. Usually tracks and trails are made in soft sediments, and sometimes they are so detailed that they have been given scientific names! They tell us how animals moved and sometimes how fast they moved, as in the case of dinosaur footprints. They tell us whether the animals moved around in herds or flocks, or as solitary individuals. Sometimes they even depict predatory events, such as a pack of predaceous dinosaurs attacking a large herbivorous one. Bodies, feet, and tails of animals are all involved in making fossil tracks and trails.

Coprolites are fossilized fecal pellets (see fig. 1h–i), and they give us a great deal of paleontological information. Shark coprolites, for example, are in a spiral shape that duplicates the spiral valve structure of the shark intestine. Sometimes coprolites contain remains of undigested food materials that may be identified and give information about the feeding habits of the animal that yielded the coprolite. A shark coprolite from the Georgia Eocene contained some of the skeletal remains of a mouse. This indicates the shark lived near land, the mouse somehow fell into the water, and perhaps even that the shark had indigestion!

Gastroliths (see fig. 1j) are fossil stomach stones that are similar to the gizzard stones of chickens in that they aid in the mechanical part of the digestive process. Dinosaur gastroliths are not uncommon and usually have a characteristic polished appearance. Gastroliths may be rocks that have been swallowed or other hard objects. Objects that have been found with fossil crocodilians have been interpreted as stomach "stones" that originated as the burned resinous knots of pine trees. Alligators swallow such "lightered-knots" in the southeastern United States today.

Dating Fossils

Fossils are dated by using *relative* and *absolute* chronological methods. Relative chronology indicates the age of the fossil relative to other fossils and the layers that contain them. Thus, in the Great Lakes region, an animal bone found in the marl layer of an infilled kettle bog and associated with an American mastodont would normally be determined to be from the late Pleistocene. This would be based on the stratigraphic position of the ancient kettle bog and the known stratigraphic occurrence of the American mastodont. To get an absolute date for this assemblage, however, we would need to submit a piece of bone from the mastodont (or the other animal), or some other organic material (such as wood) associated with these animals to a dating laboratory.

Absolute dates are determined by the study of unstable atoms of elements called *radioactive isotopes.* These isotopes break down at a completely predictable rate that is independent of any known physical or chemical change. Often in this process one element changes to another. Let's say, for instance, that in a certain igneous rock element A changes to element B by one-fourth every 5 million years. Thus if the ratio of A to B is 3:1 in that igneous rock, we know that 5 million years have elapsed since that rock solidified in its original isotopic state. Unfortunately, igneous rocks normally lack fossils, so that we must estimate the age of fossiliferous layers based on their stratigraphic relationships to dated igneous rocks.

Absolute dates on fossils can be difficult to obtain for several reasons. If the fossils are under 50,000 years old, however, carbon 14 dates are presently useful, and they are very important for dating events in the late Pleistocene of the Great Lakes region. Carbon 14 breaks down isotopically to form nitrogen 14, so that half of the carbon 14 is gone in about 5,730 years. Fortunately, many parts of animals and plants (bones, teeth, tusks, wood, seeds, peat, snail shells, and other miscellaneous bits and pieces) contain fixed amounts of carbon 14 in life.

Thus, if we analyze fossils and find that only one-half of the original carbon 14 is left, we can figure that the fossil has been dead for about 5,730 years. The drawback is that the carbon 14 method doesn't work as well beyond about 40,000 years ago because by then only a tiny fraction of the carbon 14 is left in the fossils.

Carbon 14 dates are subject to some errors. If modern roots grow into fossil wood and are not removed before the carbon 14 analysis, one can derive a date that is much too recent. On the other hand, the carbon part of a fossil has sometimes been leached out or replaced by some other element, and with no carbon there is no date. When bones are aged, the fibrous collagen portion of the bone is usually the part extracted by the laboratory for the carbon 14 date.

Carbon 14 dates are also subject to statistical errors, although these errors are much lower than they used to be. Therefore, carbon 14 dates are always presented with hedge factors. A date written as [12,400 + or − 200 B.P.] then would mean that the fossil lived between about 12,200 and 12,600 years before the present.

How Fossils Are Formed

Taphonomy is the science of the study of the death, burial, and the preservation of fossils. Sophisticated taphonomic studies demand that the fossils be recorded exactly as they are located in the sediments that surround them so that the exact orientation of the fossils with respect to the pattern of sediments around them as well as to other fossils in the deposit can be diagrammed.

Thus, grid systems of various kinds are fashioned so that this exacting information can be retrieved. The type of grid system used depends upon the nature of the sediments that enclose the fossils. Thus, a grid system used in consolidated sediments such as occur in some of the western United States would be quite different from one used in the mushy bog sediments where Great Lakes region Ice Age mastodonts and mammoths are found.

The two most important criteria for the preservation of fossils are (1) the possession of hard parts and (2) immediate burial. If immediate burial does not occur, dead animals and plants will be torn apart or entirely consumed by scavengers, and bacterial and fungal decay will do away with the leftover materials. Hard parts of these materials are usually the last to decay or weather to their constituent elements.

The rate of decay of dead organisms varies considerably, depending on the situation where the body ends up and on the climate of the area. A dead deer on the edge of a swamp in Florida is almost immediately fed upon by vultures and other scavengers, and the warm temperatures of the area facilitate rapid microbial decay of the leftover parts. But in the Great Lakes area, a deer carcass at the edge of a pond might last more than a year because of the acidic condition of the water, freezing conditions in the winter, and the much cooler summers.

In a taphonomic situation where the dead organism is quickly buried by sediments, scavengers are largely avoided, and the hard parts more or less remain associated together. Moreover, oxygen is largely excluded, and decay is greatly retarded. Finally, weathering is prevented and the process of *permineralization* may occur. Permineralization involves the impregnation of the hard parts with mineral salts such as silica and calcium carbonate. Bones are full of cavities of many sizes that may be filled by mineral salts that precipitate out of the groundwater. That is why a fossilized bone usually feels much heavier than a modern bone. We have already discussed how microorganisms may be imprisoned in chert formed from limestone and how whole animals may be preserved in tree resin that transforms into amber.

Sometimes whole communities of invertebrate animals are fossilized at one time. Examples of this phenomenon are oyster bars that may be covered by several feet of sediments after hurricanes and other storms send huge loads of sediments down coastal rivers into marine embayments. This happened in Chesapeake Bay during one of the recent hurricanes. Not only the oysters, but all of the other animal and plant inhabitants of the oyster bar community were blanketed by sediments.

Vertebrate animals are most commonly (and immediately) buried by *blankets of freshwater-borne sedments* such as those from shifting channel sands. This commonly occurred in the ancient *braided streams* of the central plains states of America. Braided streams occupy wide valleys but have very narrow, shifting channels. Thus, with every rainstorm there is the likelihood that the channel will change and that sands, muds, and silts will be spread over parts of dead animals in adjacent areas. Sometimes log jams trap dozens of large vertebrate animals; in other cases skeletal remains of small animals lying in sluggish (or slow-flowing) oxbows and pools will be covered by thin layers of sand.

Bones are sorted out based on the activity of the aquatic situation in which they occur. Large, heavy bones tend to stay put, even when the current is moderately strong. Tiny bones tend to be moved rapidly along, even by relatively slow currents. Bones that are deposited in locations where there is practically no water movement, such as in bogs in the Great Lakes region, tend to stay in place, no matter what their size or weight. Physical features of streams and seafloors also greatly affect the deposition of fossils. *Point bars* in streams influence the way that fossil bones are distributed in the streambed, whereas tides, currents and channels are important in sand and mud accumulation and thence fossil distribution on seafloors.

Fossils often accumulate in caves. Generally two kinds of cave entrances lead to the accumulation of fossils, *horizontal caves* (walk-in caves) and *chimney caves*. Obviously, chimney caves act as natural traps for animals that lack flying or climbing ability, but walk-in caves are often repositories of fossils as well. In temperate areas throughout the world, vertebrate fossils found in caves tend to have the following origins: (1) bones of small animals such as mice, rats, and shrews arranged in layers of owl pellets regurgitated by owls roosting in the cave; (2) bones of bats that died while roosting in the cave; (3) chunks of larger bones derived from large predators that brought their prey into the cave to eat; and (4) bones of animals that accidentally fell into pitfall caves.

It is important to realize that animals in caves must also be immediately buried by sediments for fossilization to occur. Some caves and rock shelters have had such slow rates of sedimentation that few vertebrate remains have been preserved as fossils there. Other caves subject to periodic floodings or other rapid influxes of sediments are rich in their fossil content.

Paleontologists have recently established that *ash falls* are very important agents of fossil preservation in many areas. This is especially evident in the plains areas of the United States where beds of ash— sometimes several feet thick—occur from Texas north almost to the Canadian border. In Nebraska, a whole group of hippolike rhinos and their young, horses, birds, and even turtles were smothered by ash-laden sediments derived from volcanic eruptions in the Rocky Mountain region.

In the Great Lakes Basin many vertebrate fossils, especially mastodonts and mammoths, have been found in the mucky and marly sediments of infilled kettle bogs. It is believed that most of these vertebrate fossils fell through unstable mats of vegetation in these situations when they were at the "quaking bog" stage. Some other ways that animals may be trapped as fossils include being trapped in quicksand or being covered by wind-blown sands. These methods of fossilization are not particularly important in the Great Lakes Basin.

Chapter 6
Collecting Fossils

Fossils are nonrenewable resources that are important scientific objects. Thus, it is important that we say something about the ethics of fossil collecting at the onset of this chapter. Fossils are important to scientists in the correlation of geological strata as well as in studies of the patterns and processes of evolution. In some instances fossils reflect in a significant way on the life patterns and habits of prehistoric humans.

To the paleontologist, fossils are never important as objects by themselves, but only in the light of their relationships to the sediments that contain them and to the other fossils that occur in those sediments. A single fossil from a critical time period can change geological and evolutionary thinking. Therefore, before an individual decides to make a private collection of fossils, he or she should realize that certain ethical considerations affect private collecting. It might be pointed out that many major museum stores, if not the majority of them, have decided that fossils are such valuable scientific resources that they will not sell them.

If one decides to collect fossils, however, it is much better to concentrate on invertebrate rather than vertebrate fossils. Invertebrate fossils may be very abundant in some situations and thus are of local cultural, educational, and recreational value. Common invertebrate fossils are useful in teaching and in giving students field and hands-on experience with scientific objects.

Mastodont and mammoth finds, rather common in some areas of the Great Lakes region, are always of great interest and importance to the local community, as they strikingly illustrate the prehistory of the area.

It is important, however, that these remains find their way to institutions where they may be maintained properly for the good of the public as well as for scientific studies.

We shall not identify specific collecting localities in the Great Lakes region but will mention general areas in the region where fossils have been found. If persons do make the decision to make private collecting trips the following strong advice is given.

1. Collect invertebrate fossils only, and these only after it has been determined that they are abundant in the area.
2. Always obtain written permission to collect fossils, whether it be on federal, state, or private lands. Be advised that it is illegal to collect fossils on many federal and state lands; and of course, trespassing on private lands is against the law.
3. Carefully record and photograph all of the stratigraphic and locational data possible with each fossil that you collect.
4. Always take significant or unusual specimens to professional paleontologists for evaluation.

Most states, and provinces in Canada, have specific laws that govern the collecting of fossils on state and provincial lands as well as regulations for federal lands. State regulations have been summarized in two publications cited in the references section of this chapter at the end of the book. Ethical guidelines for paleontological collecting are to be found in *Paleontological Collecting,* an extensive report published by the National Academy of Science in 1987 and issued to most museums and universities with paleontological programs or collections.

Where to Look for Fossils

Remember, the Great Lakes Basin has most of its fossil-bearing bedrocks buried under 20 to 100 feet of glacial silts, sands, and gravels. Also remember that an erosional interval in the Michigan Basin produced a pattern in which the youngest near-surface bedrock layers are near the center of the basin and the older rocks occur in successive peripheral layers away from the center (see fig. 5). Great Lakes region fossils are usually found in the following situations.

1. Where glacial sediments are thin or where they have been un-covered by erosion, as in some river valleys in the area. These situations are rather uncommon.
2. Where the bedrock is exposed in commercial rock quarries. One must definitely get permission to look for fossils here. Usually you must sign a liability release form with the company, and you may be required to wear goggles and a hard hat.
3. In the cores that are made when commercial companies are ex-ploring or drilling for oil or gas.
4. In sediments from water well diggings.
5. In postglacial Pleistocene stream, lake, basin, and bog fills. These deposits are likely to be in many poorly drained areas in the Great Lakes region, but vertebrate fossils are mainly restricted to the fills in the southern part of the region.

Where should the average weekend tripper in the Great Lakes region look for fossils? Material from water wells or oil well cores are normally not available to the average person. Also, vertebrate fossils are almost always absent from the glacially deposited sediments that cover most of the region. Generally, two situations are best. But let's point out that fossil-hunting trips can be unproductive even in these situations. The two situations are (1) rock quarries where many kinds of ancient plants, invertebrate shells, and Paleozoic fishes (scales, teeth, spines, and sometimes bones) might be found; and (2) low areas filled with peat and marl from early postglacial swamps, kettles, and shallow basins.

Rock quarries. Locations of rock quarries can be found by consulting the topographic maps that are available from the United States Geologi-cal Survey. Once the quarries are located, you can look at general maps of what types of bedrock are near the surface in the area (Ordovi-cian, Pennsylvanian, or whatever) and drive out and take a look. Some of these mines will be abandoned, and you will need to check who the present landowner is to get permission to collect in them. In other cases, the quarries will be active and you will need to get company permission to collect there.

How can we search for fossils in a quarry? In some cases fossils will be weathered out of the limestone or other sedimentary rocks and merely picked up off the surface. In other cases you may wish to closely inspect the exposed limestone walls for evidence of fossils, or even the large blocks of cut limestone that are sometimes lying around. Another technique is to split apart layers of shale that are sometimes present in quarries. Useful quarry tools are geological hammers, picks, and crowbars (fig. 35a–c) and a hand lens for tiny fossils. Lists of handy geological tools may be found in catalogs that are kept in most college or university geology department offices.

Postglacial swamps, kettles, and shallow basins. When the ice retreated in earnest about 14,000 years ago, the Great Lakes Basin had many more swamps, ponds, and lakes than it has today. With time, these features filled in with vegetation and finally disappeared. During one of the last stages of the infilling of a shallow basin or pond, an unstable mat of vegetation forms at the surface. This is the so-called quaking bog stage. Most of us in the Great Lakes region have at one time or another jumped up and down on mats of vegetation in modern quaking bogs and felt the eerie sensation of quivering earth beneath our feet. Pleistocene mats of quaking bog vegetation formed some of the peat layers that are harvested commercially today. The muck beneath these mats is usually in the form of a grayish or brownish gray fossiliferous marl.

Vertebrate bones, including those of mastodonts and mammoths, have often been found in the peat and/or the marl layers, often in a position somewhere between them. Many kinds of fossil plants are found in the peat layers, including stems, pieces of wood, seeds, cones, and pollen. The marl layers usually produce thousands of shells of snails and clams as well as large pieces of wood.

Tools for working in a fossil bog or shallow lake situation include (1) a long metal probe (fig. 35e) for poking down through the peat for large bones (a rock makes a "chink," a piece of wood makes a "thunk," and a large bone makes a sound somewhere in between); (2) a shovel (fig. 35d) and bags to carry marl and peat back for further examination; and (3) probably a pump, as these kinds of excavations often fill with water. Probes should be about 7 feet long with a handle at the top. Metal shops can make them with a minimum of direction. Something bright should be tied to the top of these slender probes, as they are easy to lose in the field.

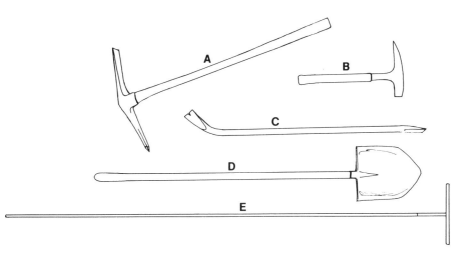

Fig. 35. Tools for collecting fossils. *A,* geological pick; *B,* geological hammer; *C,* crowbar; *D,* shovel; *E,* probe.

Collection and Preservation of Fossils

We now know that fossils in the Great Lakes region come from two main sources; exposures of bedrock in commercial rock quarries, and soft late Pleistocene sediments in low areas. Bedrock produces mainly invertebrate fossils, some plants, and a few fishes, all of Paleozoic age. The soft late Pleistocene sediments produce mainly the remains of the small plants and animals that lived in the infilling kettle or basin ponds or lakes, and occasionally the bones of large vertebrates such as mastodonts and mammoths.

Bedrock fossils. Fossils in bedrock in the Great Lakes region come mainly from limestones and shales. Sometimes these fossils merely weather out of the softer limestones and shales. In this case, you are lucky, for all the specimen usually needs is cleaning with a brush. But if the fossil is embedded in rock that is harder than the fossil, you have a long job ahead of you, as it may take hours to extract the specimen properly.

The best procedure in such cases is to try to break off a piece of the rock with the whole fossil inside, and then take the chunk to a place where the rock can be carefully chipped away from the fossil. Unfortunately, some trial-and-error work usually needs to be done by most beginning fossil collectors until they get the feel of how specific rocks react to the geological hammer. But the most important message to the novice is to *take your time!* All during the collecting procedure there is the good possibility of chipping or gouging the fossil or of breaking it into pieces.

Learning to use a geological hammer requires a certain amount of patience. One may wish to practice breaking nonfossiliferous limestones and shales into the proper sized pieces before attempting to collect the real thing. The chisel end of the hammer is the business end for worrying out chunks of rock or for splitting rocks up into proper pieces. One of the best tools to carry around is a cheap pocket knife, which is very useful in scraping away chalky limestone from fossils in quarry deposits. A crowbar is also useful for splitting shales into thin layers, in which one can often find the more delicate fossils.

Some fossil specimens are so thin and delicate that they need to be strengthened by the application of some type of cementing agent. This serves not only to strengthen the fossils but to keep them from drying out and breaking up. The cement needs to be well diluted with its own specific solvent so that it can penetrate the fossil. A common mistake is putting on such a heavy coat of cement that it does not penetrate the fossil. Some fossil cements and solvents are

Cements:	*Solvents:*
Shellac	Alcohol
Alvar	Acetone
Duco	Acetone
Polyvinyl Acetate (PVAC)	Acetone

Some precautions that go along with collecting and preserving fossils from bedrock deposits are the following.

1. Wear a hard hat when you are in a rock quarry to protect your head from falling rocks or from bumping it on rock ledges.
2. Wear goggles to protect your eyes from sharp pieces of rock, which are likely to fly up at your face when larger pieces are struck with a rock hammer.
3. Take your time!
4. Apply alvar, duco, and PVAC under a fume hood or outdoors.

When the bedrock fossil is removed, brushed, and treated with cement (if necessary), the most important part of the process is to take place. This is the labeling, cataloging, and storage phase. This will change your fossil collection from a whatnot shelf conversation piece to a scientifically valuable collection.

The label should be printed in permanent ink, fit comfortably inside the box with the fossil, and contain the following information: (1) the number you assign to the fossil, (2) the scientific name of the fossil, (3) the exact location, (4) the name of the geological formation, (5) the age and type of rock (e.g., late Ordovician limestone), and (6) the name of the collector.

The catalog should be made of fine quality paper. There the fossils should be recorded in the order of the numbers that you give them and with the inclusion of all of the data that is recorded on the label. Many collectors keep duplicate copies of catalogs in case of fire or other loss.

Fossils should be stored in well-made boxes. A fossil collection looks much nicer when the boxes are of a uniform type. Such boxes may be purchased from some pharmaceutical companies. A label should be in the box with the fossil. If possible, the fossil should have the number written directly on it in India ink; although this is impossible in the case of very small fossils or those with very shiny shells. The box should have the scientific name and the number of the fossil recorded on the outside. The fossil collection should be stored in a moderately, but not excessively, dry area, on shelves in study cabinets. The specimens may be arranged in major taxonomic groups, and then alphabetically by generic name.

Late Pleistocene fossils. The most important fossils in the Great Lakes region from many standpoints are from postglacial late Pleistocene times. The last glacier in the region left thousands of depressions, including kettles and other glacially derived basins holding leftover glacial meltwater. These developed into aquatic biotic communities and then finally filled in with inorganic and organic sediments. Each of these depressions has left a distinct sedimentary record behind that traces its biological development and the process of filling in as a series of *ecostratigraphic zones.*

These zones trace the ecological events that reflect the various successional stages in the filling of a kettle hole, pond, or shallow basin. These Great Lakes Basin features have not usually been altered by changes in drainage patterns that often make other fossil sites difficult to interpret and thus are natural laboratories for paleoecological studies.

It is important to realize that these structures contain massive accumulations of a variety of fossils that allow us to interpret the entire ecological event. Therefore, ideally, all of the ecostratigraphic zones should be carefully excavated. These zones are as follows (bottom to top).

Zone 1. This bottom zone consists of *clastic glacially derived sediments.* The common elements are sands and gravels, along with boulders and cobbles in some situations. This zone does not contain fossils and is as much as 125 feet thick in some places.

Zone 2. This zone is usually composed of relatively pure *bluish gray clay,* normally about 2 to 3 feet thick. The clay was produced chemically and physically from the parent glacial material in zone 1 above. Zone 2 represents a very early and essentially biotically sterile time in the filling in of the depression and also does not contain fossils.

Zone 3. Zone 3 is very important and usually very fossiliferous. It represents the open-water, well-aerated, biologically very diverse phase of the ecological succession of the basin. This zone is normally composed of a grayish to grayish brown colloidal (sticky) *shelly marl* about 2 to 5 feet thick. This formerly intensely biotic zone usually contains a tremendous load of fossils produced as the detrital and skeletal remains of the plants and animals that accumulated in shallow, oxygen-rich situations. A square yard of this material may contain many hundreds of freshwater shells. Fossils commonly found in zone 3 include pollen grains and spores, plant fibers, cones, stems and twigs, nuts, seeds, leaves, roots, logs, branches, bark, beaver-chewed wood, ostracods, clams, snails, beetles, and sometimes bones from large mammals.

Zone 4. This zone is composed of *dark organic peat* or *muck.* It is also an intensively biotic zone and represents the successional stage of the pond or shallow lake where mats of aquatic vegetation form over the surface of the feature. This zone may occur in the form of commercial grade peat and yields much of the commercial peat sold in the Great Lakes region and elsewhere. Zone 4 ranges from about 2 to 8 feet in thickness. Pleistocene fossils from zone 4 include pollen and spores, plant fibers, cones, stems, twigs, nuts, seeds, branches, many fewer clams and snails than in zone 3, beetles, and sometimes bones of large mammals.

Zone 5. This zone is composed of recently derived humus and topsoil, and it usually has been disturbed by humans. The dominant modern vegetation that normally grows in this zone is a willow-sedge community.

Infilled basins abound in the Great Lakes region. Some represent Ice Age deposits, while others represent more recent accumulations. The ages of these sites may be determined by either relative or absolute dating or both. The presence of an extinct Pleistocene vertebrate in a site such as a mastodont or a mammoth will confirm its Pleistocene age. Then a carbon 14 date on the bones will give it a precise date within the Pleistocene. But even if extinct Pleistocene vertebrates are not present at such sites, absolute dates may be obtained on many other components within the site, such as wood, peat, or shells. Such carbon 14 dates usually cost a few hundred dollars.

A very rewarding exercise for a group of interested people is to locate and excavate an infilled lake or bog site. Such sites are located by looking in low areas for modern willow-sedge communities; then get permission from the land owner to dig a hole there. Of course the owner should be assured that the hole will be filled up when the project is finished.

When such a site is located, a straight-sided hole about a yard wide should be dug down to the sand and gravel layer (zone 1). Then each upward layer (blue clay–marl–muck–topsoil) should be measured from the bottom to the top. Next the group should take samples of each layer; small samples of the unfossiliferous sand and clay and larger samples of the marl and peat to be picked through for fossils. There should be hundreds of small fossils in each square yard of marl or muck.

All of the various fossils in the marl should be kept separate from those of the muck or peat. Then the two layers can be compared later for content. It is likely that snails and clams will be very abundant in the marl but rare in the muck or peat. This is because the marl layer formed when the pond was open and well aerated, and the peat formed when the pond was closed over by a mat of unstable vegetation and the water in the pond had less oxygen in it.

It is best to plan such an exercise for the driest part of the summer. During wet times such holes tend to rapidly fill with water, and they need to be constantly bailed or pumped out. If the group can find a sponsor with a little money (or if it is a rock club with its own funds) it may choose to have objects carbon 14 dated. It is very exciting to await the results of such a test in the hope that the group has found a new Pleistocene site! But even if the date turns out to be only a few thousand years old, it is still a fine experience.

If large vertebrate bones are found during such an exercise, it's best to take them to a museum, or a geology or zoology department in the area for identification. Mastodont and mammoth teeth are very characteristic, and after reading this book, each person should be able to identify such finds. But other bones are more difficult to identify and need expert attention.

Fossils from late Pleistocene sites also need proper preparation, labeling, and storage. All of the fossils from marl, muck, and peat sites will be wet and soggy when they are collected and need to be dried out. Lamps with 75 or 100 watt bulbs positioned over the drying fossils will speed up the process.

Fossil wood, stems, roots, nuts, and the like, as well as vertebrate bones, will need to be strengthened by one of the cements mentioned previously in the discussion of bedrock fossils. Polyvinyl acetate (PVAC) is a good cement, but remember to dilute it well with acetone and to do the work under a fume hood or outdoors. Clam and snail shells normally do not need to be treated with cement, but they should be brushed off with small paintbrushes. Each type of fossil (e.g., snails, clams, seeds, wood, cones, bones, etc.) should be stored in a separate box. The label placed in each box with the fossils should give the date of collection, the exact locality, the proper ecostratigraphic zone (e.g., marl, peat, muck), and the name of the collector.

It is strongly advised that private collectors should not keep vertebrate bones and teeth. Teeth and tusks of mastodonts and mammoths, for instance, tend to crumble and/or flake apart and need special attention; even bones may disintegrate unless they are given proper care.

Chapter 7
Fossils of Simple Organisms and Plants

We've reviewed some basic geological concepts and terms, introduced the geology of the region, reviewed the major subgroups of the five biological kingdoms, and discussed general topics about fossils and their study. We are now ready to look specifically at fossils of some of the ancient life-forms that inhabited the region. We begin with a consideration of simple organisms (bacteria, protists, and fungi) and plants.

Bacteria

Bacteria are the simplest living things. They are called *prokaryotes* because they lack nuclei in their cells and their genetic material is merely concentrated in a circular mass. It is not surprising then that bacteria have provided evidence of the most ancient life on earth.

Cyanobacteria

Early bacteria are of the type called *cyanobacteria* and were once called blue-green algae. Cyanobacteria are photosynthetic, like plants, and can manufacture their own food in the presence of sunlight. Three and one-half billion years ago the sun blazed down on what is now a desert region in northwestern Australia and provided the energy for colonies of cyanobacteria to prosper and form *microbial mats,* from which structures called *stromatolites* (see fig. 1a) are derived. We have no other evidence of fossil life at this extraordinarily early time, but one must suppose that it consisted mainly of *nonnucleated* (prokaryotic) cells oozing along in the so-called primordial soup.

Perhaps now is the time to dwell on the enormity of this passed time. A simple but striking exhibit in the Natural History Museum in London instructs the visitor to push a button to see a hundred tiny points of light, which fill a square about the size of a postage stamp. The next button shows 1,000 points of light which fill a space less than one foot square. The next button shows 1 million points of light, and the whole room is gloriously illuminated. As a matter of comparison, 3.5 billion years equals 3,500 large rooms, each filled to capacity by 1 million tiny points of light! Cyanobacteria live today and still produce stromatolites in tropical seas! Thus, we know how the ancient stromatolites formed and can guess about the environment in which these ancient fossils lived.

Modern cyanobacteria that live in shallow inlets off the coast of western Australia produce dense microbial mats that become stromatolites. Here the summer temperatures are fiercely hot, and the salinity of the water is about twice that in regular seawater. Could this harsh environment reflect what it might have been like 3.5 billion years ago?

Microbial mats produced by the cyanobacteria form stromatolites as follows: Cyanobacteria, like all bacteria, exude a slimy substance, and they are able to glide or "ooze" slowly about. When the Australian tide comes in, particles of sediments adhere to the slime and cover the bacteria. Since the bacteria need the sunlight for their life processes, they ooze through the sediment back into the light, thus leaving the sediment underneath them. As the process repeats itself, identifiable layers of sediments are built up into moundlike structures under the mats of slimy bacteria.

In the Great Lakes Basin, structures identified as stromatolites have been found in Precambrian rocks in the Upper Peninsula of Michigan. These structures are sometimes massive, and they occur in the form of pillarlike, domelike, or moundlike (see fig. 1a) fossils. They are often seen as concentric rings exposed on the surface of limestones, dolomites, or ancient marls. These fossils formed in rocks that date back to the early Huronian portion of the Middle Precambrian from rocks that are 2 billion years old. Another area in the Great Lakes region that has produced stromatolites is the Gunflint Chert of the Lake Superior area of both Ontario and Minnesota. We will talk more about this important formation when we discuss other Precambrian bacteria.

Finally, carbonaceous material from Michigamme in the south central part of the Upper Peninsula of Michigan has produced trace fossils that occur in the form of circular or egg-shaped bodies of graphite. These have been interpreted as remains of primitive floating cyanobacteria that grew in nodular colonies. In fact, these objects have been said to compare well with such colonies of the living blue-green alga *Nostoc.* The age of the Michigamme rocks is estimated to be about 1.7 billion years.

Rod-shaped and Spherical Bacteria

Stromatolites are considered *trace fossils* because they are the by-products of the life processes of bacterial cells. Nevertheless, actual cells of bacteria have been found in the Great Lakes region in Precambrian rocks about 2 billion years old. But first, a little about the biology of bacteria. Bacteria do not reproduce sexually; lasting changes in them can only occur through *mutational* changes in the genetic material. Since mutations are usually harmful to organisms, bacteria evolved very slowly.

Natural checks on ancient populations of bacteria would have been from storms, heating, freezing, starvation (from lack of essential bacterial nutrients), desiccation in periods of drought, and from viral infections. Thus, it has been suggested that there must have been very rapid fluctuations in ancient bacterial populations because of these various factors.

It has been pointed out in the stromatolite section that all bacteria extrude a protective slimy substance. This slime appears to be one of the reasons that bacteria have lasted for so many billions of years. The oozing movements that bacteria are capable of making have fascinated biologists for years, and it has been shown that slime is essential to this mobility. In addition, this substance also protects bacteria from harmful solar radiation, and it also allows them to stick to things like rocks and animal teeth (including those of humans) where they can find essential nutrients.

Rod-shaped and spherical bacterial cells (see fig. 15c–d) are first known from the famous Gunflint Chert that occurs north of Lake Superior in the Ontario and Minnesota parts of the Great Lakes region. These rocks have been dated at about 2 billion years old. Chert is formed of tiny particles of *silica*. In Precambrian times chert formed in silica-rich waters that occurred near active volcanos. Chert formation can occur especially rapidly when hot water circulates through the cracks of recently hardened volcanic rocks. Chert is a very common Precambrian rock, because at that time organisms had not yet evolved skeletons of silica. Today chert does not form in many places because of the demands for silica as skeletal material from many kinds of organisms such as sponges and radiolarians. One of the reasons that the Gunflint Chert preserved organisms consisting of cells without hard parts is that chert is watertight; as a result the fossils did not rot and dissolve.

It is easy to collect stromatolites with a rock hammer, but looking for cells in chert is a time-consuming and often frustrating process. First, the chert must be cut into ultrathin sections. Then these sections must typically be examined for hours at a time before the rare fossil cells are found. Because bloblike, nonfossil artifacts may superficially look like cells, the microbial fossil hunter must be highly trained in the field.

Other Evidence of Early Cells

Other evidence of Precambrian life in the Great Lakes region occurs mainly in the Northern Peninsula of Michigan. Carbonaceous materials said to be derived from "simple plant cells" (probably bacteria) have been found in the 1.7-billion-year-old Michigamme rocks of the south central part of the Upper Peninsula. Some of this material is in the form of anthracitic coal. Important organic remains have been described from the Nonesuch Shale in the Ontanagon area of Michigan's Upper Peninsula. This formation is from the late part of the Precambrian and is considered to be about 1 billion years old.

Crude-oil residues from the Nonesuch indicate quite a variety of complex organic compounds that appear to be remnants of structures of microbial organisms. Carbonaceous organic material is also common throughout the copper-bearing zone. Some of the residues from the Nonesuch crude oil are similar to some of the complex organic components of *chlorophyll*. Thus it has been suggested that chlorophyll may have been present and important in the photosynthetic activities of cells at least 1 billion years ago. It has also been suggested that other tiny shreds of tissue and pieces of cell walls in the Nonesuch Shale might be from algae or fungi, but the authors of these studies are very cautious about their suggestions because of the fragmentary nature of the material.

Protists

Foraminifera, radiolarians, and diatoms (see fig. 16) are tiny protists that must be studied on a microscope slide. Fossils of these organisms are abundant in some regions, but they are not prominent in the Great Lakes Basin. A few foraminifera and radiolarians have been identified from Great Lakes Paleozoic rocks, but these have not been the subject of significant studies. It takes very specialized equipment and techniques to be able to extract, mount, and study these organisms. Common diatoms such as *Fragillaria* have been identified from late Pleistocene and post-Pleistocene bog deposits in the Great Lakes Basin.

Algae

Sedimentary rocks of early and middle Paleozoic age in the Michigan Basin may have impressions, ridges, and other distinctive marks that are called *fucoids*. Some fucoids may actually have been formed by the burrows, tracks, and trails left in soft muds by marine worms or other animals. But in other cases fucoids appear to have rootlike or stemlike structures on them. These types of fucoids have been interpreted as algal seaweeds, and it has been suggested that many of them were formed by brown algae (see fig. 17a).

Some paleontologists have suggested that some fucoids represent mats of sargassumlike vegetation that floated on the surface of Paleozoic seas. Others have suggested that other forms of fucoids represent brown algal seaweeds that were attached to the seafloor like modern kelp and that blanketing sediments compressed them into their present shapes.

If these interpretations are true, one might picture the early and middle Paleozoic seas of the Michigan Basin as having vast amounts of sargassum-like algae floating on the surface with forests of kelp attached to the bottom. These plants would have been very dominant forces in the ecology of those ancient seas. In the Great Lakes Basin fucoids are mainly found in sedimentary layers of shale and limestone that have been split apart along their bedding planes.

Fungi

The 2-billion-year-old Gunflint Chert north of Lake Superior in Ontario and Minnesota in the Great Lakes region has produced evidence of the *mycelia* of fungi. These tiny filaments occur in minutely prepared thin sections of chert. These finds are very important from an evolutionary standpoint because they represent the earliest discovery of multicellular forms of life.

Mycelia are the structures that determine the various body forms of fungi. A mycelium is composed of a meshwork of tiny tubules called *hyphae* (see fig. 18a). Fungi are unable to manufacture their own food like true plants; instead they decompose other organisms or substances by spreading their hyphae over, around, or inside of the materials or bodies upon which they feed.

It is interesting to speculate upon food chains in the Precambrian. They would be very short. Photosynthetic cyanobacteria (and perhaps other cells utilizing chlorophyll in the late Precambrian) would be the producers for the system. But the rodlike and spherical bacteria and fungal plants would have to serve the role of both consumers and reducers, for there is little or no fossil evidence of true predators during these times. Bacteria and fungi feed on other things by secreting their digestive chemicals (*enzymes*) outside of their own bodies to digest their food. Then they absorb the digested material into their bodies for maintenance and growth. In simple terms, digestion occurs externally. Predators, on the other hand, engulf or swallow their prey and digestive enzymes are secreted inside themselves, so that digestion occurs internally.

Plants

True plants differ from fungi in that they can manufacture their own food by the process of photosynthesis, where energy from the sun is captured by chlorophyll in chloroplasts in the plant cells (see fig. 14b) that transforms carbon dioxide and water into sugars for the plants. Plants that occur as fossils in the Great Lakes Basin include

Bryophytes
Lycopods
Sphenopsids
Ferns
Gymnosperms (seed ferns, cordaitalians, cycads, conifers)
Angiosperms (seed plants)

Bryophytes

Bryophytes (liverworts and mosses, see fig. 19a–b), are well represented by spores and plant parts from late Pleistocene and post-Pleistocene bog deposits in much of the Great Lakes region. *Sphagnum mosses* are particularly abundant in so-called *bryophyte beds,* where sphagnum moss species form significant mats in marls that often contain many other plant fossils and sometimes even the scats of rodents. These bryophyte beds are a part of the zone 3 assemblage of plants and animals discussed in chapter 4. Today, sphagnum mosses form a very abundant part of some of the last successional stages in the filling-in process of small ponds and lakes in the region and are a significant part of the unstable mats of vegetation that are called quaking bogs.

A typical bryophyte bed dated at about 12,500 years ago by the carbon 14 method was studied near Cheyboygan in the upper part of the Lower Peninsula of Michigan. The whole assemblage of fossil plant spores, seeds, leaves, and stems yielded species that suggested an open shrub vegetation very similar to what one would find in the tundra today. Scats (fecal pellets) of northern species of voles were found within the sticky mats of sphagnum mosses. Eight species of mosses were identified as well as several unidentified species of liverworts.

Lycopods

Lycopods are called the club mosses and scale trees. The living lycopods or club mosses are small plants only a few inches high (see fig. 20a), but the fossil lycopods or scale trees formed tree-sized plants that were important members of coal-swamp forests. Two of the most important ancient lycopod or scale trees are *Sigillaria* and *Lepidodendron*

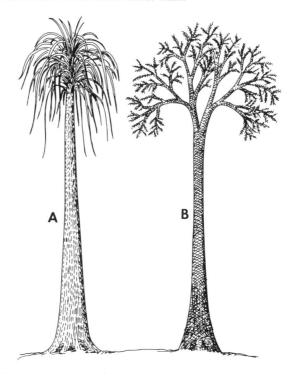

Fig. 36. Artist's reconstruction of Great Lakes Basin Pennsylvanian lycopod trees. *A, Sigillaria; B, Lepidodendron.*

(fig. 36a–b). *Sigillaria* is well known because the earliest known fossil reptiles were found in fossil *Sigillaria* stumps excavated from Pennsylvanian deposits in the Bay of Fundy in Nova Scotia. These stumps were in an upright position in the sediments where they were found, so it is not known whether the small reptiles fell into the cavities of the stumps and were trapped there, or whether they were using the stumps as sheltering places.

Lycopods have small, bladelike leaves. When the fossil tree-sized lycopods lost their leaves, leaf scars or *scales* (fig. 37) were formed. Reproduction in fossil lycopods was by tiny spores that were contained in spore cases that looked like small pods and are called *sporangia*. These cases occur on leaf stems near or on the main trunk of the plant. These case-bearing stems often grew together to form structures that looked like cones.

Both *Sigillaria* and *Lepidodendron* are found in Pennsylvanian rocks

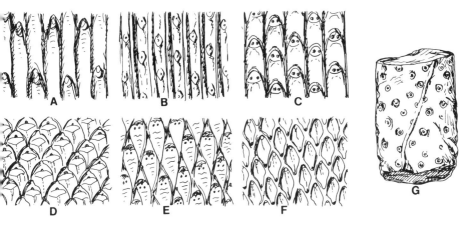

Fig. 37. Leaf scars (scales) and underground stems (stigmaria) of Great Lakes Basin Pennsylvanian lycopods. *A–C*, leaf scars of three forms of *Sigillaria*. *D–F*, leaf scars of three forms of *Lepidodendron*. *G*, underground stem (stigmarium) of *Lepidodendron*.

in the Michigan Basin, and spores of the latter genus are common in Mississippian rocks of the basin. Fine examples of both of these genera have been found in quarries in the southern peninsula of Michigan near Lansing. The leaf scars or scales of *Sigillaria* are lined up vertically and go straight up the trunk (fig. 37a–c). The leaf scars of *Lepidodendron*, on the other hand, are arranged in spiral rows around the trunk (fig. 37d–f).

Small lycopod fossils are also found in Pennsylvanian rock formations in the Michigan Basin. An enjoyable thing to do, if you are captivated by fossils, is to find some of the so-called living fossils to get an idea of what some of the ancient plants looked like. *Selaginella* and *Lycopodium* (see fig. 20a) are small plants called club mosses or ground pines that grow in sandy forests in the Great Lakes region today whose stems and leaves look remarkably like the Pennsylvanian *Bothrodendron*.

Although the stems of *Sigillaria* and *Lepidodendron* are very distinct, the rootlike structures, or *root organs,* of the two genera cannot be told apart and are collectively called *stigmaria* (fig. 37g). Actually stigmaria are underground stems that have taken on the function of roots. Stigmaria are often found in clays under coal beds, so that it has been suggested that the trunks and leaves of these "roots" contributed to the formation of the coal beds above them.

We know that some of these scale trees reached heights of over 110 feet in the Pennsylvanian and had a diameter of about 20 inches, so they must have played one of the dominant roles in the ecology of the coal-swamp forests of the Pennsylvanian. We have mentioned that the club moss or ground pine *Lycopodium* resembles some of the smaller Pennsylvanian lycopods. *Lycopodium* occurs in the form of fossil spores in late Pleistocene and post-Pleistocene bog deposits in the Great Lakes Basin.

Sphenopsids

The sphenopsids are called horsetails or scouring rushes. Like the lycopods, the sphenopsids were a dominant group of plants in the coal-swamp forests of the Pennsylvanian period; some were treelike forms growing over 50 feet high, with a diameter of about two feet. The sphenopsids are also similar to the lycopods in that they have a small modern representative, the horsetail *Equisetum* (see fig. 20b) that is an abundant, simple plant of sandy areas in the Great Lakes region.

We have already discussed pulling apart and putting back together the jointed stems of modern horsetails. The ancient sphenopsids were also jointed (fig. 38a–c), and these joints occurred both in the trunks and in the stems. Sphenopsid trees (fig. 38a) differed from true trees in that their trunks and stems were hollow and had very thin walls. These ancient hollow stems and trunks often filled with mud and sand that formed natural casts that are rather common fossils in some parts of the Great Lakes region.

The jointed sections of sphenopsid trees have characteristic vertical striations or ridges alternating with grooves. The genus *Calamites* (fig. 38a–b) is an important treelike sphenopsid of the Great Lakes Basin, with several species that are defined on the basis of differing structures in the trunks and stems. Figure 38c represents an underground stem of *Calamites* found in Pennsylvanian rocks near Lansing, Michigan.

The classification of fossil sphenopsids has been difficult because it has been difficult to find associated trunks, stems, leaves, and reproductive bodies. For example, the genus *Calamites* was originally named on the basis of a fossil trunk. But leaves and twigs were given two additional generic names, *Asterophyllites* and *Annularia,* and a reproductive body was given a third generic name, *Macrostachya.* Actually, all of these leaves, twigs, and reproductive bodies belong to *Calamites.*

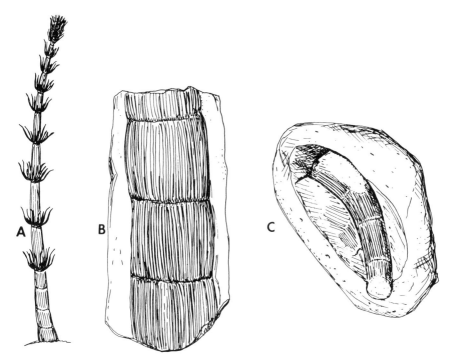

Fig. 38. Great Lakes Basin Pennsylvanian sphenopsids. *A,* artist's reconstruction of *Calamites,* a sphenopsid tree; *B, Calamites* stem in matrix; *C, Calamites* underground stem in matrix.

Sphenopsids reproduce by means of tiny spores that are borne on some-what conelike bodies called *sporangia* that occur on the ends of the stems and their branches.

Some important Great Lakes sphenopsids include the several species of the treelike *Calamites* as well as the various parts of *Calamites* named *Asterophyllites, Annularia,* and *Macrostachya,* and the smaller shrubby genus *Sphenophyllum. Calamites* has been recorded from as early as the Mississippian in the Michigan Basin of the Great Lakes region, but sphenopsids do not really become abundant until the Pennsylvanian. The clay quarries near Lansing in the Lower Peninsula have most consistently produced sphenopsid fossils in the Michigan Basin. Spores of modern horsetails, *Equisetum,* have been found in late Pleistocene and post-Pleistocene bog sites in the Great Lakes region.

Ferns

True ferns are very common in the modern flora of the Great Lakes region, but they are not at all common in the ancient flora of the area. One fossil found in Pennsylvanian rocks in the Michigan Basin is troublesome. *Rhacopteris* has fernlike parts, but it is not known if it had reproductive spores on the underside of its leaves or if it had large reproductive bodies on the ends of its leaves like the *seed ferns* that follow. Nevertheless, ferns have been positively identified on the basis of spores found during palynological studies of the Jurassic red beds of the Michigan Basin. These red beds are buried beneath the surface and were discovered within the cores of well-drilling samples in southern Michigan. Spores of modern kinds of ferns are common in late Pleistocene and post-Pleistocene bog deposits in the Great Lakes region.

Gymnosperms

Gymnosperms are plants that have true seeds rather than spores, but as we have seen, they lack ovaries that protect and provide nutrients for the seeds. Ancient gymnosperms in the Great Lakes region are represented by the primitive seed ferns, *cordaitalans,* and *cycads* as well as by the more advanced conifers.

Seed Ferns

All of the seed ferns (pteridosperms) are extinct, but several of them were common in the Pennsylvanian rocks of the central part of the Michigan Basin. The seed ferns (fig. 39a–b) look very much like true ferns in that they have lacy foliage, but they differ from ferns in that their reproductive bodies are contained in structures that look like seeds at the ends of the leaves. Stems of seed ferns were woody, and the plants occurred in the form of low shrubs or trees.

Fossils may be recognized by the fact that they have compound leaves with leaflets that are arranged on both sides of a common axis (fig 39b). The leaflets have a rather thicker appearance than those of true ferns. It is not known with certainty whether the seed ferns were ancestral to the higher gymnosperms or whether they were a so-called dead-end group, not closely related to any subsequent plants. The common seed fern genus that occurs in the Pennsylvanian rocks of the

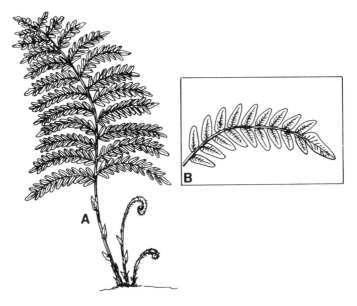

Fig. 39. Great Lakes Basin Pennsylvanian seed ferns. *A*, artist's reconstruction of a seed fern plant, *Neuropteris*; *B*, compound leaf of *Neuropteris*.

central part of the Michigan Basin is *Neuropteris*. This genus appeared in the form of several species.

Cordaitalans

This is another group of extinct primitive gymnosperms that includes treelike forms; it was one of the dominant plants of the coal-swamp forests in the Pennsylvanian (fig. 40a–b). Some scientists believe that the cordaitalans gave rise to the modern conifers, but others classify them with the conifers. At any rate, the woody stems and trunks of these extinct plants closely resemble those of living conifers. But cordaitalians had a large central pith area in their trunks that decayed rapidly after the death of the plant and often became filled with mud or sand. This material led to the formation of natural casts of the internal parts of the trunks of cordaitalans, and these fossils are common in some Great Lakes Basin Pennsylvanian deposits.

Many of these plants reached tree size, and some had large straplike leaves with parallel veins up to a yard long (fig. 40b); they are structur-

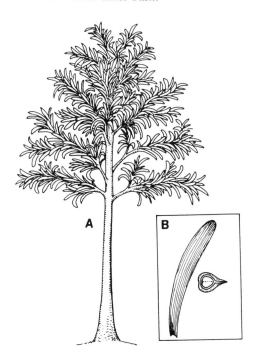

Fig. 40. *A,* artist's reconstruction of the Great Lakes Basin Pennsylvanian cordaitalian, *Cordaites; B, left,* leaf and *right,* seed of *Cordaites*

ally comparable to modern leaves of cattail plants, but the cordaitalan leaves occurred in spiral whorls on the secondary branches of the plant. Cordaitalans reproduced by means of distinctive heart-shaped seeds that often had winglike structures on them to aid in their dispersal by the wind. These seeds developed on short leafless stems among clusters of leaves. The genus that occurs in the Great Lakes region is *Cordaites,* common in the Pennsylvanian rocks of the central part of the Michigan Basin.

Cycads

Living cycads (see fig. 21a) are plants of the tropics and subtropics that look like stubby palm trees with bulbous trunks. Living cycads have huge cones. Extinct cycads were important parts of the vegetation of the Mesozoic during the heyday of the dinosaurs. The only record of cycads from the Great Lakes region is from spores that have been identified from the late Jurassic red beds of the central part of the Lower Peninsula of Michigan.

Conifers

Conifers (see fig. 21d) are very important parts of the modern vegetation of the Great Lakes region, and they become increasingly dominant as one travels northward. Conifers bear their seeds on cones and occur mainly in the form of trees and shrubs. The leaves are needlelike or scalelike. In the Great Lakes region, ancient conifers are represented by pollen from the late Jurassic red beds of the central part of the Lower Peninsula of Michigan. Late Pleistocene and post-Pleistocene conifers are represented by stems, wood, leaves, cones, and pollen.

Angiosperms

Angiosperms, including both *monocots* and *dicots* (see fig. 22a–b) are the other modern dominant group of plants in the Great Lakes region, where they occur in the form of trees, bushes, shrubs, grasses, sedges, wildflowers, and water plants. The seeds of angiosperms are protected and provided with nutrient material by an ovary that is attached to a flower. Angiosperms are first known from the Cretaceous (although ancestral forms may occur in the Triassic); but in the Great Lakes region, angiosperms are not known until they are found in late Pleistocene or post-Pleistocene deposits. In these deposits, angiosperms are known on the basis of seeds, stems, wood, leaves, and pollen.

Late Pleistocene and Post-Pleistocene Vegetation

The development of late Pleistocene and post-Pleistocene vegetation in the Great Lakes region is not only important in its own light, but also as it relates to the reinvasion of animal species into the area after the retreat of the last Pleistocene ice sheet. These vegetational events have been particularly well studied in southern Michigan, mainly on the basis of pollen. When the ice sheet retreated (see fig. 11), it left a blanket of sterile mud, sand, and gravel. In order to establish stable biological communities, plants and animals had to establish a foothold in these areas. Thus, the story of the reinvasion of formerly uninhabitable lands in the Great Lakes region is the story of the formations of stable biological communities.

Records of plant life in southern Michigan during the temporary withdrawals of the glacier about 40,000 years ago (Cherry Tree substage) in Kalkaska County and about 24,000 years ago (Plum Point substage) in Muskegon County, indicate a boreal or a subboreal climate with open forests that were dominated by spruce and pine. Tamarack and probably white cedar were prominent in the swamps of the time; with sedges, cattails, and disturbed-ground herbaceous plants found in marshy and well-drained areas.

When the ice sheet began to melt away in earnest about 14,800 years ago, the earliest records in southern Michigan (and in northern Indiana) indicate sparse but unquestionable evidence of tundra vegetation. Marshes and muskegs were characteristic of the lowlands and the wetlands. By 13,000 years ago, nearly half of the Lower Peninsula of Michigan was deglaciated. Almost all of the well-drained landscape had scattered stands of pioneer trees (juniper, aspen, ash, spruce) and sun-tolerant shrubs such as willow, silverberry, and crowberry. But it is not known for sure whether this early deglaciated landscape was essentially treeless tundra, or whether it was an open forest of spruce, tamarack, and mixed deciduous trees.

From 12,500 to about 11,800 years ago southern Michigan (and northern Indiana) had a boreal forest that was dominated by spruce trees, but with areas of open woodland or boreal parkland. In the north, boreal parkland dominated the area, and tundra vegetation occurred in the open-ground communities along the ice front and on exposed slopes and hills. Between 11,000 and 9,900 years ago there were changes in the pollen records. At about 10,600 years ago, jack pine and red pine began to replace spruce in southwestern lower Michigan, and by 10,000 years ago white pine began to occur. Early kinds of hardwood trees such as birch, blue beech, and elm became abundant during this time period.

In summary, by 10,000 years ago the forest vegetation in southern Michigan had become more diverse, with mixed forests of white and red pine, yellow and paper birch, aspen, oak, white ash, red and white elm, and blue beech. In fact, the paleoecological changes that occurred during the transitional stages between 10,600 and 9,500 years ago have helped Great Lakes region scientists to define the end of the Ice Age in the area.

By 9,900 years ago the glacial ice was gone from Michigan except for the northern edge of the Upper Peninsula. In the southern part of the state and in Indiana a mixed hardwood forest existed, dominated by birch, ash, blue beech, elm, and oak, with lesser amounts of hickory, walnut, butternut and basswood and small amounts of white pine. In central lower Michigan, however, a poorly delineated pine-spruce-hardwood forest was present, with spruce particularly abundant in the "thumb" area of Michigan. For some reason, spruce-pine forests seem to have persisted longer here than elsewhere at similar latitudes. Interestingly, the pine period ended between 9,800 and 9,000 years ago in southern Michigan and not until about 8,000 years ago in the thumb.

For years there was scientific controversy about just when the Pleistocene, or Ice Age, ended and the Holocene, or Recent, age began. But now almost everybody agrees that the Pleistocene ended about 10,000 years ago. Some scientists, however, contend that it is pointless to argue about when the Pleistocene ended and the Holocene began because we are still in the Pleistocene with another ice age coming down the road!

Here we will use the term *Holocene* to designate the time between 10,000 years ago and now. During the early to middle Holocene new plants invaded Michigan. Hemlock reached North Manitou and Beaver Islands by 7,000 years ago and Sault Ste. Marie by 6,400 years ago. These plants reached central lower Michigan around 5,800 years ago and the interior of the Upper Peninsula by 5,000 years ago, but they did not reach the interior of northwest lower Michigan until about 4,200 years ago.

American beech probably spread into Michigan from Ontario; it arrived in Lapeer County in the thumb area by about 8,000 years ago and the interior of the southern Lower Peninsula by about 7,600 to 7,100 years ago. American beech reached northern Michigan about 4,000 years ago and got to the eastern part of the Upper Peninsula between 2,900 and 2,300 years ago.

Based on the vegetational changes, a framework for temperature changes in the Holocene has been worked out for Michigan and the surrounding regions. There was a long-term increase in temperature from 9,000 years ago until at least 2,500 years ago. But cyclic changes in the vegetation, which consisted of dry oak forests being replaced by moister forests and vice versa, occurred in southern Michigan during this time. Basing their judgment on both plant and animal evidence, most scientists recognize that a *hypsithermal* or "warmest Holocene period" occurred about 5,500 years ago.

Between about 3,400 and 3,000 years ago, a major vegetational change occurred in the Upper Peninsula of Michigan, when northern hardwood forests expanded, as birch, hemlock, and maple mixed with white pine. Evidence indicates that several plant pathogens were active agents of destruction of certain elements of the forests even before the invasion of America by Europeans. In fact, indications are that a pathogen killed off hemlock (*Tsuga canadensis*) in North America about 4,500 years ago and that it did not become reestablished until about 2,500 years ago in northern Michigan according to fossil evidence.

The climate became moister and cooler again from about 3,000 to 1,500 years ago, and this produced changes in the vegetation. In southern Michigan beech-maple forests expanded, while oak-hickory and prairie-oak grassland retreated. Moreover, white pine expanded southward in central Michigan. Several climatic fluctuations occurred between 1,500 years ago and the present as warm and cool periods alternated. When European settlers came, some dramatic changes took place, as revealed by the pollen record. Forest tree pollen decreased, and "weed pollen," especially ragweed, increased.

In summary, late Pleistocene vegetation began to develop in the Great Lakes region about 15,000 years ago in areas formerly denuded of life when the last ice sheet began to retreat for the final time. By 13,000 years ago about half of Michigan was deglaciated, and tundra vegetation occurred in southern Michigan. From about 12,500 to 11,800 years ago boreal forest had established itself in southern Michigan and northern Indiana. By about 10,000 years ago the ice was gone from Michigan, except for some in the northern part of the Upper Peninsula, and hardwood forests reached southern Michigan. The period from 10,000 years ago to present saw fluctuations between beech-maple and oak-dominated communities, with a warm spell, or hypsithermal, about 5,500 years ago.

Chapter 8
Fossil Invertebrates

Invertebrate animal phyla that have hard parts and thus have a good fossil record in the Great Lakes region include

Poriferans (sponges)
Cnidarians (including corals)
Bryozoans
Brachiopods
Mollusks
Arthropods (including trilobites)
Echinoderms
Hemichordates (including graptolites)

Sponges

Fossil sponges are rare in the Great Lakes region and mainly consist of bits and pieces of sponge spicules (see fig. 23b).

Cnidarians

Class Hydrozoa
Class Anthozoa

Cnidarians are abundantly represented in the Great Lakes region by extinct stromatoporoids of the class *Hydrozoa* and by extinct fossil corals of the class *Anthozoa*. Hydrozoans have two stages, a non-free-swimming stage called a *polyp* (see fig. 23c) and a swimming jellyfish or *medusa* stage (see fig. 23d). The living hydrozoans do not have hard parts, but the fossil stromatoporoids (which some workers think might not be cnidarians at all) do secrete hard parts. Anthozoans are characterized by having the polyp form dominant and having this polyp secrete a limy exoskeleton.

Stromatoporoids (fig. 41a) are extinct colonial organisms that secreted limy exoskeletons, which in turn contributed greatly to fossil reef formation in the Great Lakes region. They are classified here as hydrozoan cnidarians, but they have been classified as sponges from time to time and even as algae! The problem is that the soft-bodied parts of the colony are unknown, and there are no real modern counterparts of stromatoporoid colonies.

The living, breathing part of any coral is a tiny jellylike animal called a polyp. Polyps are able to form a calcium carbonate exoskeleton for themselves called a *corallum* that contributes to the formation of the definitive coral structure. The *solitary* corals or *horn* corals (fig. 41b) consist of a single individual polyp that builds a horn-shaped structure. The *reef-building* (*tabulate*) corals (fig. 41c–f) build a structure composed of many individuals in which the coralla are joined together or fused in various ways to form a massive structure. Colonial reef-building corals were very important in the Devonian and the Silurian in the Great Lakes Basin, where they built up extensive limestone reef deposits in several areas. These reefs were also composed of other animals, such as stromatoporoids, bryozoans, and brachiopods.

Some solitary or horn corals of the Great Lakes Basin consist of the middle Silurian *Dinophyllum,* the middle Devonian *Acrophyllum* (fig. 41b), and the early Pennsylvanian *Lophophyllum*. Some colonial or reef-building corals of the Great Lakes Basin consist of the middle Silurian *Halysites, Catenipora,* and *Syringopora* (fig. 41f), and the middle Devonian *Cylindrophyllum, Favosites* (fig. 41c and e), *Striatopora,* and *Hexagonaria* (fig. 41d), the Petoskey stone of Michigan. So you see, the Petoskey stone, which is the designated state stone of Michigan, is not a stone at all, but a fragment of a coral colony formed by the adherent exoskeletons of tiny animals!

The middle Silurian reefs of the Niagaran series of rocks in Ontario, Canada, are world famous. In fact, they have provided the standard for the study of middle Silurian reefs for the entire Great Lakes region.

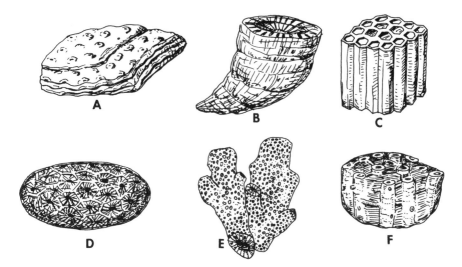

Fig. 41. Great Lakes Basin Devonian stromatoporoids and corals. *A*, typical stroma-toporoid. *B, Acrophyllum,* a horn coral. *C–F,* reef-building (tabulate) corals. *C* and *E*, two forms of *Favocites. D, Hexagonaria,* the Michigan "Petoskey stone." *F, Syr-ingopora.*

Reefs are important in that they indicate the overwhelming biological contribution to the formation of limestone in the world, and in that subsurface reefs often contain oil and gas. Fossil reefs in the Great Lakes region are common in the middle Silurian deposits of the area, but they also occur to a lesser extent in the early Silurian and in the middle Devonian.

A modern reef is formed by lime-secreting corals and their symbiotic algal partners along with other marine plants and animals that play somewhat smaller parts in reef construction. The massive accumulations of fossils in the Niagaran reefs show that ancient reefs formed in essentially the same way as do the modern ones. Since the coral animals are dependent upon algae that need sufficient light for photosynthesis, modern reefs are most common in clear, rather shallow water, where the sun's rays can penetrate effectively. Anyone fortunate enough to see the beautiful coral reefs that live off the Florida Keys can attest to how clear and clean the water is.

Modern reef-building is further constrained by the fact that the coral polyps can grow effectively only in water that freely circulates, is well oxygenated, and has abundant nutrients. Finally, modern reefs are only abundant in water with a temperature range from about 75 to 90 degrees F. Ancient Silurian reefs were mainly built up by organisms that had essentially the same requirements of clear, shallow, well-oxygenated, equably warm water, with plenty of available nutrients.

Silurian reefs were hard formations that pushed up from the ocean floor, as do modern reefs. The organisms that formed the framework of the Silurian reefs were stromatoporoids, extinct corals, and algae; all of which secrete exoskeletons of calcium carbonate. *Favosites* and *Syringopora* (fig. 41c, e, and f) were especially important reef-building corals in the Great Lakes region. It is important to note that the framework provided by the reef builders becomes filled in by the skeletons of other organisms and that this tends to bind the whole mass together.

Bryozoans

Compared to some of the larger corals, bryozoans don't look like much. Actually, the soft little bryozoan animal is more highly evolved in many ways than the coral polyp. The bryozoan animal (fig. 42a) lives in an exoskeleton that it secretes called a *zooecium*. A zooecium looks like a tiny tube or cup and is usually composed of calcium carbonate, but some bryozoans secrete a chitinous zooecium. The bryozoan animal has both a mouth and an anus (an anus is lacking in coral animals), and it has a ciliated structure called a *lophophore* that allows it to gather food particles. Food passes from the lophophore into the stomach and intestine, where it is digested; then the undigested material passes out the anus. A coelom, or lined body cavity, as well as reproductive organs of both sexes, is present in the bryozoan animal.

Bryozoan zooecia are usually solidly packed together to form colonies of a wide variety of shapes, including clublike branching forms, netlike forms, mosslike forms, or odd-looking lacy forms. Bryozoans mainly are marine, but some freshwater species exist, some of which make pests of themselves by clogging up water pipes in buildings. Bryozoan colonies have little holes that represent the openings where the little animals stick their lophophores out to gather food. Bryozoans can be distinguished from corals if one looks at the bryozoan skeleton in cross section and notes that the separate zooecia do not have the tabular or septal parts found in corals.

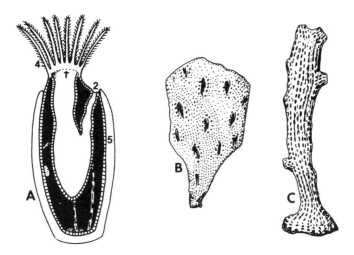

Fig. 42. Bryozoans. *A*, diagrammatic bryozoan animal indicating the mouth (1), anus (2), coelom (black area), and lophophore (4). The animal lives in an exoskeleton that it secretes, called a zooecium (5). Great Lakes Basin Devonian bryozoan colonies: *B, Ceramella; C, Euspilopora.*

Bryozoans often encrust the skeletons of other organisms such as coral heads, brachiopod shells, or even the carapaces of slow-moving crabs. Although small, they are very important contributors to coral reefs. Bryozoans are most common in the Great Lakes Basin in Devonian deposits. Some Great Lakes Devonian bryozoan genera are *Fenestella, Sulcoretopora, Ceramella* (fig. 42b), *Euspilopora* (fig. 42c), *Streblotrypa,* and *Acanthoclema.* Freshwater bryozoans are occasionally found in late Pleistocene or Holocene lake or bog deposits.

Brachiopods

Brachiopods are marine shellfish that occur as individuals rather than as colonies. The soft parts of brachiopods (fig. 43a) are somewhat more complicated than those of bryozoans and much more complicated than those of corals. A calcareous (sometimes chitinous) shell composed of two parts or *valves* is secreted by the brachiopod animal. Brachiopods are bilaterally symmetrical, with the plane of symmetry passing through the shell rather than between the two valves of the shell.

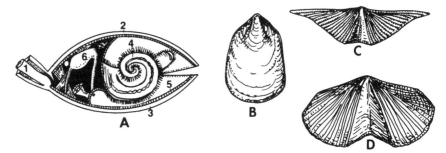

Fig. 43. Brachiopods. *A*, diagrammatic view of a brachiopod showing the pedicle (1), brachial valve (2), pedicle valve (3), lophophore (4), mantle (5), and stomach (6). *B*, the Great Lakes Basin Ordovician *Lingula*. *C*, the Great Lakes Basin Devonian *Mucrospirifer*. *D*, the Great Lakes Basin Devonian *Paraspirifer*.

A complex system of muscles opens and closes along the *hinge line*. The body of the brachiopod animal is enclosed by a soft tissue called the *mantle*. The animal has a coiled, ciliated structure called the *lophophore* that causes water to circulate into the mantle cavity, bringing with it nutrients and oxygen for respiration. Brachiopods are held to the bottom or other firm objects on the seafloor by a stalk called the *pedicle* which usually comes from one valve or the other (fig. 43a). The valve that bears the pedicle is called the *pedicle* valve; the other valve is called the *brachial* valve because it has structures that support the lophophore. In some brachiopods, however, the pedicle arises from both valves at the hinge line.

The brachiopod animal has a mouth, a stomach, and an intestine, but it lacks an anus. Undigested material is channeled back out the mouth. Brachiopods are unaware of this unpleasant situation, however, as they have no brain. Some brachiopods valves link together by means of toothlike structures that occur along the hinge line. These kinds are called *articulate* brachiopods. Other kinds of brachiopods lack these toothlike structures and are thus called *inarticulate* brachiopods. Brachiopods may be distinguished from mollusks with two valves (bivalved mollusks) on the basis that each of the two valves that make up the brachiopod is shaped differently, but the two valves that make up the mollusks are mirror images of one another.

The modern brachiopod genus *Lingula* is famous as a living fossil, as it goes back to the early Paleozoic. Nevertheless, modern brachiopods are not nearly as common as they once were in the middle and late Paleozoic, when the group reached its greatest diversity. Brachiopods are such strictly marine animals that they have been extensively used as indicators of the marine origin of the sedimentary rocks in which they occur. Moreover, they were so abundant in some situations that they probably contributed significantly to limestone formation in these areas.

Brachiopods are rather abundant fossils in some parts of the Great Lakes region and are rather easily collected in certain rock quarries. Some common brachiopod genera in the Great Lakes region include the middle Ordovician *Lingula* (fig. 43b), the late Ordovician *Dalmanella*, the middle Silurian *Pentameroides* and *Leptatrypa*, the middle Devonian *Mucrospirifer* (fig. 43c) and *Paraspirifer* (fig. 43d), and the early Pennsylvanian *Juresania*.

Mollusks

Mollusks are exceedingly important fossils in the Great Lakes Basin. They are not only important in the Paleozoic seas, but they occur by the millions in late Pleistocene and post-Pleistocene bog deposits. Mollusks have a short, unsegmented body with both a mouth and an anus (see fig. 25a). The upper part of the body is soft and lies inside an envelope called the mantle. A muscular foot occurs on the lower part of the body. Each of the four classes that we shall discuss has variations on this basic structural plan. The shell of mollusks is secreted by the edge of the mantle and is composed of calcium carbonate and chitin. Often, a shell is not present.

Four classes of mollusks occur as fossils in the Great Lakes region.

Class Amphineura
Class Gastropoda
Class Pelecypoda
Class Cephalopoda

The classes of mollusks will be discussed separately because each one of them is very distinct.

Amphineurans

Amphineurans are easily identified in that their shell consists of eight overlapping plates (fig. 44a), which may be composed of chitin or calcium carbonate. The body has a large foot, but the head lacks eyes and antennae. Food is scraped off the surface of the hard bottom or other structures by a *radula* that is armed by minute teeth. These animals crawl along the seafloor on their foot and have been around since the Cambrian. Modern amphineurans are called *chitons.* Fossil amphineurans are rare in the Great Lakes region.

Gastropods

Gastropods may be at once distinguished from amphineurans on the basis of their shell and head. Gastropods (fig. 44b–d) have a shell composed of a single unit (that is, if a shell is present), and have eyes and antennae on their heads (see fig. 25b). The shell of gastropods is composed of calcium carbonate and chitin that is secreted by the mantle and usually spirally coiled. Gastropod shells are coiled in a left or a right pattern. Thus, students of gastropods talk about "left-handed" and "right-handed" shells—in a most anthropocentric way.

In some gastropods the opening to the shell may be effectively closed by a stiff plate called the *operculum.* This adaptation is especially useful for terrestrial snails in times of drought because it keeps the soft inner parts from drying out. In most of these forms the animal is further sealed in the shell by a mucoid substance that hardens around the edge of the operculum.

Gastropods have been crawling around on the ocean bottoms on their big foot since Cambrian times. But many terrestrial forms presently occur, including the slugs (some of respectable size) that have lost their shell entirely. Snail fossils are very important in late Pleistocene and post-Pleistocene bog deposits in the Great Lakes region.

The shells of gastropods are composed of calcium carbonate in the form of the mineral aragonite, which tends to dissolve away in seawater over the eons. Thus, fossils of Paleozoic gastropods often occur in the form of internal casts. Some Paleozoic gastropod genera of the Great Lakes region include the middle Ordovician *Maclurites* and *Fusispira* (fig. 44b), the middle Devonian *Loxonema* (fig. 44c) and *Acanthonema,* and the early Pennsylvanian *Worthenia.* Late Pleistocene and post-

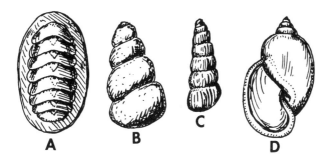

Fig. 44. Amphineurans and gastropods. *A,* a typical amphineuran. *B,* cast of the Great Lakes Basin Ordovician gastropod *Fusispira. C,* the Great Lakes Basin Devonian gastropod *Loxonema. D,* the Great Lakes Basin Devonian Pleistocene gastropod *Physa.*

Pleistocene snails that are common fossils in bog deposits in the Great Lakes are *Physa* (fig. 44d), *Helix,* and *Planorbis.*

Pelecypods

Pelecypods may be distinguished from other fossil and modern shellfish in that the exoskeleton is made up of two *valves* that are mirror images of one another (fig. 45a). One exception to this is the oyster, where the shell is designed so that the animal will stick to the bottom and one valve is bigger than the other. Pelecypods also have a big ventral foot (see fig. 25a), and they do quite a bit of crawling on it in their seafloor and freshwater habitats. Some forms, such as the delicious scallops, can swim about for short periods by clapping their valves together.

Pelecypods have well-developed gills and a pair of tubes called *siphons* that pull water in and out of the *mantle cavity.* This activity brings in food and oxygen and carries out waste products. Large muscles in the front and back of the shell close the valves, and when these muscles relax, an elastic ligamentlike structure pulls the valves apart. The muscles leave prominent scars on the shell after the animal dies.

The pelecypod shell is composed of chitin and calcium carbonate that occurs in two mineral forms. The inner layer is called "the mother of pearl" and like gastropod shells is composed of *aragonite.* The middle layer is composed of the mineral variety of calcium carbonate called *calcite.* The outer layer is formed of chitin, and its function is to protect the two inner layers from being dissolved away by water. The

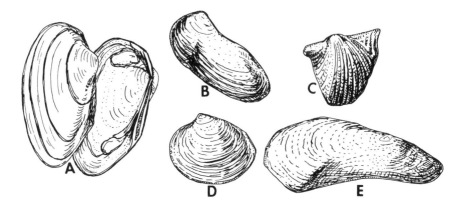

Fig. 45. Pelecypods. *A*, two halves of the Pleistocene and Holocene clam *Anodonta*. Great Lakes Basin Paleozoic pelecypods: *B*, the Ordovician *Cuneamya; C*, the Devonian *Conocardium, D, Paracyclas;* and *E, Liromytilus.*

chitin typically rots away after the animal dies and usually is not preserved in fossil forms of the animal—not even in those of late Pleistocene and post-Pleistocene fossils.

Pelecypods occur in all kinds of aquatic situations, both in freshwater and in salt water. The common names for these animals are clams, mussels, and oysters. Clams and mussels are both bivalves, with each valve a mirror image of the other. It seems the name *clam* is usually applied to the saltwater forms and the name *mussel* is usually applied to freshwater forms, but this usage is somewhat inconsistent.

For instance, the zebra mussel is a saltwater "clam" that was introduced to the modern Great Lakes by hitching rides on ocean-going ships. These animals stick together in masses and cause great human consternation by clogging all kinds of water intakes. Ironically, zebra mussels seem to be clearing up the murky water of some Great Lakes ports, especially those of Lake Erie.

In general, saltwater pelecypods have much thicker shells than their freshwater equivalents, but again, this is not always the case. Freshwater pelecypods occur by the millions in late Pleistocene and post-Pleistocene bog deposits in the Great Lakes region and are very important fossils in these situations. Some common pelecypod fossil genera from the region are the middle Ordovician *Cuneamya* (fig. 45b), the late Ordovician *Anomalodonta*, the middle Devonian *Conocardium* (fig. 45c), *Paracyclas* (fig. 45d), and *Liromytilus* (fig. 45e), the Mississippian *Sanguinolites,* the early Pennsylvanian *Naiadites,* and the late Pleistocene and post-Pleistocene *Anodonta* (fig. 45a) and *Piscidium.*

Cephalopods

The cephalopods are the most active and highly evolved of all of the mollusks. Comparing the lowly chitons with modern squids and octopuses would be like comparing *Amphioxus* with humans. Modern cephalopods such as squids have evolved (in their own way) eyes that are comparable to those of modern vertebrates. Unlike the chitons, snails, and slugs crawling slowly along on their single foot, squids are active predators that hunt in packs, darting here and there to catch fish with great dexterity. The members of squid "wolf packs" are able to communicate with each other during the hunt by color-change signals.

Cephalopods may be immediately distinguished from other mollusks by the fact that the mouth is circled by tentacles that bear sucking discs or hooks, and by their well-developed head and eyes. Moreover, when shells are present, they are internally divided by *septa.* We tend to think of modern cephalopods as soft-bodied animals such as squids and octopuses, but one living form, the chambered nautilus, and many fossil forms developed shells. Of the shelled cephalopods that occur as Paleozoic fossils, the *nautiloids* and *ammonoids* are the two groups well represented in the Great Lakes region. Some of their fossils get large enough to make you grunt when you pick them up.

Nautiloids

Nautiloids have a calcareous shell that may be straight or curved (fig. 46a–b). The shell is divided internally by septa that are visible on the external part of the shell in most fossils as structures called *sutures.* Nautiloids have *simple* sutures. The septa divide the nautiloid shell into chambers. The animal inside the shell always occupies the chamber that was formed last. We know what the soft parts of nautiloids looked like because we have been able to study the living genus *Nautilus,* which has a chambered shell so beautiful that it has inspired poetry. The nautiloid animal had a mouth that was armed with teeth and surrounded by tentacles. There were two pairs of gills that were housed

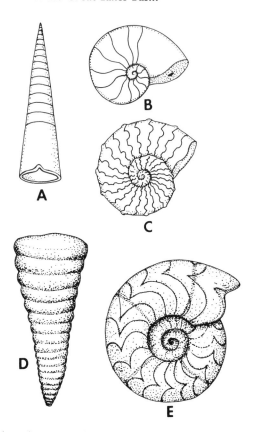

Fig. 46. Nautiloids and ammonoids. *A,* typical straight nautiloid shell. *B,* typical curved nautiloid shell. *C,* typical curved ammonoid shell. *D, Stokesoceras,* nautiloid internal shell (siphuncle) cast from the Silurian of the Great Lakes Basin. *E, Munsteroceras,* ammonoid internal shell (siphuncle) cast from the Mississippian of the Great Lakes Basin.

in the mantle cavity. A large *crop* was an important part of the digestive system.

Very often, the fossils of nautiloids occur as the internal casts of the chambered shells. Some Paleozoic nautiloid fossils of the Great Lakes Basin include the middle Silurian *Stokesoceras* (fig. 46d), the middle Devonian *Alpenoceras,* the early Mississippian *Cycloceras* and *Endolobus,* and the early Pennsylvanian *Pseudorthoceras.*

Ammonoids

Ammonoids also have a calcareous shell that may be straight or coiled; the shell is divided into chambers internally by septa that are usually visible on the outside of fossil shells as sutures. Ammonoids have *complicated* or *wrinkled* sutures (fig. 46c). All ammonoids are extinct, but we assume that they had soft parts that were similar to the living genus *Nautilus* and the extinct nautiloids. We also assume that the soft-bodied animal occupied the last-formed chamber of the shell, as did the nautilus animal. Some Paleozoic ammonoid fossils of the Great Lakes include the Mississippian genera *Imitoceras*, *Munsterocerus* (fig. 46e), and *Merocanites*.

Arthropods

The arthropods are the most specialized and diversified group of all of the invertebrate animal phyla.

Subphylum Trilobita
Subphylum Chelicerata
Subphylum Crustacea
Subphylum Uniramia (includes insects)

We have briefly discussed the most important groups of arthropods in chapter 3. All of these groups have been found fossilized, some in certain unusual situations. Insects and spiders have been preserved in amber, and shrimp have sometimes been preserved in very fine sediments.

Arthropod fossils in the Great Lakes region include trilobites, eurypterids, ostracods, and a strange crustacean called a rhinocarid. Trilobites and ostracods are common and the eurypterids regionally common in the area. Arthropods have segmented bodies and jointed appendages that are modified for all sorts of different activities. They have highly developed circulatory, excretory, and breathing systems, and they secrete an exoskeleton of chitin that is structurally different in the different groups.

Trilobites

Trilobites seem to be everyone's favorite invertebrate fossils. Since trilobites have been extinct since the Permian, we cannot say much about their soft parts. Possibly their habits were somewhat like those of the king crabs (see fig. 26b), but we are not completely sure of that. The trilobites have an exoskeleton composed of dense chiton that covers the top of the body. This exoskeleton is called the carapace, and it is divided into three side-to-side parts called *lobes* that run parallel to one another (fig. 47a). The lobe that runs down the center of the body is called the *axial* lobe. The lobes that run down the body on either side of the axial lobe are called the *pleural* lobes.

The body of trilobites is further divided into segments that run from front to back. Several of these segments are fused together at the front of the body to form the head, or *glabella*. The head has eyes that are divided into many small *facets* like the compound eyes of insects. Thus, extinct trilobites probably saw a mosaic of light and dark spots, which translated into a picture in the tiny brain of the animal. The head also had a pair of sensory antennae. Some segments in the head region and all of the segments behind the head had a pair of appendages, each of which split into branches at its end. These are called *biramous appendages*.

The segments of the body behind the head region or glabella form the main part of the body, called the thorax. The segments of the thorax are hinged together in such a manner that the animal could roll up in a ball the way the crustacean pill bugs do today. This no doubt protected the trilobites from some animals that might want to bite, pinch, or rasp at their vital parts. In fact, sometimes whole fossil trilobites or their shed exoskeletons have been found in the rolled-up position. Finally, several segments at the back end of the trilobites body are fused together to form a tail or *pygidium,* which varies in size and shape among the different genera.

Trilobites, like crabs, lobsters, and crayfish, shed their exoskeletons during periods of growth; and like these modern animals probably spent a secretive time as soft-shelled trilobites. After death, the different trilobite parts, glabellae, thorax and thorax segments, pygidia, and legs tended to come apart, so that pieces of trilobites are much more common fossils than the whole carapace. Trilobites probably were mainly bottom crawlers, but it has been suggested that some of them were fair

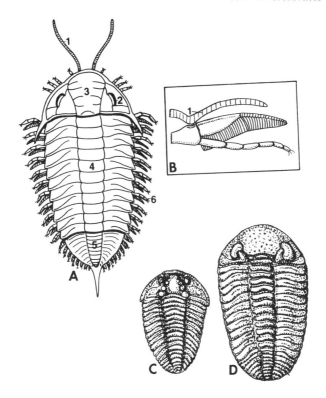

Fig. 47. Trilobites. *A.* generalized trilobite showing antenna (1), eye (2), glabella (3), thorax (4), pygidium (5), and biramous appendage (6). The three rows of plates are called lobes; the outside are pleural lobes and the middle the axial lobe. *B,* enlarged view of a biramous appendage showing its relationship to a segment of the pleural lobe (1). *C,* the Great Lakes Basin Ordovician trilobite *Flexicalymene. D,* the Great Lakes Basin Devonian trilobite *Phacops.*

swimmers. Some trilobite genera from the Paleozoic rocks of the Great Lakes Basin include the middle Ordovician *Ogygites, Ceraurus,* and *Flexicalymene* (fig. 47c) and the middle Devonian *Trimerus, Calymene,* and *Phacops* (fig. 47d).

Chelicerates

The chelicerates are represented in the Great Lakes region by fossil water scorpions or eurypterids. Chelicerates also include such animals as ticks, spiders, and scorpions. All chelicerates are divided into two parts called a forebody and a hindbody (see fig. 26b), and all have four pairs of walking legs, some of which have been modified for grasping things, handling particles of food, or swimming.

Eurypterids (fig. 48a) had a jointed body and a distinct head region with large lateral eyes. Some of them had their front walking legs modified to form a pair of scorpionlike pincers located at the front end of the animal. At the back end of the body there was either a rounded or pointed tail called a *telson*. Both balancing legs and swimming legs were present in eurypterids, and some of the swimming legs had paddles.

Some eurypterids were rather small animals that probably fed on other smaller animals, but others reached a length of almost 10 feet and were among the largest invertebrate animals that ever lived. It has been suggested that some of the giant eurypterids were probably top predators in the early Paleozoic. It has even been postulated that armored plates in early vertebrates evolved as protection against eurypterid attacks.

Fossil eurypterids are only locally common, and it has been suggested that they were freshwater animals. If this is so, it may account for their rather rare occurrence in the Michigan Basin Paleozoic sedimentary rocks, which were mainly laid down in seawater. Excellent eurypterid fossils, however, are known from both Ordovician and Silurian deposits in New York. A late Silurian eurypterid, *Erieopterus,* is common in New York State but is rare in the Michigan Basin.

Crustaceans

Crustaceans are segmented animals that have two pairs of antennae on the second and third segments of their bodies and pincers or jaws on the fourth one. The exoskeletons of crustaceans are usually segmented and are always composed of chitin. Ostracods (fig. 48b–d) are the only fossil crustaceans that are abundant in the Great Lakes region, where they are common in many Paleozoic sedimentary rocks and also occur in late Pleistocene and post-Pleistocene bog deposits. Ostracods are microscopic animals the size of small seeds, and they have a bivalve shell that makes them look like tiny clams.

The bodies of the animals (fig. 48b) have shortened, somewhat shrimplike appendages, and for this reason ostracods are often called "seed shrimps." Ostracods have tiny eye spots and a jaw structure rather

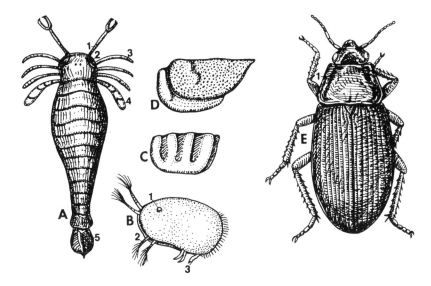

Fig. 48. Chelicerates, Crustaceans, and Insects. *A,* generalized eurypterid showing pincer (1) modified from walking legs, eyes (2), walking leg (3), swimming leg (4), and telson (5). *B,* generalized ostracod (seed shrimp) showing eye spot (1), antenna (2), and leg (3). Great Lakes Basin Ordovician ostracods: *C, Quadrijugator; D, Levisulculus. E,* ground beetle showing the hardened front wings called elytra (1).

than pincers. A brood pouch for eggs occurs in the back part of the shell. You will need a microscope and other specialized equipment to be able to identify and prepare a collection of fossil ostracods. Some fossil ostracods from the Great Lakes region including the Ordovician genera *Quadrijugator* (fig. 48c), *Levisulculus* (fig. 48d), and the Devonian genus *Phlyctiscapha.*

A strange group of poorly known, extinct arthropods called the *rhinocarids* have been included with the crustaceans, but they could actually represent a distinct class. Rhinocarids have been found from the middle Devonian of northern Ohio.

Insects

Insects are arthropods with three pairs of walking legs and usually with one or two pairs of wings on the thorax. Several important groups of insects have been identified from late Pleistocene and post-Pleistocene deposits in several areas in the Great Lakes region. Fossils of insects usually occur as the hardened chitinous parts of the animals. Beetles (fig. 48e) are very important late Pleistocene fossils in the region and are useful in indicating climatic changes. The hardened front wings (*elytra*) are the most commonly found beetle fossils.

Echinoderms

Echinoderms appear to have an exoskeleton, but it really is an *endoskeleton* because their skeletons (including even the spines of the prickly groups) are covered by a very thin skin (*epidermis*) composed of living cells. This endoskeleton is calcareous and takes quite a variety of shapes. Adult echinoderms tend to be radially symmetrical, with the body parts arranged around a central axis like the spokes of a wheel.

There are usually five major parts that radiate out from this central axis. These parts may be fused, as in most echinoderms, or extend outward as arms, as in brittle stars and starfishes (fig. 49d). The echinoderms have a unique water vascular system, a pipelike system containing a ring around the central axis that sends "pipes" out the five radiating parts and down into tiny soft tube feet that are worked hydraulically. Four classes of echinoderms are regularly found in rocks of the Great Lakes region, the crinoids are the most common.

Class Cystoidea
Class Crinoidea
Class Edrioasteroidea
Class Asteroidea

Echinoderm fossils are important because they indicate that the sedimentary rocks that contain them were laid down in a marine environment.

Cystoids (Includes Blastoids)

Cystoids (fig. 49a) are an ancient extinct group of echinoderms that were typically attached to the seafloor by a stem called a *column*. The main body of the animal was composed of a structure called the *calyx* that usually had a regular number of *calcareous plates* bound together in a symmetrical manner. The cystoid calyx lacks the bunch of seg-

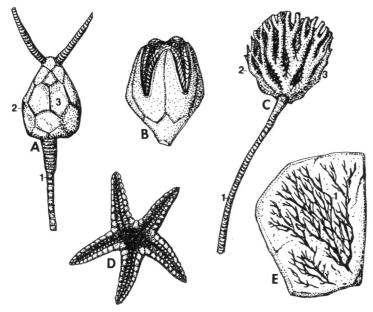

Fig. 49. Echinoderms and Graptozoans. *A,* the Great Lakes Basin Ordovician cystoid *Pleurocystites,* showing the column or stem (1), and the calyx (2) composed of individual calcareous plates (3). *B,* the Great Lakes Basin Devonian "blastoid" *Hyperoblastus. C,* the Great Lakes Basin Devonain crinoid *Euryocrinus,* showing the column or stem (1), the calyx (2), and an individual arm (3). *D,* the Great Lakes Basin Ordovician starfish genus *Protopalaeaster. E,* the Great Lakes Basin Ordovician graptolite *Dictyonema;* the threadlike structures (1) bear the thecae that contain the living graptolite animals.

mented arms (fig. 49c) found in the crinoids and the five prominent food grooves that are found in edrioasteroids. Some fossil cystoid genera from the Great Lakes Basin are *Pleurocystites* (fig. 49a) from the middle Ordovician, *Lipsanocystis* from the middle Devonian, and the "blastoid" genus *Hyperoblastus* (fig. 49b) from the middle Devonian.

Crinoids

The crinoids or "sea lilies" occur in the seas today as well as in ancient rocks. The modern ones are more abundant in some areas than it was once thought, and they form lush crinoid gardens in some tropical seas. Crinoids typically have a stem or column with a calyx on top that is composed of a regular number of calcareous plates fused together in a symmetrical way and with many segmented arms (fig. 49c). Crinoids are common finds in most Paleozoic strata in the Great Lakes area, with the most abundant fossils consisting of pieces of the jointed crinoid stems. Crinoid genera from the Great Lakes region include the attractive middle Devonian genera *Proctothylacocrinus, Euryocrinus* (fig. 49c), and *Corocrinus*. A scientific name like that of the first genus is one reason students preparing for a biological career should be taught to divide words into syllables!

Edrioasteroids

Edrioasteroids are a unique extinct group of echinoderms with a body or *test* that is composed of an indefinite number of irregular plates and that has five prominent *food grooves* that are wrapped around the test as if they were octopus arms grabbing something. The middle Ordovician Great Lakes region genus *Edrioaster* is not common.

Asteroids

Asteroids are the familiar starfishes that are abundant in modern oceans, but that were not very common in the Paleozoic rocks of the Great Lakes region. Starfish normally have five radiating arms and tiptoe slowly along by means of their hydraulically controlled tube feet. Figure 49d shows the Middle Ordovician starfish genus *Protopalaeaster*.

Hemichordates

The hemichordates were once included with the true chordates because they had a short rodlike structure that was mistaken for a notochord. Hemichordates are now put into an invertebrate phylum of their own. These animals resemble chordates in that they have paired gill slits and a short nerve cord on the underside of the body. The only hemichordates that are known as fossils in the Great Lakes Basin are the *graptolites* of the class Graptozoa. The individual graptolite animals lived in little chitinous chambers called *thecae,* which occurred along threadlike structures. Graptolites are extinct, but their skeletal structures resemble those found in living hemichordates called pterobranchs. Figure 49e shows a branching colony of the graptolites *Dictyonema* from the middle Ordovician of the Great Lakes region.

Chapter 9
Fossil Vertebrates

The characters of the phylum Chordata and its subphyla, as well as those of the major vertebrate classes, have been discussed in chapter 3. This chapter will deal with important vertebrate fossils of the Great Lakes Basin.

Phylum Chordata
Subphylum Vertebrata
Class Agnatha
Class Placodermi
Class Chondrichthyes
Class Osteichthyes
Class Amphibia
Class Reptilia
Class Aves
Class Mammalia

Agnathans

The agnathans or jawless fishes are the earliest known vertebrates. They occur first as bits of phosphatic primitive bonelike material from the late Cambrian. Then, in the early Ordovician of the United States, Greenland, and Spitzbergen, more bits and fragments of these ancient verebrates are found. For a long time scientists argued about whether the first vertebrates evolved in freshwater or salt water, but now it is

141

generally agreed that they evolved in nearshore saltwater habitats. That is because these earliest fossils occur with trilobites, conodonts, and brachiopods, all saltwater forms.

The main characteristic of the agnaths is that they lack jaws. But they are otherwise very primitive vertebrates, and to call them fishes, at least in the sense of the modern ones swimming about today, is somewhat of an exaggeration. The ancient armored agnathans of the early Paleozoic seas are collectively called ostracoderms. This is a common name, not a scientific name. The modern, slimy, unarmored lampreys and hagfishes are also agnathans (jawless fishes) and are the closest relatives of the ancient ostracoderms.

Ostracoderms

Almost all ostracoderms are covered by armor plates composed of bony tissue. Internal skeletal parts such as vertebrae and ribs have never been found; thus it is assumed that the internal skeleton was cartilaginous. Most ostracoderms were filter feeders. One group of ostracoderms, called *osteostracans,* consisted principally of bottom crawlers (fig. 50a). These animals were flattened from top to bottom with the eyes on top and a small round mouth on the bottom of a bony head shield. Just behind the head shield were a pair of prop- or flaplike structures (sometimes called pectoral fins) that probably pushed the animals through the mud. The body was composed of smaller bony plates, and the tail was directed upward rather than downward, as in many other ostracoderm groups. When this type of tail swishes back and forth in flattened animals such as these, it tends to nose them downward and keep them on the bottom. Along each lower side of the head shield and in the middle of the top of the head shield, some bottom-crawling ostracoderms had enlarged water-sensory structures that were connected to the brain that gave the animal information about currents and pressure changes and might have warned them about approaching eurypterid predators.

An excellent preparation of the brain of a fossil bottom crawling ostracoderm shows that both the brain and the major sense organs associated with it were very similar to those of modern lampreys, even to the point of having two semicircular canals in the inner ear rather than three, like other vertebrates.

Another group of ostracoderms, called *anaspids,* was flattened from

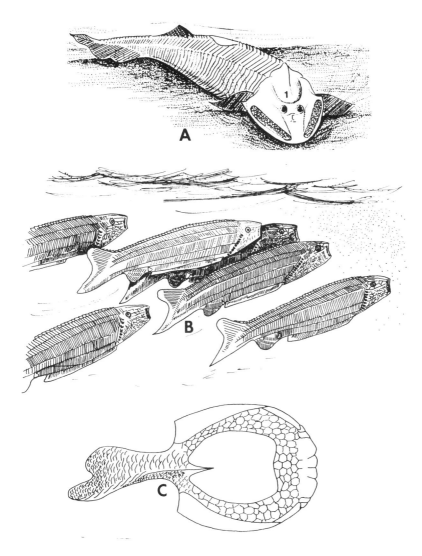

Fig. 50. Ostracoderms. *A,* a flattened, bottom-feeding, osteostracan ostracoderm with a large head shield (1) and an upturned tail. *B,* compressed, surface-feeding, anaspid ostracoderms with downturned tails. *C,* a blind, heterostracan ostracoderm. (Drawings by Donna R. Holman.)

side to side and had the tail directed downward rather than upward (fig. 50b). Tail action in a compressed body like this should nose the animal toward the surface; thus it has been suggested that these little ostracoderms fed on tiny organisms or bits of organic matter trapped in the surface film. The bony plates covering these animals were small, further suggesting a more active animal than the bottom-crawling group.

A very important group of ostracoderms are called the *heterostracans*. Heterostracan ostracoderms are not only the earliest known vertebrate, but they went on to be the most diverse group of ostracoderms. Some of them were blind (fig. 50c) and are thought to have done their filter feeding in turbid water. Some had a long tubular "snout" at the end of the head shield and a small mouth at the end of the snout.

Another group of heterostracans had a very large barrel-shaped body, and it is believed that these animals had developed some kind of a pumping mechanism to pull water into the mouth. Other heterostracans had sledlike runners on the bottom of the body that possibly could have allowed them to glide along the top of the mud.

Early heterostracan ostracoderm skeletal parts (fig. 51b) have been found in the Great Lakes region from middle Ordovician rocks on St. Joseph Island, Ontario, in the north channel of Lake Huron. These skeletal fragments represent a genus named *Astraspis,* which probably looked something like *Pteraspis* (fig. 51a). The small bony plates (fig. 51b) representing *Astraspis* have very distinctive, tiny, crownlike tubercles on them.

Lampreys

Most jawless vertebrates died out at the end of the Devonian period, but some gave rise to the modern jawless vertebrate groups, the lampreys and the hagfishes. Lampreys are common in the Great Lakes region today. Native lampreys are small creatures that do not have a negative impact on the Great Lakes ecosystem. But the large sea lamprey that was introduced into the Great Lakes accidentally through the St. Lawrence Seaway greatly impacted the fishery in the area; in fact, this one primitive agnathan practically brought commercial fishing in the Great Lakes to a standstill for awhile.

Lampreys differ from ostracoderms in their total absence of bones. They have a slimy, eel-like body with no pectoral fins, but with dorsal

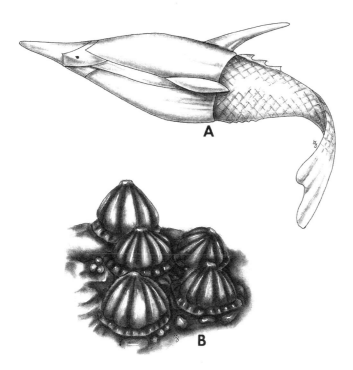

Fig. 51. Heterostracan ostracoderms. *A,* artist's reconstruction of *Pteraspis,* a common heterostracan ostracoderm. *B,* tubercles from *Astraspis,* a heterostracan from the middle Ordovician of St. Joseph Island, Ontario. (From J. A. Holman, *Michigan's Fossil Vertebrates* [East Lansing: Michigan State University Museum, 1975].)

fins and a primitive tail fin. An important feature in lampreys is that the gills lie inside of the throat region (*pharynx*) and the skeletal cartilages that support the throat. It is assumed that this was also the situation in the ostracoderms. In all of the higher vertebrate groups, however, the gills lie outside the throat region and its supporting skeletal cartilages or bones. The lamprey and ostracoderm condition supposedly exists because both groups eat tiny particles of food or liquid food that do not injure the delicate gill tissues as they pass through the throat.

The mouth of lampreys has evolved into a circular sucking disc that is used to attach to the fishes upon which it feeds. The lamprey has a rasping tongue that it uses to drill a hole into the fish to which it has attached. Its saliva has an anticoagulent in it that promotes fluid flow from the fish into the lamprey. The sea lamprey (fig. 52) usually ends

Fig. 52. A sea lamprey attacking a lake trout. (Drawing by Donna R. Holman.)

up killing the fish it attaches to, especially if it is a soft-scaled fish such as the native lake trout of the Great Lakes. The small native brook lampreys normally do not kill the fish they attach to and sometimes just get a free ride on them.

Why So Few Early Fish Fossils in the Great Lakes Region? We have already asked and answered the question, "Why have no dinosaur remains been found in the Great Lakes region?" We might also ask the question, "Why have so few early Paleozoic fish remains been found in the region?" The answer is rather simple. Most early Paleozoic fishes apparently lived in freshwater habitats until the middle and late Devonian, when they reinvaded the seas. Since most Paleozoic rocks in the Great Lakes region represent saltwater habitats, there is no really good record of fishes in the region until middle and late Devonian times.

Placoderms

Placoderms represent a very strange group of early jawed fishes; they were called "the funny fishes" by the late and influential vertebrate paleontologist A. S. Romer. Placoderms may be defined in a simplified way, as early armored fishes with jaws, but it is possible or even probable that some of the placoderm groups are not closely related to one another. One character that unites most of the placoderm groups is the fact that the armor is composed of two parts, a head shield that protects the brain and sense organs and a thoracic shield (fig. 53a) that protects the front part of the body.

Placoderms are the only class of vertebrates that has all of its species extinct. They evolved in freshwater habitats and appear for the first time in the fossil record in the Silurian. An important character (other than the presence of jaws) that indicates that placoderms are more closely related to higher fishes than to the jawless fishes is that the delicate gill tissues occur outside of the throat or pharyngeal region. Here they are protected by the gill arch skeleton from possible abrasion by large chunks of shelly or bony food that pass through the throat.

On the Importance of Jaws. The first vertebrates with jaws are known from the Silurian a long time after jaws evolved. No earlier fossils are known that represent transitional stages from jawless to jawed forms. Nevertheless, based on studies of the gill arch skeleton and its innervation in agnathous fishes, it appears that jaws evolved from a structure in the mouth in front of the gill arches called a *velum.*

Jaws allowed fishlike vertebrates to become much more diverse in their feeding habits and to exploit many different new ecological situations. Large objects could now be eaten, and those forms that developed cutting edges or teeth on their jaws could bite off and swallow large pieces of plants and animals. Fishes soon became specialized as scrapers, crunchers, slicers, and suckers. All and all, the evolution of jaws allowed for a large *adaptive radiation* to take place in fishes that could have never occurred in the jawless ostracoderms. This adaptive radiation led to the so-called age of fishes in the Devonian.

Great Lakes Basin Placoderms

The placoderms are divided into about nine or ten groups by most paleontologists, and their relationships have been portrayed in several ways by recent systematic studies. The most dominant group of placoderms, the *arthrodires* (fig. 54b), are well represented in the Great Lakes region and include some spectacular species. Placoderms range from very small forms with tiny nibbling jaws to huge predators that lived in the late Devonian seas that existed near what is now Cleveland,

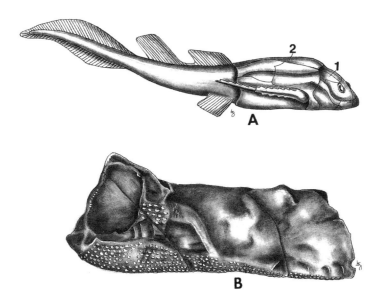

Fig. 53. The placoderm *Bothriolepis*. *A,* artist's reconstruction of *Bothriolepis,* an antiarch placoderm from the middle Devonian of the Great Lakes Basin, with head shield (1) and thoracic shield (2) indicated. *B,* plate from the side of the thoracic shield of *Bothriolepis* of the type found in the middle Devonian of the Michigan Basin. (From J. A. Holman, *Michigan's Fossil Vertebrates* [East Lansing: Michigan State University Museum, 1975].)

Ohio. Other placoderms superficially resembled modern cartilaginous ratfishes, while stll others looked something like modern stingrays or banjo fish. In the next paragraphs we will discuss the structure and diversity of the two common Great Lakes region fossil placoderm groups, the *arthrodires* and the *antiarchs.*

The arthrodires are divided into two groups, a more ancestral group called the *arctolepids* and a more derived group called the *brachythoracids.* Arctolepids have a relatively long thoracic shield that is closely connected to the head shield. The eyes tend to be at the tip of the head shield in these forms. In the brachythoracids (fig. 54b) the thoracic shield is much shorter and is connected to the head shield by a ball-and-socket joint that would have allowed the head region to move up and down independent of the thoracic shield. The eyes usually occur farther back in the head shield in these forms.

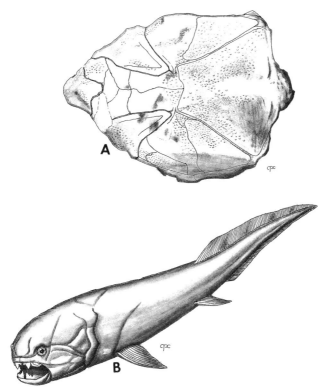

Fig. 54. The placoderm *Protitanichthys. A,* plate from the head shield of *Protitanichthys,* an arthrodiran placoderm from the middle Devonian of the Michigan Basin. *B,* artist's reconstruction of *Protitanichthys.* (From J. A. Holman, *Michigan's Fossil Vertebrates* [East Lansing: Michigan State University Museum, 1975].)

These modifications in the brachythoracids tend to indicate that they were faster and more mobile forms than the more primitive arctolepids. Arctolepids mainly are found as fossils in the freshwater early Devonian beds, whereas brachythoracids are characteristic of the middle and late Devonian. Brachythoracids began to invade brackish water in the middle Devonian and then made a full invasion of the sea in the late Devonian, when some became the top marine predators of the time. Some paleontologists have argued that the arctolepids are the advanced forms and the brachythoracids are primitive. But earlier distribution of the arctolepids in the fossil record and the more active and mobile body style of the brachythoracids would suggest the contrary.

Arctolepid arthrodires are represented in the Great Lakes region by forms such as *Arctolepis* and *Holonema,* which have been found as fossils in the middle Devonian rocks of the Michigan Basin. *Arctolepis,* a primitive form, had a body that was somewhat flattened from side to side and had the typical arctolepid head shield with the eyes at the very front end of the shield. The relatively elongate thoracic shield was armed by two huge, immovable *pectoral spines* that are lacking in the brachythoracid arthrodires. The head shield fitted snugly into the thoracic shield, and there was no ball-and-socket joint between the two. *Holonema,* on the other hand, had a body that was somewhat flattened from top to bottom and is thought to have been a slower form that lived on the bottom. *Holonema* is believed to have been a divergent branch off the primitive arctolepid stock.

Brachythoracid arthrodires are represented in the Great Lakes region by middle Devonian forms such as *Protitanichthys* (fig. 54b), and *Titanichthys, Dunkleosteus* (fig. 55), and *Trachosteus* that occurred both in the Michigan Basin rocks and in the famous Cleveland Shales in northern Ohio. *Protitanichthys* reached the size of an adult sturgeon, and *Dunkleosteus* was gigantic, the most spectacular of all of the placoderms.

Dunkleosteus was called *Dinichthys* for years and still bears that name in some books and museum labels. *Dunkleosteus* had a head shield and thoracic shield that together reached a length of about 10 feet. The posterior region of *Dunkleosteus* is not well known, but known posterior regions of related brachythoracid genera suggest that it must have had paired fins, a dorsal fin, and an uplifted tail. In the brachythoracids related to *Dunkleosteus* the head and thoracic shield section of the animal made up about 25 percent of the total length of the placoderm; thus, by projection, *Dunkleosteus* would have been about 40 feet long from the tip of its head shield to the end of its upturned tail!

The armor plates that formed the two shields of *Dunkleosteus* were decorated by small bumps (*denticles*), and the individual plates of the shields were arranged singly in the middle of the shields and in pairs on the sides of the shields. These bones are not at all comparable to the bones in the skulls of modern bony fishes. Grooves in the bony plates indicate that a *lateral line system* was present in *Dunkleosteus.* Lateral line systems are important in modern sharks, bony fishes, aquatic salamander larvae, and frog tadpoles, where they act as sensory organs for detecting currents and other movement and pressure changes

Fig. 55. *Dunkleosteus,* the giant arthrodiran placoderm of the late Devonian Cleveland Shales, resting on the bottom and about to capture a fish that came too near the open jaws.

in the aquatic environment. *Dunkleosteus* had two large eyes with a surrounding ring of bony plates to protect the eyeballs.

Toothy projections occurred on both the upper and the lower jaws. These were not real teeth, but they were very sharp bony ridges that appear to have been able to cut and crunch at the same time and must have been devastating to other Paleozoic creatures. The back end of the head shield surrounded and protected the delicate gills. The thoracic shield surrounded the body behind the head, and it formed the typical brachythoracid ball-and-socket joint with the head region. It has been suggested that the up-and-down head movement made possible by this joint was associated with pushing water through the gill region. So it was apparently a modification for breathing rather than for feeding.

One can picture this huge creature lying on the bottom of a late Devonian sea with its steel-trap jaws open, its bony rimmed eyes staring ahead, and its head bobbing slowly up and down. Then—swoosh—*Dunkleosteus* lunges forward, the jaws snap shut, and some unfortunate Paleozoic fish that wandered too near the giant in ambush is obliterated. It seems unlikely that *Dunkleosteus* would have been an effective swimmer for any extended period of time, considering the heavy armor that encased the anterior part of its body. Rather, it must have been more like a horseless knight in armor, having adequate defensive armor and offensive weapons, but without much agility.

Compared to the arthrodires, the *antiarchs* (see fig. 53) were the runts of the placoderm world and had tiny jaws made up of transverse bony plates. The head shield was reduced in size, and the eyes were directed upward. The thoracic shield was flattened on the bottom but tended to come to a peak at the top, especially in the genus *Pterichthyodes*. This type of body plan strongly indicates a bottom-crawling mode of life. This existence is further suggested by the presence of prominent, movable pectoral "arms" at the front of the thoracic box that allowed the little placoderms to oar their way along the bottom.

Some antiarch fossils were preserved with traces of their internal soft parts intact. It is known that their intestines had an internal spiral valve like those of living sharks and lungfishes. Moreover, there was a pair of saclike structures in the back of the throat region that have been interpreted as lungs. Perhaps the ecological role of the antiarchs was that of "sea rodents" nibbling away at rock-encrusting plants and tiny invertebrate animals. Surely, their small size must have been helpful to them in some ways, as it is difficult to imagine a 40-foot *Dunkleosteus* bothering with a 6-inch *Pterichthyodes*!

Bothriolepis (see fig. 53) is the common antiarch of the Great Lakes region, where it occurs in the middle Devonian rocks of northern Ohio as well as in Michigan Basin rocks. This placoderm was about 16 inches long and was more flattened from top to bottom than in *Pterichthyodes*. Moreover, its thoracic shield did not peak as much as those of *Pterichthyodes* and it lacked scales on its trunk and on its tail. Some of the armored catfishes on sale at pet stores look strikingly like some of the antiarch placoderms, but of course they are not related to them.

Ptyctodont placoderms (fig. 56) are a far cry from the heavily armored arthrodires and antiarchs we have just discussed. In the ptyctodonts the head shield is reduced to a small shield at the back of the head region, and the thoracic shield is quite short. This frees the back part of the body for efficient swimming. Ptyctodonts resemble living ratfishes (cartilaginous fishes related to sharks) in several ways. The tail is reduced to a narrow filamentlike structure, as in ratfishes. Ptyctodonts also have tooth plates rather than true teeth, and odd structures called claspers on the front fins, as in ratfishes. Finally, the overall body shape, with an enlarged head region tapering into a narrow body, is similar to ratfishes.

Nevertheless, paleontologists think that all of these developments occurred independently in ptyctodonts and that they are not ancestral to ratfishes. Certainly the presence of a head shield and a thoracic shield, even in a reduced condition, indicates that ptyctodonts should be included among the placoderms. This is a very specialized group of placoderms, and even though they have been characterized as bot-

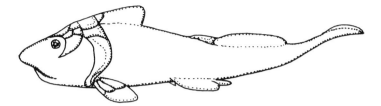

Fig. 56. Artist's reconstruction of the ptyctodont placoderm *Ctenurella*. Fragmentary remains of other ptyctodont placoderm genera have been found in Paleozoic rocks of the Michigan Basin.

tom feeders, they must have been much better swimmers than the more heavily armored forms. They certainly needed to be pretty good swimmers to be able to escape the predatory arthrodires. Genera such as *Ptyctodus* and *Eczematolepis* are ptyctodonts that have been found as fossils in middle Devonian strata of the Michigan Basin.

Chondrichthyes

All living fishes except for the jawless lampreys and hagfishes are either sharklike fishes or bony fishes. There is no fossil evidence that either of these major groups evolved from any known ostracoderm or placoderm group. Fossils of sharks and bony fishes are first known from the upper Silurian. Here sharks are represented by *dermal denticles,* and bony fishes are represented by overlapping scales.

Based on the structure of their jaws, it is believed that both of these groups had a common ancestor. In both sharks and bony fishes the jaws have the shape of meat cleavers. The "handle" of the cleaver bears the teeth, while the "blade" of the cleaver lies behind the teeth. Moreover, in both groups the teeth occur in "families" that originate on the inner surface of the jaw and then rotate into biting position as they mature.

As far back as their fossil record goes, both sharklike and bony fishes were good swimmers with well-developed paired fins. Sharklike fishes, however, have an internal skeleton of cartilage rather than bone, have a huge oily liver, and lack the swim bladder that developed in bony fishes. Some cartilage in the sharklike fishes may become very hard and brittle and looks superficially like bone. But this is a process of calcification (deposition of limy calcite in cartilages) rather than the *ossification* process that produces true bone by the synthesis of calcium phosphate, collagen fibers, and mucoid gels.

Two groups (subclasses) of sharklike fishes are known, the *elasmobranchs* and the *holocephalans,* or ratfishes. These groups differ from one another in several ways, including the general form of the body and especially the teeth. But both of them produce their calcified cartilages in the same way and have such similar reproductive structures that it is believed that they had a common ancestry. Both elasmobranchs and ratfishes are represented by fossils in the Paleozoic strata of the Great Lakes Basin.

Elasmobranchs

The elasmobranch group contains ancient sharklike fishes that may not fit our idea of what sharks should look like, as well as modern shark and ray types. Some of the least sharklike of these fishes are the cladoselachian, xenacanth, and ctenacanth groups discussed below.

Cladoselachians

The oldest remains of sharks are teeth from the last part of the middle Devonian and are called *cladodus* teeth (fig. 57a–c). Cladodus teeth are very easy to recognize and consist of a long central *cusp* that sits on a broad base that houses one or more pairs of lateral points. These teeth were given the name *Cladodus,* but the fish they belonged to was unknown at the time. Later, the Cleveland Shales of the Great Lakes region yielded some interesting late Devonian nodules or *concretions* that provided excellently preserved specimens of the fish that produced the cladodus teeth. This primitive shark was named *Cladoselache* (fig. 58), the genus from which the whole group took its name.

The Cleveland Shale concretions contained calcified skeletal cartilages; impressions of the body outline; impressions of the skin; and even impressions of soft tissues such as muscles and kidneys of *Cladoselache,* and it was shown that this fish looked much different than modern sharks. First, the head is much different. In modern sharks the part of the braincase behind the eyes is very short, and the mouth is located toward the bottom of the head. In *Cladoselache* the part of the braincase behind the eyes is long, and the mouth opens at the front end

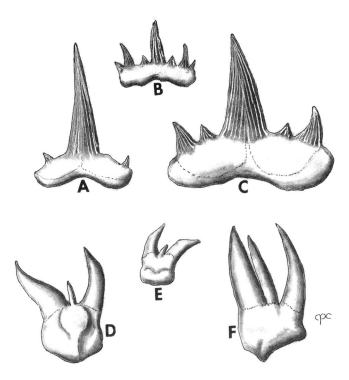

Fig. 57. Primitive shark teeth. *A–C,* "cladodus" teeth belonging to the primitive cladoselachian shark *Cladoselache* of the late Devonian of the Cleveland Shales. *D–F,* "diplodus" or "dittodus" teeth typical of xenacanth sharks. (From J. A. Holman, *Michigan's Fossil Vertebrates* [East Lansing: Michigan State University Museum, 1975].)

of the head. *Cladoselache* had a pair of large eyes as in modern sharks, but unlike modern sharks the eyeballs were circled by a layer of denticles.

The jaws of *Cladoselache* were partially supported on the braincase by a modified gill skeletal structure, whereas most modern sharks have the jaws fully supported from the braincase by this structure. Behind the head there was a unique, very stout spine, followed by two unpaired fins on the top of the back. The tail fin is symmetrical from the outside, but inside the spinal cord turns upward into the top lobe of the tail fin.

Paired fins occurred on the belly of *Cladoselache.* The pair of front fins were very large with broad bases and had very little maneuverability. The pair of back fins were much smaller and also were not very

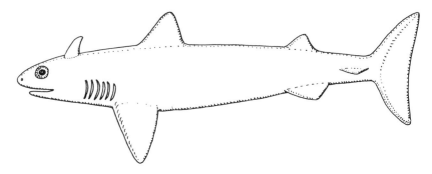

Fig. 58. Artist's reconstruction of the primitive cladoselachian shark *Cladoselache* of the Cleveland Shales.

maneuverable. Specimens of *Cladoselache* range from about 2 to 4 feet in length, and thus they were fairly large predators. But they lived in the same Upper Devonian habitats as *Dunkleosteus* and must have in turn been preyed upon by that monster of the northern Ohio Paleozoic seas.

Xenacanths

Xenacanths are a primitive group of sharklike fishes that are considered by most paleontologists to represent a side branch of shark evolution. These animals, unlike almost all of the other elasmobranchs, were mainly freshwater forms. The xenacanths also had very distinctive teeth called *diplodus* or *dittodus* teeth (fig. 57d–f) when they are found by themselves. These teeth tended to be only loosely attached to the xenacanth jaws, with each tooth composed of three parts consisting of a central short cusp with two longer, more pointed cusps on either side. The cusps emerge from a knoblike or buttonlike base.

Xenacanths (fig. 59b), have been found in the early Pennsylvanian rocks of the Michigan Basin. Xenacanths had a head with a long braincase and a terminal mouth. The jaws were also only partially braced to the braincase by an element from the gill skeleton. Xenacanths also had a spine (fig. 59a) that occurred directly behind the head, but it was long and movable and had two rows of little denticles on it. A long dorsal fin ran down the back. The tail tapered to a point and turned slightly upward at the end.

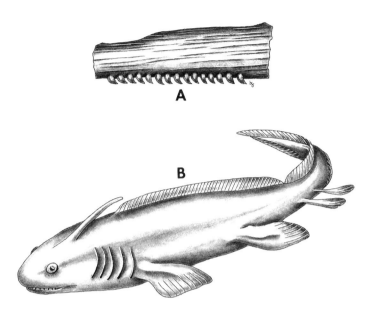

Fig. 59. Xenacanth sharks. *A*, xenacanth spine fragment of the type found in the early Pennsylvanian rocks of the Michigan Basin. *B*, artist's reconstruction of a xenacanth shark. (From J. A. Holman, *Michigan's Fossil Vertebrates* [East Lansing: Michigan State University Museum, 1975].)

A pair of well-developed fins of about equal size at the front of the animal were much more maneuverable than those of *Cladoselache*. A unique shark character of xenacanths was the presence of two pair of finlets near the back end of the animal near the anus. Some workers have suggested that the diplodus-type tooth of xenacanths evolved from the cladodus (*Cladoselache*) type (fig. 57a–c) by the reduction of the middle cusp and the emphasis on the side cusps. Perhaps these changes were related to new kinds of food that were being eaten by xenacanths in freshwater.

Ctenacanths

Ctenacanth sharks are considered by many paleontologists to be the most important of Paleozoic sharks because they are the thought to be the ancestral group for all of the modern sharks, as well as their relatives, the skates and the rays. *Ctenacanthus* (fig. 60a) is represented in middle Devonian as well as early Mississippian strata in rocks of the

Michigan Basin. *Ctenacanthus* resembles the very primitive form, *Cladoselache,* in having cladodus-type teeth, a long braincase, the same position of its mouth, and jaws supporting the braincase in a similar way. But they resemble modern sharks in other structures, including the structure of the fins and the spines associated with the unpaired fins on the top of the body.

The spines (fig. 60b) have an external coating of enamel, and the spines are set in deeply between the muscle bands on the back of the animal. Each spine is held in place by a large triangular cartilage. The anterior paired fins have two new skeletal cartilaginous supports called the *mesopterygium* and the *proterygium* that are similar to the ones found in the modern sharks and rays. The body of ctenacanths was covered by a sandpapery skin infused with tiny dermal denticles, as in modern sharks, and calcifications occurred in some of the cartilages. The tail was similar to modern sharks in that the top lobe of the tail fin was the longest and swung sharply upward, as did the vertebral column inside the tail fin.

Holocephalans

Modern holocephalans are strange, deepwater oceanic creatures called ratfishes that some people find unattractive. Paleozoic holocephalans are not as odd looking as modern ratfishes, but they had all of the major characteristics of the group. In holocephalans, unlike the sharks, the upper jaw is not supported on the braincase in any way by elements of the gill arch skeleton and is firmly fused to the braincase. Sharks have gill slits that open to the outside, but ratfishes have the gills covered by a fleshy flap called the *operculum.* A slitlike mini gill slit called the *spiracle* that occurs in sharks is absent in adult ratfishes. In ratfishes the dentition is composed of tooth plates on the jaws rather than individual teeth. These tooth plates are not replaced.

In the Great Lakes region the genera *Helodus* (fig. 61a) and *Psephodus* (fig. 61b) have been found in late Mississippian rocks of the Michigan Basin; and a structure representing an odd group of holocephalans called the cochliodonts also has been found in late Mississippian strata of the basin. *Helodus* is a well-known ancient holocephalan. It had the upper jaw immovably fused to the braincase as in modern ratfishes, but its head was much smaller. The body tapered toward the tail as in modern ratfishes, but not as much; and rather than being a ratlike

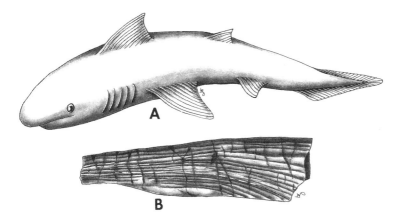

Fig. 60. Ctenacanth sharks. *A,* artist's reconstruction of the ctenacanth shark *Ctenacanthus* from the Devonian and Mississippian of the Michigan Basin. *B,* fin spine of *Ctenacanthus* of the type found in the Michigan Basin. (From J. A. Holman, *Michigan's Fossil Vertebrates* [East Lansing: Michigan State University Museum, 1975].)

whiplash, the tail had a lobe on it that tipped upward as in ctenacanth and modern sharks.

Osteichthyes

We finally come to the last group of fishes, the Osteichthyes. This group contains fishes with a well-developed internal skeleton of bone. The major groups we will consider here are the *acanthodians* (formerly called the spiny sharks), the lobe-finned fishes, and the rayfinned fishes. Zoologists used to classify the acanthodians as placoderms, mainly because they could not think of anywhere else to put them. Today they argue about whether to put them in a class by themselves or with the other bony fishes in the class Osteichthyes. Here, we shall very tentatively include them with the bony fishes of the class Osteichthyes for reasons we shall soon give.

It has already been stated that there is no evidence that bony fishes (including acanthodians) evolved from any particular ostracoderm or placoderm group and that bony fishes and cartilaginous fishes probably had common ancestors. Acanthodians are known from the early Silurian. The other bony fishes are first known from the late Silurian based

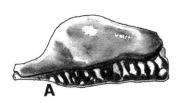 

A

B

Fig. 61. Holocephalan fish teeth of the crushing type found in the late Mississippian rocks of the Michigan Basin. A, *Helodus;* B, *Psephodus.* (From J. A. Holman, *Michigan's Fossil Vertebrates* [East Lansing: Michigan State University Museum, 1975].)

on a handful of the type of fish scales that overlap one another in life. Although bony fishes evolved early in the Paleozoic, they really did not diversify until the end of the Cretaceous period. But the rayfinned bony fishes have so absolutely dominated the seas and freshwaters in the Cenozoic era or Age of Mammals that this era might as well be called "The Age of Rayfinned Bony Fishes."

Acanthodians

Here are our reasons for tentatively including the acanthodians with the bony fishes of the class Osteichthyes. The acanthodians are neither covered with heavy dermal armor like that of the ostracoderms or placoderms, nor are they covered with sandpapery skins like sharks. In fact, in some areas of the body, such as around the fins and the head, acanthodians have scales that resemble the scales of the class Osteichthyes. Moreover, they resemble both the sharks and Osteichthyes in having an upper jaw shaped like a meat cleaver.

Acanthodian spines are first known from the early Silurian, but whole fishes are not known until the late Silurian. The most unique feature of the acanthodians are their *fin-spines,* which support numerous pairs of paired fins (fig. 62a). Moreover, they had a gill cover or operculum composed of many individual bones, rather than of a single plate, as in the Osteichthyes. In addition, their teeth lacked enamel, and their tooth replacement took place in a different way than in Osteichthyes, in that the teeth grew in from the front and were worn away

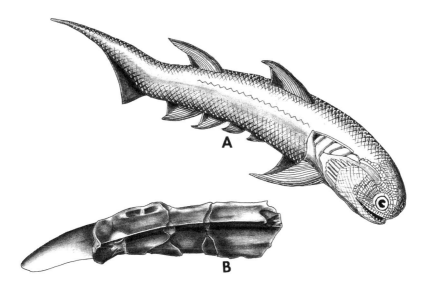

Fig. 62. Acanthodian fishes. *A,* artist's reconstruction of the common acanthodian *Climatius. B,* end of the fin spine of *Machaeracanthus* of the middle Devonian of the Michigan Basin. (From J. A. Holman, *Michigan's Fossil Vertebrates* [East Lansing: Michigan State University Museum, 1975].)

posteriorly. The acanthodian braincase was ossified, but not as completely ossified as in Osteichthyes. Acanthodians of the Great Lakes region include such forms as *Machaeracanthus* (fig. 62b) and *Onychodus* from middle Devonian strata of the Michigan Basin and *Gyracanthus* from late Mississippian strata of the basin.

Lobe-finned Fishes

Lobe-finned fishes may be immediately distinguished from acanthodians and rayfinned fishes by the lobe at the base of the fins. The reason for this swollen condition is that the lobes contain muscles and bones that are similar in many ways to those in the limbs of the *tetrapods* (four-legged vertebrates). Thin, flexible rays extend from the lobe to support the rest of the fin area. These flexible rays are used to maneuver.

Lobe-finned fishes also have well-developed lungs and *internal nostrils.* Lungs supplement the gills when the water gets stagnant. The internal nostrils allow these fishes to breathe with just the tip of the nose breaking the surface of the water. This way they can get oxygen without gulping air at the surface, which tends to attract predators.

There are two very different kinds of lobe-finned fishes, the lungfishes (fig. 63a) and the crossopterygians or "crossopts" (see fig. 31a). Ancient lungfishes have a variable number of outer (dermal) skull bones, the braincase is composed of a single unit, and the dentition is in the form of tooth plates. Ancient crossopts, on the other hand, have a regular number of stable dermal skull bones, the braincase is composed of two movable units, and they have rows of single teeth called labyrinthodont teeth. Labyrinthodont teeth are so named because they have complex wrinkles on their outer surfaces. The crossopts are an important group of fishes because they are believed to have given rise to the tetrapods (four-legged vertebrates).

Modern lungfishes occur today in Africa, South America, and Australia. The African and South American lungfishes are eel shaped and have filamentous fins and slimy bodies. They often crawl around in the mud with their heads elevated, looking more like snakes than fishes. But when their pond dries up, they burrow into the mud and writhe around until they excavate a flask-shaped burrow. They coat this burrow with a slimy mucous that hardens to form a protective cocoon that saves the fish from desiccation until the pond fills up again with rainwater. Modern Australian lungfishes look more like some of the larger ancient forms (fig. 63a) and probably act like them as well. Australian lungfishes live in rivers, have well-developed lobe fins, are "fish-shaped," and have large scales.

Crossopterygians are known only on the basis of ancient fossil forms, except for the coelacanth, a living fossil that lives in deep seawater near Madagascar. This very large predatory fish was not discovered by scientists until 1945, although local people had been familiar with it for many years. When a scientist was finally able to see a modern coelacanth, he was moved to tears.

Lobe-finned fishes in the Great Lakes region are mainly represented by a few unidentified fossil specimens from the early Pennsylvanian rocks of the Michigan Basin. A fossil lungfish burrow (fig. 63b) has also been excavated from these strata. It seems only a matter of time until more of these specimens are collected in the region and are documented by publications. The difficulty is that one must find freshwater deposits, and most Paleozoic deposits in the region are saltwater ones.

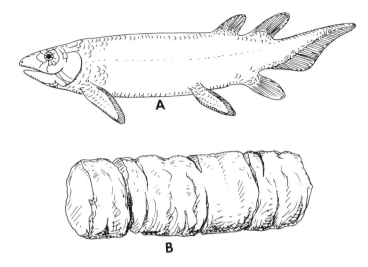

Fig. 63. Lungfishes. *A,* artist's reconstruction of the Devonian lungfish *Dipterus; B,* lungfish burrow from early Pennsylvanian rocks near Lansing, Michigan.

Rayfinned Fishes

Rayfinned fishes lack the lobe that occurs at the base of the fins in the lobe-finned fishes. Rayfinned fishes also lack lungs and internal nostrils, so that forms such as garpikes and bowfins that use their air bladder as a primitive lung must gulp air at the surface of the water. Rayfinned fishes are divided into two groups, the primitive *chondrosteans* that are primarily a Devonian, Mississippian, and Pennsylvanian group, and the *neopterygians* that originated in the Paleozoic but had an extensive radiation in the late Mesozoic, and became the dominant fishes of the Cenozoic period.

Chondrosteans

Chondrosteans (fig. 64a) have thick, shiny, rhomboidal scales called *ganoid* scales, the vertebral column turns upward into the upper lobe of an asymmetrical tail, the upper jaw is very long and is connected to the bones of the cheek region, and the internal skeleton is not very bony. Chondrosteans are commonly called the ganoid fishes. Two living representatives of these primitive rayfinned fishes that live in the Great Lakes region are the sturgeons and the garpikes.

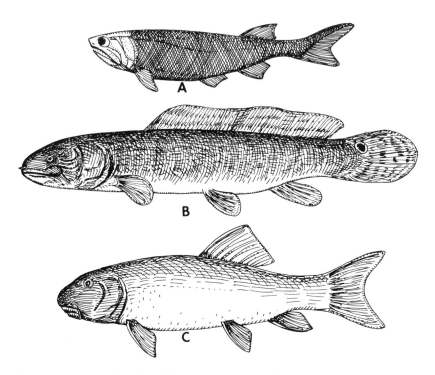

Fig. 64. Ancient and modern fishes. *A,* artist's reconstruction of *Cheirolepis,* an ancient chondrostean palaeoniscoid fish. *B,* the modern bowfin (*Amia calva*), a primitive neopterygian fish. *C,* the modern white sucker (*Catostomus commersoni*). Both *B* and *C* occur in the modern fauna of the Great Lakes Basin today. *Catostomus* sp. has been identified from the late Pleistocene of the Great Lakes Basin.

Paleozoic chondrostean fishes were mainly a freshwater group; thus Paleozoic chondrostean fish fossils are mainly found in the rather rare freshwater or brackish water deposits in Pennyslvanian strata of the Michigan Basin. Several kinds of chondrostean fishes called *palaeoniscoids* have been collected from these rocks in the central Michigan area, but none of them have been carefully studied or written about. Palaeoniscoids are immediately distinguishable from most other fishes by their covering of very large, thick, rhomboidal, and very shiny ganoid scales.

Neopterygians

The neopterygians represent fishes that have progressed beyond the chondrostean condition. Primitive neopterygians (formerly called "holosteans") are represented in the modern fish fauna of the Great Lakes region by the bowfin (fig. 64b) that is common in some shallow, weedy lakes and ponds in the southern part of the region. Advanced neopterygians have thin, overlapping scales called *cycloid* or *ctenoid* scales; a tail that is symmetrical both on the outside and the inside; an upper jaw that is not only not connected to the cheekbones, but often is not even a functional part of the mouth; and a very bony internal skeleton.

Neopterygian fishes occur in Pleistocene sites in the Great Lakes region ranging from the Sangamonian interglacial age until the late Wisconsinan glacial age. These fishes belong to several different families and all represent species living today in the Great Lakes region.

Cyprinidae (minnows). The word *minnow* usually suggests a small bait fish you put on the end of a fishhook; but in western North America and in Europe some cyprinids reach a large size. Minnows are very abundant in the Great Lakes region today and are represented by scores of species. Most minnows are either forage feeders or vegetarians, but some will eat small animal prey. The European carp is a cyprinid that has been widely introduced into the Great Lakes region, where it is often considered a pest. Minnows, unidentified specifically, have been reported from the Pleistocene middle Wisconsinan (Cherry Tree substage) near Port Huron, Michigan, and from the Indian Trail Caverns late Pleistocene postglacial site in northwestern Ohio.

Catostomidae (suckers). Suckers are freshwater fishes with a downturned mouth. Some of them may reach several pounds in weight, and they are a common fish in all parts of the Great Lakes region, where they are often smoked and eaten. White sucker (*Catostomus commersoni*, fig. 64c) has been found associated with a mastodont in a late Pleistocene postglacial bog site in the central part of the Lower Peninsula of Michigan.

Ictaluridae (catfishes). Catfishes have naked skins, spines, and "whiskers" called *barbels*, and they are quite familiar to most people. Catfish spines are rather structurally complicated; a single one resides on the back, behind the head; and a pair of them (*pectoral spines*, fig. 65a) occur just behind the head on either side of the body. These spines tend to fossilize and because of their complex structure can often be identified to the specific level. Fossils representing catfishes, *Ictalurus* (fig. 65b), have been reported from the Pleistocene Sangamonian interglacial stage near Toronto.

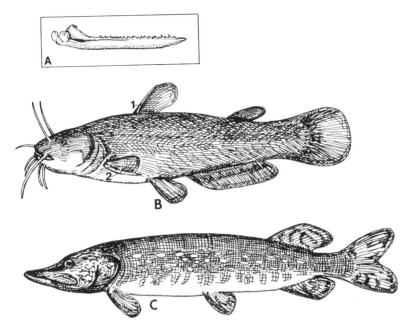

Fig. 65. Bullheads and pike. *A*, pectoral spine of the modern yellow bullhead catfish, *Ictalurus natalis*. *B*, modern *Ictalurus natalis,* showing the position of dorsal (1) and pectoral (2) spines. *C*, modern northern pike, *Esox lucius.* Both *B* and *C* occur in the modern fauna of the Great Lakes Basin. *Ictalurus* sp. and *Esox* sp. have been reported from the late Pleistocene of the Great Lakes Basin.

Esocidae (pike and pickerels). This family of elongate, toothy predators is very common today in the Great Lakes region, and it includes the muskies and northerns that are popular with fishermen. Fossils representing pike, *Esox* (fig. 65c) have been found in the Pleistocene Sangamonian interglacial stage near Toronto.

Gasterosteidae (sticklebacks). The spiny little sticklebacks (fig. 66a) are common fishes in the northern parts of both North America and Europe. They are abundant in the modern fauna of the Great Lakes region. Stickleback reproductive antics have fascinated animal behaviorists for many years. Sticklebacks have been reported from the Pleistocene middle Wisconsinan (Cherry Tree substage) near Port Huron, Michigan.

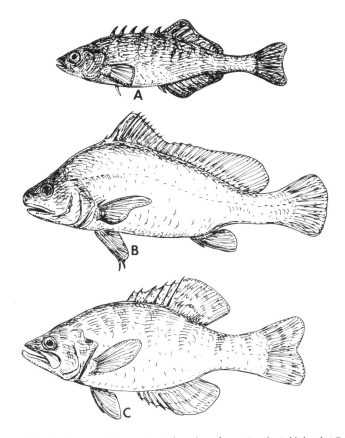

Fig. 66. Stickleback, drum, and crappie. *A,* brook or five-spined stickleback (*Culaea inconstans*). *B,* freshwater drum (*Aplodinotus grunniens*). *C,* white crappie (*Pomoxis annularis*). All of these fishes occur in the late Pleistocene and modern fauna of the Great Lakes Basin.

Sciaenidae (drumfish and croakers). This eminently edible group of fishes is largely marine, but the freshwater drumfish (fig. 66b) is widespread in the United States and is quite common in some parts of the southern Great Lakes region today. Freshwater drum tooth plates and ear structures called *otoliths* often fossilize, and both are useful in the identification of these animals. Freshwater drumfish fossils, *Aplodinotus grunniens,* have been reported from the Pleistocene middle Wisconsinan (Cherry Tree substage) near Port Huron, Michigan.

Centrarchidae (sunfishes). This family, particularly popular with fishermen all over, contains the large- and smallmouth basses, the bluegills, crappies, and sunfishes, as well as the rock and warmouth basses. These fishes are common in most of the warmer waters of the Great Lakes region today. Crappie, *Pomoxis* (fig. 66c), has been found associated with a mastodont in a late Pleistocene postglacial site in the central Lower Peninsula of Michigan.

Tetrapods

All of the remaining fossil vertebrates to be discussed are called tetrapods in that all of them have (or their ancestor had) paired limbs instead of paired fins. Most paleontologists believe that the tetrapod ancestor was one of the crossopterygian fishes (see fig. 31a), but some hold out for a lungfish (see fig. 63a) ancestry. The earliest tetrapods appear in late Devonian times, and some of them had more than five "fingers" and/or "toes."

The why of the origin of the tetrapod limb has been the subject of several hypotheses or educated speculations. One hypothesis stresses the need to develop limbs to get out on land to escape aquatic predators. Another suggests that crossopterygian fishes used their lobe fins to struggle from dried-up ponds or swamps to ones that still contained water. A third hypothesis points out that limbs and "fingers" and "toes" might have evolved in the water as a means for the animals to anchor themselves to vegetation while waiting in ambush for prey.

Amphibians

Amphibians are vertebrates that lack a land egg (*amniote egg*). Most must return to the water to reproduce, but a few have evolved an elaborate way to hatch a jelly-coated egg on land. Amphibians were the earliest tetrapods, and some of the ancient Paleozoic ones were much larger than their modern survivors. Other Paleozoic amphibians were much smaller. Some looked like snakes, others had bizarre boomerang-shaped heads, while still others look like salamanders or rather large-headed lizards.

Lissamphibians

All of the modern amphibians are put in one subclass, the *Lissamphibia*, that is thought to have a common ancestor somewhere back in the late Paleozoic. Lissamphibians have unique teeth composed of two parts, a base called a *pedicel* and a *crown* that sits on top; unique structures in the eye and the ear; a unique skin used for breathing that often contains specialized mucous and poison glands; and specialized fat bodies associated with their reproductive organs. This group contains the caecilians, salamanders, and frogs (including toads and treefrogs).

Caecilians (fig. 67a) are tropical animals that look like big earthworms; they have a long legless body ringed with grooves from front to back. The head of caecilians usually has tiny eyes the size of pinheads on it, a mouth that contains two rows of very sharp teeth, and protrusible, sensory tentacles between the eyes and the nostrils. The caecilian tentacle is a unique structure in tetrapods and is innervated by former eye nerves and moved by former eye muscles.

Caecilians spend most of their lives in underground burrows, and their eyes have degenerated to the point that they merely register the presence of light rather than a picture. In fact, some species have eyes that are completely covered over by the bones of the skull! The skull of caecilians is composed of a few bones fused together to ram through the soil; where the animals search for worms, other caecilians, or small snakes to eat. The first fossil caecilians are known from Jurassic rocks in Arizona. These animals had most of the structures of modern caecilians, but they had small somewhat salamander-like legs! Caecilians have left no fossil record in the Great Lakes region.

Salamanders (fig. 67b) are much more conventional-looking tetrapods than caecilians or frogs and resemble small scaleless lizards. They have looked that way for a long time, as Jurassic salamanders very closely resemble some of the modern ones. Salamanders are rather common in the Great Lakes region today, especially in the southern parts. Most of them live in moist places on land but must return to the water where they lay jelly-coated eggs during breeding. These eggs hatch into larvae with external gills that allow them to breathe in the water until they transform into the adult form. The red-backed salamander common in wooded areas throughout most of the region, however, lays its eggs on land under moist logs or piles of leaves. These eggs

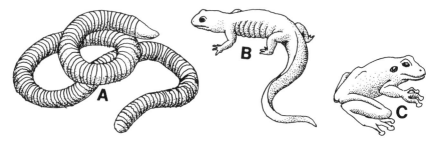

Fig. 67. Lissamphibians. *A,* terrestrial caecilian; *B,* mole salamander; *C,* treefrog. (Drawing by Merald Clark.)

hatch into miniature replicas of the adult. The largest salamander in the region, the mudpuppy, spends all of its life in the water, and fishermen describe it as looking like "a bullhead with legs."

Thus far, the only fossil salamanders that have been unearthed in the Great Lakes region are some as yet unidentified vertebrae and limbs from the Indian Trail Caverns late Pleistocene site in northwestern Ohio. Other cold-tolerant species of salamanders should eventually turn up in some of the late Pleistocene postglacial deposits in the area. One of the reasons that fossil salamanders have not been found may be that their bones are very tiny and therefore overlooked by people digging up mastodonts and mammoths.

Frogs and toads (fig. 67c) have bodies that are quite modified for jumping (frogs) or hopping (toads). The vertebral column is very short, but the hip girdle is especially well developed and modified to support a long pair of jumping or hopping legs. The skull of frogs and toads is also highly modified from the original tetrapod condition; it is composed of relatively few bones and has very large eye sockets. In fact, many true frogs have such large eyes that they use the backs of them to help push large prey down their throats!

Frogs and toads are common in the Great Lakes region today, and all of them must return to the water in the spring or early summer to reproduce. The males make various clacking, chirping, trilling, or guttural calls to the females to entice them to the breeding ponds, where the eggs are laid and fertilized externally.

The eggs hatch into larvae called tadpoles that look more like tiny bulbous fishes than tetrapods. Tadpoles usually transform into froglets or toadlets by the end of the first summer; but in the Great Lakes region

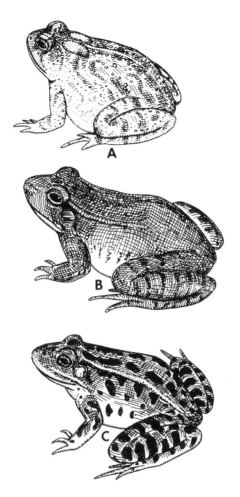

Fig. 68. Toads and frogs. *A,* American toad (*Bufo americanus*); *B,* green frog (*Rana clamitans*); *C,* leopard frog (*Rana pipiens*). All of these species occur in the late Pleistocene and modern fauna of the Great Lakes Basin.

some of the larger species such as the bullfrog or the green frog may spend two or three years as tadpoles. Some of the northern frogs are quite cold-tolerant, and one would expect to find these species in late Pleistocene and post-Pleistocene deposits of the region. But only a handful of frog/toad fossils have been reported from sites that are reliably dated.

Order Anura (toads and frogs)

Bufonidae (bufonids and toads). An American toad, *Bufo americanus* (fig. 68a) was reported from an organic layer in a water well beneath late Wisconsinan glacial lake sediments in the southwestern part of the Lower Peninsula of Michigan. Another toad referred questionably (*Bufo* sp., *?B. americanus*) was reported from a cave in Halton County, Ontario. This cave was thought to be of possible Illinoian glacial age, based on mammalian remains there.

Ranidae (ranids). Two species of ranid frogs, the green frog, *Rana clamitans* (fig. 68b) and the bullfrog, *Rana catesbeiana*, were reported from the same mastodont site in the late Wisconsinan Two Creeks substage in the southeastern part of the Lower Peninsula of Michigan. Some paleontologists, however, have expressed some concern about the identification of the bullfrog bones and have suggested that all frog bones of the mastodont site probably represented green frogs.

A leopard frog, *Rana pipiens* (fig. 68c), was reported from a mastodont site in northwestern Indiana. This site has not been carbon 14 dated, but it is almost certain that it represents the late Wisconsinan part of the Pleistocene. Unidentified large and small species of frogs were reported from the Indian Trail Caverns late Pleistocene postglacial site in northwestern Ohio.

It is not surprising that the American toad, the leopard frog, and the green frog were among the first animals that reinvaded postglacial Michigan in the Pleistocene, for each of them is a hardy, cold-tolerant species. One cannot help but think that more frog and toad bones will come to light in the region when sediments from mastodont sites are carefully sieved through screens.

Reptiles

Reptiles are the earliest animals with a type of egg (amniote egg) that allowed them true independence from the water. Some ancient, thick-skinned amphibians ventured into pretty dry situations, and a few amphibians live in desert and semidesert areas today. But most of these animals need at least a temporary pond to start their tadpoles in. In fact, some spadefoot toads that live in semidesert areas are only able to breed about once every two or three years, when it rains enough to make a puddle of water.

The amniote egg is named after one of its important internal membranes called the *amnion*. Reptiles, birds, and mammals are called amniotes because all of them are attached to amniotic tissues when they are embryos. Amniotic tissues form an amniotic sac containing the amniotic fluid. This fluid keeps the embryo from drying out, protects the embryo from shock (when the eggs are moved around), and keeps the delicate embryonic tissues from sticking together.

Other amniote egg membranes enclose food (yolk) for the developing embryo, while still others take care of the breathing and excretory problems. Finally, a calcareous shell supports the embryo and embryonic tissues on land. When vertebrates hatch from an amniote egg, they are much larger and more completely developed than when they hatch from aquatic eggs.

The true invasion of the land by reptiles was a significant evolutionary event that allowed complex vertebrate communities to develop, communities that for the first time featured giant herbivores (*megaherbivores*), with large predatory carnivores feeding upon them and large scavengers to clean up after the carnivores. The first unquestionable reptiles are known from the early middle Pennsylvanian; their fossils were found in the upright stumps of the lycopod genus *Sigillaria* (see fig. 36a). These first reptiles were small lizardlike animals and were modified for eating insects. Later in the Pennsylvanian and in the Permian there was an adaptive radiation of reptiles that produced the first large, true land herbivores as well as mammal-like carnivores with huge heads and a doglike gait.

In the Triassic, reptiles called *thecodonts* became important and eventually evolved into the first dinosaurs at the end of the period. Dinosaurs radiated spectacularly in the Jurassic and the Cretaceous periods and dominated the land for about 145 million years. Several dinosaur groups arose and declined during these times, and most of them existed in megaherbivore-carnivore-scavenger communities. Dinosaurs became extinct at the end of the Cretaceous.

Several groups of reptiles returned to the sea and were especially important in the shallow inland seas that were extensive in both the Jurassic and the Cretaceous. These animals also became extinct at the end of the Cretaceous.

Modern reptiles are only a remnant of the groups that existed in the past, consisting of *turtles, crocodilians, lizards* (including *worm* lizards), *snakes,* and the *tuatara* of several islands in the New Zealand area. Of the surviving reptiles, crocodilians are the most closely related to the dinosaurs. Modern reptiles tend to decrease in diversity as one travels northward. Nevertheless, reptiles occur in moderate numbers in the Great Lakes region and are one of its important natural resources. But very few ancient reptile fossils are known in the area because of the Lost Interval that basically wiped out all of the sedimentary record from the Permian to the end of the Quaternary.

There are some fossil records of reptiles in late Pleistocene and postglacial deposits in the Great Lakes region, but these are spotty and some are questionable. For instance, several reptile fossils have been reported from lake and bog deposits that are of very doubtful Pleistocene age. These records are often reported only as "from lake sediments" or from "beneath muck" or "beneath peat," and these kinds of occurrences are not always indicative of Pleistocene or even of early post-Pleistocene age.

To be considered a valid Pleistocene fossil, a bone should meet at least one of the following three criteria: (1) It should be at least 10,000 radiocarbon years old or associated with some object that is 10,000 radiocarbon years old; or (2) it should be in stratigraphic context with an extinct Pleistocene vertebrate such as a mastodont or a mammoth; or (3) it should occur beneath glacial sediments of known Pleistocene age. Only a few reptiles have been reliably identified from the late Pleistocene of the Great Lakes region.

Order Testudines (turtles)

Turtles are certainly living fossils, as they were a well-established group before the first dinosaurs evolved, and some of the turtles that lived with the dinosaurs would be very difficult to distinguish from living ones. No other vertebrate has a shell as structurally perfect as that of turtles; and it seems that once the shell was perfected, the animals underwent very little structural change.

Turtles are considered to be one of the earliest branches of early amniote evolution and have physiological, genetic, embryonic, and structural differences that distinguish them from other reptiles, birds, and mammals. In spite of its relatively northern latitude, the Great Lakes

Fig. 69. Snapping turtles and painted turtles. *A*, snapping turtle (*Chelydra serpentina*). *B*, painted turtle (*Chrysemys picta*). *C*, two plates from the lower shell (plastron) of a painted turtle recovered from the late Pleistocene of a mastodont site in southeastern Michigan. Both species of turtles occur in the late Pleistocene and modern fauna of the Great Lakes Basin. (*A* and *B* from J. A. Holman and J. H. Harding, *Michigan's Turtles* [East Lansing: Michigan State University Museum, 1977]; *C* from J. A. Holman and D. C. Fisher, Late Pleistocene turtle remains [Reptilia: Testudines] from southern Michigan, *Michigan Academician* 25 [1993]: 491–99.)

region is, compared to many other regions in the world, well represented by turtle species. Michigan, for instance, has 11 species of turtles, whereas in central western Europe there is only one species, and it is presently uncommon.

Chelydridae (snapping turtles). Remains of a snapping turtle, *Chelydra serpentina*, (fig. 69a), have been reported from the Indian Trail Caverns late Pleistocene postglacial site in northwestern Ohio. Snapping turtles are a cold-tolerant species that extends northward to the area of the Great Slave Lakes in Manitoba today; thus it is not surprising that it occurs as a late Pleistocene fossil in northwestern Ohio.

Emydidae (emydids). A painted turtle, *Chrysemys picta* (fig. 69b), is represented by two shell bones (fig. 69c) from a mastodont site in southeastern Michigan. One can count growth rings on the shells of painted turtles in the same manner one counts tree rings to determine age. Male painted turtles are smaller than females; thus it was determined that one large young turtle found was a female and one old small one was a male. It was also determined, by comparing age-size data in the fossils with data from modern painted turtles in different habitats, that the fossil turtles lived in a moderately enriched habitat.

This painted turtle site does not have a carbon 14 date, but it is believed that it represents a time from about 12,000 to 11,000 years before the present. The vegetation in southeastern Michigan at this time consisted mainly of spruce and jack pine, which suggests a very cool postglacial climate. The painted turtle find, then, is not surprising.

Painted turtles today are among the most cold-tolerant turtles in the world and, along with the snapping turtle, range farther north than any other American turtle. Painted turtles have many adaptations that indicate they might be among the earliest reptilian species to have reinvaded deglaciated areas. These adaptations involve being active at lower temperatures than many turtles, being able to have some of their tissues frozen solid without permanent damage, and having the hatched baby turtles able to overwinter in the nest.

A Blanding's turtle, *Emydoidea blandingii* (fig. 70a), is known from a site in Ontario north of Lake Erie near the town of Innerkip. This site may represent a very warm Wisconsinan interstadial period or possibly may be of Sangamonian (last interglacial) age. Blanding's turtles are a rather cold-tolerant species and occur in the Upper Peninsula of Michigan today. This species has also been found in the Indian Trail Caverns late Pleistocene postglacial site in northwestern Ohio.

Trionychidae (softshell turtles). A softshell turtle (fig. 70b) represented by a right femur (fig. 70c) from a mastodont site near Lansing in the central part of the Lower Peninsula of Michigan is puzzling, as it was not found directly associated with the mastodont. The mastodont had been dated by the carbon 14 method at about 11,000 years before the present, and stratigraphic comparisons indicated that the softshell turtle might have been about 10,000 years old. If this is true, the climate might have improved enough by this time to have allowed for the reinvasion of this species, a form that is definitely not as cold tolerant as painted and snapping turtles.

More turtle fossils and hopefully other reptilian fossils will turn up

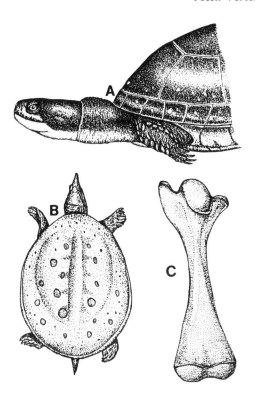

Fig. 70. Blanding's and softshell turtles. *A,* Blanding's turtle (*Emydoidea blandingii*). *B,* spiny softshell turtle (*Apalone spinifera*). *C,* the right femur of a spiny softshell turtle that may be about 10,000 years old taken near a mastodont site near Lansing, Michigan. Both species of turtle occur in the late Pleistocene and modern fauna of the Great Lakes Basin. (*A* and *B* from J. A. Holman and J. H. Harding, *Michigan's Turtles* [East Lansing: Michigan State University Museum, 1977]; *C* from J. A. Holman and D. C. Fisher, Late Pleistocene turtle remains [Reptilia: Testudines] from southern Michigan, *Michigan Academician* 25 [1993]: 491–99.)

in late Pleistocene sites in the Great Lakes region when sediments from extinct vertebrate sites are carefully picked through or sieved for small vertebrate remains. On the other hand, it may be that turtles and other reptiles were few and far between in the cool postglacial Great Lakes region. One only has to go as far south as central Ohio, Indiana, and Illinois to find several turtles in some late Wisconsinan deposits; and a late Wisconsinan site in southwestern Indiana has a rich herpetofauna, typical of the area today, and contains several "southern" reptile species as well.

Birds

Birds are warm-blooded (*endothermic*) amniotes with feathers. Birds evolved from small dinosaurs at least by late Jurassic times, and according to some vertebrate paleontologists, they may have appeared much earlier. Modern birds, of course, are common in the Great Lakes region, but fossil birds are rare and confined to late Pleistocene sediments. As in the case of many fossil reptiles reported as Pleistocene fossils from the region, birds bones have been identified from certain peat and lake bed deposits that have not been reliably dated. The three following fossil bird records are thought to be from reliable Pleistocene deposits in the Great Lakes region.

Order Galliformes (gallinaceous birds)

Phasianidae (pheasants, grouse, turkeys, and quail). A bird record consists of bones of a grouse (not specifically identified) from a cave fauna from Halton County, Ontario. Other faunal units in the cave suggest that the deposit might be of the Illinoian glacial age.

A turkey, *Meleagris gallopavo,* has been identified on the basis of bones from the Indian Trail Caverns late Pleistocene postglacial site in northwestern Ohio.

Order Anseriformes (waterfowl)

Anatidae (swans, geese, and ducks). The bone of a lesser scaup duck (*Aythya affinis,* fig. 71) was found under rather unusual circumstances. The find was made during the digging of a water well in the west central part of the Lower Peninsula of Michigan. The bone was found at a depth of about 145 feet among wood fragments and pollen that indicated vegetation dominated by jack pine and spruce. A carbon 14 date of about 25,000 years before the present was obtained on the wood layer. This indicated that the duck occurred in Michigan at about the time of the Plum Point substage (glacial withdrawal stage) of the late middle Wisconsinan.

Fig. 71. Lesser scaup ducks (*Aythya affinis*). This species occurs both in the modern fauna of the Great Lakes Basin and from a site about 25,000 years old in the Lower Peninsula of Michigan. (From J. A. Holman, *Michigan's Fossil Vertebrates* [East Lansing: Michigan State University Museum, 1975].)

Mammals

Mammals are first known from the late Tertiary period about the same time that the first dinosaurs appeared in the fossil record. The earliest mammals were derived from small members of a mammal-like reptile group called the *cynodonts*. Mammal-like reptiles were important members of the land fauna in the late Permian, but they began to decline in the Triassic when a group of reptiles called thecodonts (which ultimately gave rise to the dinosaurs) began to expand. If you wish to imagine what the earliest mammals looked and acted like, try to picture

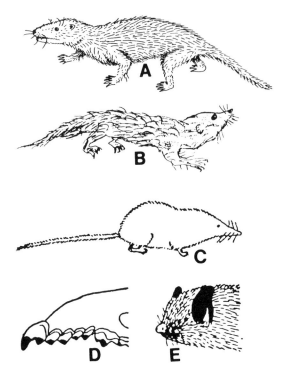

Fig. 72. Early mammals, insectivores, and bats. A and B, two conceptions of the appearance of one of the very earliest mammals, *Morganucodon*, of the late Triassic period. C, masked shrew (*Sorex cinereus*), an insectivore of the modern Great Lakes region. D, rostrum of a masked shrew showing pigmented teeth. E, head of little brown bat (*Myotis lucifugus*). (B, sketch by the author; C–E, W. H. Burt, *Mammals of the Great Lakes Region* [Ann Arbor: University of Michigan Press, 1957].)

a mouse-sized hybrid between an opossum and a shrew. These animals undoubtedly had twitchy little faces, beady eyes, a body only sparsely covered with hair, and a scraggly tail (fig. 72a–b). Their activities were probably mainly nocturnal, for if they had been active in the daytime, they would have been eaten by small dinosaurs.

Many adaptations that carry over from the earliest mammals to the mammals of today are the result of these early nocturnal habits, and many mammals are still nocturnal. The whiskers (*vibrissae*) of mammals occur not only on the face but on the legs of some mammals such as squirrels. Vibrissae are sensory hairs that help the animals move about in the dark. The lack of color vision in most mammals is also attributed to a nocturnal existence. Finally, warm-bloodedness (*endothermy*) itself is an adaption to cooler temperate, alpine, and nocturnal temperatures.

For about 145 million years mammals remained small and mainly nocturnal, as they had to avoid small dinosaurs as well as birds and large lizards through the Jurassic and the Cretaceous. But finally, about 65 million years ago, the dinosaurs became extinct and the way was opened for the mammals to make their way into the sun. The first radiation of mammals took place very early in the Tertiary period and produced the first mammalian communities dominated by large herbivores and their predators. Both of these groups evolved very rapidly from small mammals left over from the Cretaceous and consisted of large, ungainly, small-brained herbivores and equally dimwitted carnivores to feed upon them.

A relatively short time later in the late Paleocene and early Eocene, the ancestors of modern herbivores, carnivores, rodents, and other familiar mammalian groups evolved and quickly began to outcompete the earlier large forms. These groups continued to diversify and achieve large size in the Oligocene, and some new groups were added as well. In the Miocene, grasslands expanded greatly and replaced forests in many parts of the world. During this time hoofed herbivores diversified at an amazing rate, and by late Miocene times megaherbivores such as elephants, rhinos, and hippos were abundant.

In the Pliocene a general extinction began that was to culminate at the end of the Pleistocene (Ice Age). This extinction affected most of the megaherbivores, many other large herbivores, and the carnivores and scavengers that fed upon them. Today, humans and their domestic animals have largely taken the place of the great mammalian communities of the Tertiary and Pleistocene. This system still depends on grasses such as rice, wheat, corn, oats, and barley for its survival.

One of the most important features of mammals is their teeth. Mammals have only two sets of teeth, unlike fishes, amphibians, and reptiles, where the teeth are continually replaced. In mammals, milk teeth are succeeded by the permanent teeth, and when these are worn down the mammal is toothless. The advantage to this system is that a very complicated *occlusion* occurs. This means that the teeth in the upper and lower jaws fit together in a very complex way. Occlusion allows mammals to be such efficient processors of food that it is usually pulverized before it enters the throat. The problem side of this arrangement is that each little cusp of each tooth must fit into every little depression of the tooth with which it occludes, or there is a chewing or biting problem. Recalling experiences with imperfect, newly fitted dental crowns allows one to realize the importance of perfect alignment of cusps and cusp receptors.

Teeth are the most important mammalian fossils. This is because the surfaces of mammalian teeth often have very complicated patterns on them that allow specific identifications to be made. Moreover, teeth are the hardest tissues in the mammalian body and are more likely to be preserved than any other structures. Problems in the identification of mammalian teeth vary. For instance, it is quite easy to tell a mastodont tooth from a mammoth tooth, but one needs to be an expert to be able to distinguish the teeth of the different species of mammoths. The tiny teeth of mice are easy to distinguish from those of shrews and bats, but identifying species of any of these groups can be an arduous task.

The following section deals with fossil mammals that have been identified from the Great Lakes region. All of these represent late Pleistocene finds.

Order Insectivora (insectivores)

The insectivores comprise a group of mammals that are very primitive and that were present in the Cretaceous along with the dinosaurs. Familiar types of insectivores include shrews (fig. 72c), moles, and the European hedgehog. The insectivores are not known for their intelligence. They have small tubular brains and a primitive flat-footed way of scurrying about. The food consists mainly of invertebrate animals, but sometimes small vertebrates are eaten.

Soricidae (shrews). Shrews are among the smallest mammals in the world. Probably the best characterization of shrews was given by the late vertebrate paleontologist John Guilday, who said that a shrew looks like a mouse that got its nose caught in a pencil sharpener. Shrews are voracious animals that eat all kinds of other little creatures up to the size of mice and small snakes. But shrews are also prey for many small predators, such as owls, snakes, and sometimes even large frogs.

The teeth of shrews (fig. 72d) are very characteristic in that they are capped with a dark red color. This color occurs on the teeth of most fossil shrews as well. An interesting study showed that this reddish pigment is even harder than tooth enamel and that it is associated with

chewing up things like earthworms that have sand grains in their digestive tracts. Shrews are common in the modern fauna of the Great Lakes
region. Fossil material assigned to the genus *Sorex* (fig. 72c), but not
assigned to species, has been found at the Pleistocene late Wisconsinan
(Cherry Tree substage) near Port Huron, Michigan; and *Sorex* (red-
toothed shrew), *Microsorex* (pigmy shrew), and *Blarina* (short-tailed
shrew) have been reported from the Indian Trail Caverns late Pleistocene postglacial site of northwestern Ohio.

Order Chiroptera (bats)

Bats are some of the most specialized of all mammals in their structural
modifications associated with flight. These modifications must have occurred early, as bats very similar to modern ones are known from the
Eocene. Bats are closely related to insectivores and may have evolved
from them.

Vespertilionidae (vespertilionid bats). Fossils of the little brown bat
(*Myotis lucifugus*, fig. 72e) are known from a cave in Halton County,
Ontario, that is thought to be of possible Illinoian age on the basis of
other faunal associates. *Myotis* sp. has been reported from the Indian
Trail Caverns late Pleistocene postglacial site of northwestern Ohio.
Bats are frequent cave fossils, as they often roost in caves during the
daylight hours.

Order Carnivora (carnivores)

True carnivores of the order Carnivora quickly replaced the less well
adapted, clumsy creodont carnivores early in the Tertiary. The earliest
true carnivores were animals that looked something like the civet cats
of the Old World or the fishers and martins of the New World. Carnivores are distinguished by several adaptations. The teeth are differenti-
ated into little incisors at the front of the mouth for nipping, followed
by canines for stabbing and slashing, and cheek teeth that are specialized for shearing and grinding. An upper and lower pair of cheek teeth
that are especially adapted for shearing are termed *carnassials*.

It's instructive to watch a dog process a fresh bone. When the animal
wants to shear off the cartilaginous end parts of the bone, it shifts the
bone around to the corner of its mouth, where the carnassials get the
job done. Some interesting kinds of carnivores evolved in the middle

part of the Tertiary, including the large "bear dogs" (neither bears nor dogs) and, later on, bone-crushing dogs that developed broadened cheek teeth for this purpose. These animals soon became extinct.

Modern carnivores are divided into three groups or suborders. These are the *feloids* (often called aeluroids), *arctoids*, and *otaroids*. Feloids include (1) the primitive viverrids, which consist of the mongoose and civets and their relatives; (2) all of the cats, large and small; (3) an extinct group called the sabertooths (incorrectly called saber-toothed tigers); and (4) the hyenas.

Arctoids include (1) the mustelids, which consist of animals like otters, skunks, weasels, badgers, and fishers; (2) canids, including domestic dogs and doglike animals such as wolves, foxes, and coyotes; (3) ursids, the bears; and (4) procyonids, which include raccoons, coatis, ringtail cats (not cats), and pandas. Finally, the otaroids include seals and sea lions.

Mustelidae (mustelids)

Mustelids are very common small predators in the Great Lakes region today, especially in northern areas. The ermine (*Mustela erminea*) has been found in the late Wisconsinan (Cherry Tree substage) near Port Huron, Michigan, and from the Indian Trail Caverns late Pleistocene postglacial site in northwestern Ohio. Today these animals occur widely in Alaska, Canada, and the northern United States.

The martin (*Martes americana*, fig. 73a) has been identified from the Indian Trail Caverns late Pleistocene postglacial site in northwestern Ohio. Today, in eastern North America, the pine martin occurs mainly north of the Great Lakes in Canada. Thus, a cooler climate is indicated for northwestern Ohio during the time the martin lived there.

The striped skunk (*Mephitis mephitis*) has been found as a fossil from a cave in Halton County, Ontario, near Toronto. Based on other fauna members, it is believed that this might be an Illinoian glacial age deposit. This skunk has also been identified from the Indian Trail Caverns late Pleistocene postglacial site of northwestern Ohio.

Ursidae (bears)

Bears have been around since the Miocene. At present, black bear is the only species that occurs in the Great Lakes region; but in the late

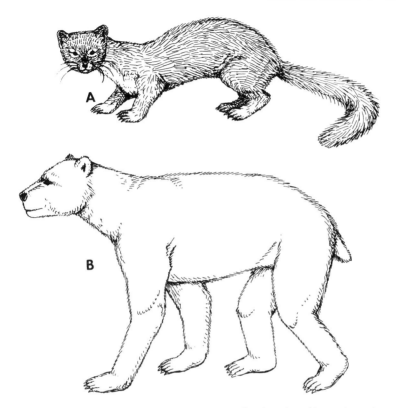

Fig. 73. *A,* martin, and *B,* artist's reconstruction of a short-faced bear (*Arctodus simus*). Both of these animals are found in the late Pleistocene of the Great Lakes region. The short-faced bear was a top predator.

Pleistocene the black bear, the grizzly bear, and the extinct short-faced bear have been recorded. The black bear (*Ursus americanus*) has been recorded from the postglacial late Wisconsinan of the Lower Peninsula of Michigan, from the early Wisconsinan of the Toronto region of Ontario, and from the Indian Trail Caverns late Pleistocene postglacial site in northwestern Ohio. Black bears are omnivores that store up fat during the summer, which enables them to hibernate in cold northern regions. The fact that there is only one valid Pleistocene record for this species in Michigan seems strange, considering that it is not rare in the northern part of the state today.

There is only one record of the grizzly bear (*Ursus arctos*) as a fossil from the Great Lakes region and this is from the middle Wisconsinan of Woodbridge, Ontario, near Toronto. This is an important record, since *Ursus arctos* occurs in North America today only in the northern Rocky Mountain area of the United States and then northward and westward to the Arctic. The grizzly (also called the brown bear) is much larger than the black bear and can occasionally be dangerous to humans. The earliest fossil record of *Ursus arctos* is from the middle Pleistocene of China. The species eventually migrated to North America over the land bridge between Siberia and Alaska. The Toronto grizzly record indicates a colder climate than occurs in the area at present.

The short-faced bear (*Arctodus simus,* fig. 73b) is an important extinct species that has been found at the Indian Trail Caverns late Pleistocene postglacial site in northwestern Ohio. This bear was very different from modern North American bears. The short-faced bear had a short body with long legs, and its face was short and had a wide muzzle. The short-faced bear was much more of a predator than are modern bears. It is believed that many of the broken pieces of mammalian bone found in North American Pleistocene cave sites represent the prey of short-faced bears. This carnivore ranged from Alaska to Mexico (excluding southeastern United States) until it became extinct at the end of the Pleistocene. Some believe that the short-faced bear became extinct because it could not compete with the grizzly and brown bears that invaded North America from Eurasia.

Procyonidae (procyonids)

This family contains the familiar raccoons of North America as well as the ringtail cats of the Southwest and the coatis of Mexico and Central America. Raccoons (*Procyon lotor*) have been identified as fossils from the Indian Trail Caverns late Pleistocene postglacial site in northwestern Ohio.

Order Rodentia (rodents)

Rodents range in size from tiny mice to the giant beavers of the Pleistocene that were two-thirds as large as a black bear (fig. 74). Most rodents are small; being able to live within a few square yards of habitat has its advantages. Other rodent adaptations are important as well. One of these is their very high reproductive rate. Mice can produce several litters of young per year, so that one pair can produce thousands of

Fig. 74. *Upper,* giant beaver (*Castoroides ohioensis*) group scene. *Lower,* giant beaver skull with incisor tooth indicated (1). Giant beavers occur in the Pleistocene of the Great Lakes Basin. (From J. A. Holman, *Michigan's Fossil Vertebrates* [East Lansing: Michigan State University Museum, 1975].)

progeny in a very short time. The other one is that they have very specialized teeth.

Rodents have a pair of incisor teeth (front teeth) that have a layer of hard enamel on the front of the tooth and a layer of softer dentine on the back. Thus, as the animals gnaw away, a very sharp edge is honed between the enamel and the dentine. These teeth are so effective that rats in apartment buildings have been known to gnaw through water pipes! The incisors are ever growing and must occlude well enough that the lower pair doesn't grow up through the palate and penetrate the brain. Most museums with large mammal collections have rodent skulls representing animals that died in this way.

Behind the incisors, a space where the canines have been lost is called the *diastema*. Behind the diastema rodents have grinding teeth called *cheek teeth*. The cheek teeth of rodents tend to have simple cusps in the seed-eating and omnivorous species and complex cusps in the grass-eating species (fig. 75a). The gnawing teeth and the grinding teeth of rodents function independently of one another. Next to humans, the house mice (*Mus musculus*) and rats of the genus *Rattus* are probably the most successful modern mammals. These animals live everywhere in the world where humans occur.

Several rodents have been identified from Pleistocene sites in the Great Lakes region; some of them represent forms that do not occur in the area today. One of these is the spectacular extinct giant beaver.

Sciuridae (squirrels)

The earliest known rodent *Paramys* from the late Paleocene probably looked very much like a modern squirrel. Squirrels are very abundant animals in many areas of the world, and of course, are a prominent part of the modern fauna in the Great Lakes region, where most areas have at least six or seven species. Generally, squirrels are categorized as tree squirrels (including flying squirrels), or ground squirrels and marmots (including woodchucks).

Three kinds of tree squirrels were identified from the sediments of the Indian Trail Caverns late Pleistocene postglacial site in northwestern Ohio. These are the eastern chipmunk (*Tamias striatus*), the red squirrel (*Tamiasciurus hudsonicus*), and either the fox squirrel or the gray squirrel (*Sciurus* sp.). All of these animals occur in the fauna of northwestern Ohio today.

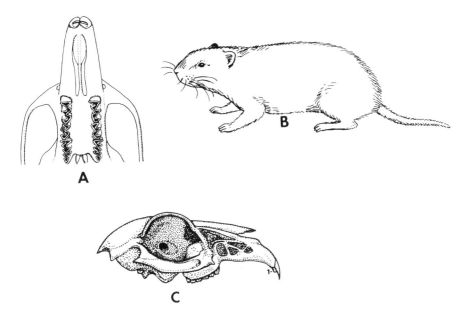

Fig. 75. Voles and rabbits. *A*, palatal view of tooth pattern of a generalized vole. *B*, the southern red-backed vole, *Clethrionomys gapperi*. *C*, rostrum of a young eastern cottontail rabbit (*Sylvilagus floridanus*), showing secondary incisors (1) and the perforated rostral area in front of the eye. Voles and rabbits occurred in the Pleistocene of the Great Lakes Basin.

Many people do not realize that woodchucks are in the squirrel family. Woodchucks (*Marmota monax*) live in rather large holes in the ground and get a bad reputation when they dig their holes around houses. Woodchuck fossils have been recorded from the Don Formation of the Sangamonian interglacial stage near Toronto, Canada, and from the Indian Trails Cavern late Pleistocene postglacial site in northwestern Ohio. Woodchucks occur both in the Toronto area and in northwestern Ohio today.

Castoridae (beavers)

Modern beavers are known from both the Old and the New World, but the giant beaver is known only from the Pleistocene of North America. The modern beaver (*Castor canadensis*) is the largest modern North American rodent and is very widespread in Alaska, Canada, and the

United States. Beavers and beaver dams are very common in the Great Lakes region, especially in the northern parts. Beavers have a great impact on the environment in that their dams impound ponds that support all kinds of aquatic animals and plants. Modern beavers have been identified from the Indian Trail Caverns late Pleistocene postglacial site in northwestern Ohio.

The extinct giant beaver (*Castoroides ohioensis*) may be the largest rodent that the world has ever known, as some of them reached two-thirds the size of a black bear. Fossil giant beavers are known from the Pleistocene of North America from Alaska to Florida, but they were most common in areas just south of the Great Lakes Basin. Nevertheless, giant beavers are known from the Great Lakes Basin from as early as the Sangamonian interglacial age, in the Don Formation near Toronto, to late Wisconsinan postglacial sites in several areas. In Michigan, at least, all of the records are confined to the southern half of the Lower Peninsula. We shall discuss this southerly distribution of extinct Pleistocene vertebrates later, under the section concerning mastodonts and mammoths.

The typical fossil that may be immediately identified as part of a giant beaver is an incisor tooth (fig. 74). These teeth are usually black in front and yellowish or brownish in back. The numerous thin grooves on the front portion of the tooth are quite diagnostic.

The giant beaver has often been depicted as merely a giant edition of the modern beaver, *Castor canadensis*. It has been shown in illustrations with a flattened tail along with the stumps of huge trees it has cut down. It was reasoned that an animal the size of a giant beaver might have felled giant trees, because it is known that modern beavers can fell cottonwood trees 2 or 3 feet in diameter! It was also believed that giant beavers could have created massive dams that impounded huge bodies of water. Fossil studies of giant beaver, however, show that it differed from the modern beaver in several important ways. First, the giant beaver had shorter legs than the modern beaver. Moreover, the structure of the bones of the tail shows that the giant beaver had a round tail rather than a flat tail like the modern one.

A study of the teeth in the two animals shows that the cheek teeth or molars are more like those of a very large rodent that occurs in South America today (the capybara, or water hog) than those of the modern beaver. The incisors are also different in the giant form. As previously mentioned, the incisors have thin grooves on their front surfaces, while the front surfaces are smooth in the modern beaver. In addition, the giant form has both the upper and the lower incisors tapering to a blunt point, whereas in modern beavers the tips of the incisors are wide and have a chisel-like edge for cutting down trees.

Finally, the brain of the modern beaver is relatively large and wrinkled on the surface, indicating an animal capable of complex behavior patterns such as building dams and social interactions. But a brain cast of the giant beaver showed that the brain was relatively small and that it was smooth on the outside. This strongly indicates that the giant beaver must have had much less complicated behavior patterns than its modern relative.

It appears that the best way to picture the life of the giant beaver is as a large, clumsy, water hog, meandering about in marshes and ponds, looking for aquatic vegetation to eat. It certainly seems very unlikely that giant beavers cut down trees or built dams or even that they had as complicated a social life as the modern beaver.

Fossil finds of giant beavers indicate that it inhabited lakes and ponds that were bordered by swamps. It has been suggested that the large hind feet were webbed. There has been no proven association with humans at any known site, so that it has been suggested that it became extinct because of habitat changes at the end of the Pleistocene and because of competition with the modern beaver.

Muridae (rats, mice, and voles)

This huge rodent family includes most of the common animals that we refer to as mice and rats in North America and includes such forms as the deer mice, wood rats, voles, cotton rats, and the muskrat.

Deer mice have simple-cusped cheek teeth that are adapted for an omnivorous or seed-eating diet. The deer mouse (*Peromyscus maniculatus*) has been recorded as a fossil from a cave in Halton County, Ontario, near Toronto. The conclusion that the cave may represent the Illinoian glacial age is based on other vertebrate remains. A deer mouse or white-footed mouse (*Peromyscus* sp.) has been recorded from the Indian Trail Caverns late Pleistocene postglacial site of northwestern Ohio.

Voles have cheek teeth with complicated surface patterns (fig. 75a), and many of them eat grasses. Several species have been identified from the Pleistocene of the Great Lakes region, most of which today occur north of the Pleistocene localities where they were found. These northern records of voles indicate colder climates in the Pleistocene in areas where they have been reported as fossils.

The southern redback vole (*Clethrionomys gapperi*, fig. 75b) has been identified from the Indian Trail Caverns late Pleistocene postglacial site in northwestern Ohio. Today, this species lives in the northern part of the Great Lakes region south to the southern two-thirds of Wisconsin and the northern third of Michigan.

The Greenland collared lemming (*Dicrostonyx groenlandicus*) has been reported from the late Wisconsinan (Cherry Tree substage) near Port Huron, Michigan. Today the Greenland collared lemming inhabits Alaska, northern Canada, and Greenland.

The meadow vole (*Microtus pennsylvanicus*) is common throughout the Great Lakes region today and has been recorded as a fossil from the late Wisconsinan (Cherry Tree substage) near Port Huron, Michigan, and from a late Wisconsinan postglacial age deposit near Lansing, Michigan, where it was found in association with a mastodont.

The yellow-cheeked vole (*Microtus xanthognathous*) has been recorded from the late Wisconsinan (Cherry Tree substage) near Port Huron, Michigan, and from the Indian Trail Caverns late Pleistocene postglacial site in northwestern Ohio. Today this species occurs in northern Canada and Alaska.

The heather vole (*Phenacomys intermedius*) has been reported from the Indian Trail Caverns late Pleistocene postglacial site in northwestern Ohio. This vole occurs only in the northwestern United States today.

The northern bog lemming (*Synaptomys borealis*) has also been reported from the late Wisconsinan (Cherry Tree substage) near Port Huron, Michigan, as well as the Indian Trail Caverns late Pleistocene postglacial site in northwestern Ohio. Today, this species occurs in extreme northeastern United States, Canada, and Alaska.

The *muskrat* or "ditch rat" (*Ondatra zibethicus*) is common in the Great Lakes region today. It has been reported as a fossil from a cave in Halton County, Ontario, near Toronto that may represent the Illinoian glacial age; from a site in the southeastern part of the Lower Peninsula of Michigan, where it was associated with a mastodont; and from the Indian Trail Caverns late Pleistocene postglacial site in northwestern Ohio.

Dipodidae (birch mice, jumping mice, and jeroboas)

The jumping mice are appealing little creatures with very long tails and hind feet. A jumping mouse (*Zapus* sp.) has been recorded from the late Wisconsinan (Cherry Tree substage) near Port Huron, Michigan. The genus *Zapus* occurs in Alaska, Canada, and about the northern two-thirds of the United States today.

Erethizontidae (New World porcupines)

A porcupine (*Erethizon dorsatum*) has been reported from the Indian Trail Caverns late Pleistocene postglacial site in northwestern Ohio. Today, these spiny rodents occur in the northern and eastern parts of the Great Lakes region but do not occur in Ohio.

Order Lagomorpha (lagomorphs)

Lagomorphs were once classified as rodents, and fossil evidence indicates that rodents and rabbits may have had a common ancestor. Rodents have hundreds of species and rabbits relatively few, but each rabbit species is usually more widespread. Rabbit skulls have an extra pair of incisors behind the main pair, and each side of the rostrum is full of a labyrinth of holes and struts (*fenestrated* condition, fig. 75c). The teeth of rabbits are much simpler than those of rodents. Two families of lagomorphs have been found in the Pleistocene fossil record in the Great Lakes region.

Leporidae (hares and rabbits)

The snowshoe hare (*Lepus americanus*) has been found as a fossil from a cave in Halton County, Ontario, near Toronto, that is thought to possibly represent the Illinoian glacial age of the Pleistocene. Today, snowshoe hares occur in Alaska, Canada, and the northern United States, ranging southward in the major mountain chains from east to west. The eastern cottontail rabbit (*Sylvilagus floridanus*) has also been found from the cave in Halton County. Today, eastern cottontails range from southern Canada through the United States to northern Mexico.

A fossil that represents either a hare or a rabbit, but that could not be identified to the generic or the specific level, was collected at the late Wisconsinan (Cherry Tree substage) site near Port Huron, Michigan; and other fossil material that represents an unidentified "rabbit" was collected at the Indian Trail Caverns late Pleistocene postglacial site in northwestern Ohio.

Ochotonidae (pikas)

Pikas are small rabbitlike animals, except that they have short ears and no visible tail. They presently occur in Alaska, Canada, the northwestern United States, and southward in the United States in the Rocky Mountains. Fossil remains that represented a very large pika (*Ochotona* sp.), but that could not be specifically identified, were found in a cave in Halton County, near Toronto. This fossil material is similar to fossil remains found in Illinoian deposits in Maryland and West Virginia.

Ungulates

Ungulates are probably best defined as large mammalian herbivores (vegetarians). All of the various groups of ungulates tend to have similar kinds of adaptations that go along with eating plants for a living. The major adaptations involve the teeth, the limbs and limb girdles, the horns on their heads, and the digestive system.

Modifications of the teeth of ungulates are as follow. The incisor teeth are usually large and important for cropping up grasses and other types of vegetation; but the canines tend to be reduced or absent, leaving a space called a diastema. We have also seen this condition in rodents and rabbits. The molar or cheek teeth tend to develop grinding surfaces on them. The most primitive ungulates had low-crowned teeth with simple cusps (fig. 76a) and the most advanced ones have high-crowned teeth with very complex patterns of enamel on them (fig. 76b). There are several stages in between; and in several forms all of the teeth continue to grow and be worn down throughout the lives of the animals.

The teeth of ungulates, especially the more complicated cheek teeth, are very important when they occur as fossils, and many of them can be identified to the specific level. Tusks are specialized types of teeth that may develop either from incisors or canines, but they never develop from cheek teeth.

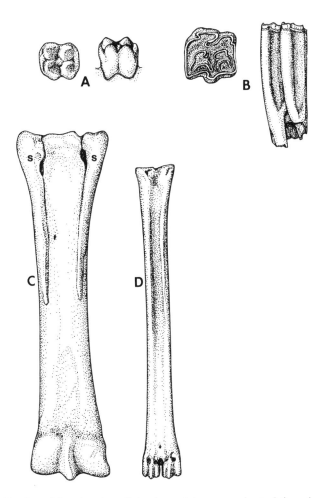

Fig. 76. Teeth and fused metapodials of ungulate mammals. *A, left,* surface and *right,* side view of the low-crowned tooth of a peccary, a piglike ungulate. *B, left,* surface and *right,* side view of the high-crowned tooth of a horse. *C,* metapodial (cannon bone) of a horse showing the fused splint bones (*s*) on either side of the main bone; these three bones represent the fused middle three bones of the original five. *D,* metapodial (cannon bone) of a deer; this bone represents the fused third and fourth bones of the original five.

The limbs of ungulates tend to occur directly under the body and to move only in a forward or a backward direction. The bones that correspond to those in the thick part of the hand and foot behind the fingers and toes in humans (*metapodials*) tend to become very long and reduced in number as well as the digits (toes) that are attached to them (fig. 76c–d).

The elongation of these metapodials creates an efficient third joint in the limbs that greatly increases the stride of ungulates and allows some of them to run like the wind. Primitive ungulates often had five toes, but in more advanced forms the number becomes reduced to four or three toes. Then, in the most advanced forms such as deer and horses, the number of toes is reduced to two (deer) or one (horses). Ungulates started out primitively with claws on the end of their toes and ended up with hooves.

The *clavicle* (collarbone) that connects the front limb skeleton to the body skeleton is lost in advanced ungulates, so that there is nothing but "flesh" between the shoulder and the body skeleton. This allows the animals to run faster, but it is taken advantage of by the bullfighter when he makes his hopefully fatal thrust.

Horns tend to develop on the heads of many advanced ungulates. These are used in defense against large predators, for male-to-male battles over females, or for the defense of territories. Ungulate horns have various origins and structure and a bewildering variety of shapes. Fossil horns are often very good elements for the identification of many ungulate species.

The more primitive ungulates have simple digestive systems, but the advanced grass-eating kinds may have several chambers in the stomach region of their digestive tracts in order to process grasses effectively. Grasses have a high silica content and are difficult for many animals to digest. Helpful bacteria occur in some of these extra chambers to assist in the breakdown of grasses; and primary grass material is often regurgitated as a cud to be further chewed, swallowed, and reprocessed.

Ungulates are divided into four groups:

Archaic ungulates (extinct very early forms)
South American ungulates (strange, extinct South American forms)
Modern ungulates (familiar odd-toed and even-toed forms)
Subungulates or African ungulates (sea cows, coneys, "elephants")

The Great Lakes region is represented by fossils of two of these four groups, the modern ungulates and the subungulates.

Modern Ungulates

The modern ungulates are divided into two orders, the perissodactyls (horses and relatives) and artiodactyls (cows and their relatives). Perisso-dactyls are called odd-toed ungulates because the main axis of the foot goes through what was primitively toe number 3. No fossil perisso-dactyls have been found in the Great Lakes region. Artiodactyls are called even-toed ungulates because the main axis of the foot passes between what were primitively the third and the fourth toes. There are three very interesting artiodactyl families represented by fossils in the Great Lakes region.

Order Artiodactyla (Even-Toed Ungulates)

The three Great Lakes region artiodactyl families represented by fossils are the peccaries of the family Tayassuidae, the deerlike animals of the family Cervidae, and the cowlike animals of the family Bovidae.

Tayassuidae (peccaries)

Piglike mammals appeared in the early Oligocene epoch of the Tertiary about 35 million years ago. Two families of piglike mammals are living today; the true pigs of the Old World, from which the domestic pig is descended, and the peccaries in the New World. Peccaries differ from Old World pigs in several ways. Their cheek teeth have fewer of the little lines or striations that occur on the enamel layers of their Old World cousins, and their canines (stabbing teeth) are always directed up and down and rub against one another like shears.

Recognizable piglike features in peccaries include, among other things, cloven hooves and a hog nose. Peccaries do not live in the Great Lakes region today but occur in the southwestern United States, southward through Mexico and Central America, and into South America. Peccaries run in packs, and their shearing canines are razor sharp. Packs of modern peccaries have been known to attack intruders. Living peccaries have a mixed diet of vegetable and animal matter and do a lot of rooting around in the soil to get their food.

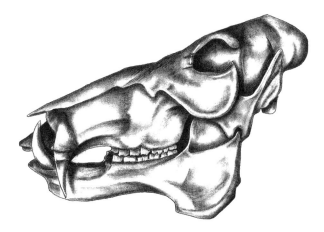

Fig. 78. Skull of a flat-headed peccary (*Platygonus compressus*) from the late Pleistocene of the Lower Peninsula of Michigan. (From J. A. Holman, *Michigan's Fossil Vertebrates* [East Lansing: Michigan State University Museum, 1975].)

The fossil peccary found in the Great Lakes region is the extinct flat-headed peccary, *Platygonus compressus* (figs. 77 [color] and 78). The genus *Platygonus* ranged throughout both North and South America during the Pleistocene and was represented by several species ranging in size from those as large as European wild boars to those as small as the little collared peccary of the southwestern United States. *Platygonus compressus* supposedly lived mainly in the prairies and the plains. Thus, one might wonder why it occurred in the Great Lakes region in late Pleistocene postglacial times. The hypothesis is that it lived in open grasslands that may have been near the edge of the glacier, and peccaries have often been pictured in association with mammoths. A close relative of the flat-headed peccary, Wagner's peccary of Paraguay, is adapted for living in open areas interspersed with woody shrubs.

The flat-headed peccary has never been found in direct association with humans in North America. It has been suggested that its extinction was due to vegetative changes resulting in the loss of habitat near the end of the Ice Age, as well as its competition for food with the black bear. Fossil peccaries are rare in the Great Lakes region and are represented by scattered finds. One of these finds was near Belding in the middle of the Lower Peninsula of Michigan, and another was from the banks of the Huron River in Ann Arbor, Michigan. These finds were about 100 years apart, but both were of remarkably well-preserved

Fig. 77. Flat-headed peccaries (*Platygonus compressus*) in the snow in the late Pleistocene of the Great Lakes Basin

Fig. 79. Wetland scene in the late Pleistocene of the Great Lakes Basin depicting a Scott's moose (*Cervalces scotti*) and a giant beaver (*Castoroides ohioensis*)

Fig. 81. Woodland musk oxen (*Bootherium bombifrons*) in a defensive circle in the late Pleistocene of the Great Lakes Basin

Fig. 88. Scene depicting a Jefferson mammoth (*Mammuthus jeffersoni*) in the Great Lakes Basin during the late Pleistocene

Fig. 90. Scene depicting American mastodonts (*Mammut americanum*) in an upland habitat in the Great Lakes Basin during the late Pleistocene

Fig. 91. Artist's conception of mastodonts rooting for salt in southern Michigan during the late Pleistocene. (Painting by Cam Wood.)

Fig. 92. Artist's conception of a Precambrian seashore in the upper Great Lakes Basin. Stromatolites and bacterial sludge are the only living material in the scene.

Fig. 93. Artist's conception of a predaceous worm attacking an early chordate in a Great Lakes Basin Cambrian sea

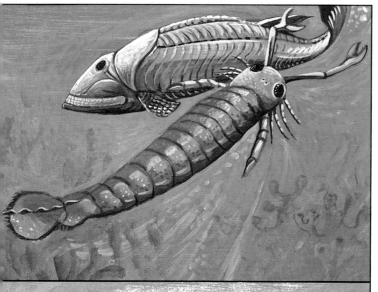

Fig. 94. Artist's conception of a eurypterid (water scorpion) attacking a bottom-dwelling ostracoderm in a Great Lakes Basin Silurian Sea

Fig. 95. Artist's conception of an active *Dunkleosteus* attacking a cladoselachian shark in a Devonian sea in the Cleveland, Ohio, area

Fig. 96. Artist's conception of a coal-swamp scene in the early Pennsylvanian in the Lansing, Michigan, area. Lycopod and sphenopsid trees, as well as giant insects and a labyrinthodont amphibian, are shown.

specimens, including complete skulls (fig. 78). This species has also been identified on the basis of many individuals from the Indian Trail Caverns late Pleistocene postglacial site in northwestern Ohio.

Cervidae (deer, moose, wapiti, and caribou)

This family includes those artiodactyls that have antlers that are shed every year. Members of the Cervidae that occur in the Great Lakes region today are caribou, deer, elk, and moose. Five species of Cervidae, two of which are extinct, occur in the Pleistocene of the Great Lakes region.

The only elk (wapiti) (*Cervus elaphus*) that occur in the Great Lakes region today consist of a population that has been successfully reintroduced into the upper part of the Lower Penninsula of Michigan. Elk are quite large deer, reaching a height at the shoulder of about 5 feet. Males weigh up to about 900 pounds, but females only get to be about 600 pounds. Male elk develop very large spreading antlers late in the summer.

Modern elk shun thick forests, possibly because of their very wide rack of antlers, and prefer rather open woods. Several finds of fossil elk have been made in late Wisconsinan postglacial sites in the southern part of the Lower Peninsula of Michigan. Holocene finds of elk are much more common than Pleistocene finds in the Great Lakes region.

The extinct Scott's moose (*Cervalces scotti*) (figs. 79 [color] and 80) is often called the stag moose. Scott's moose is known from rather fragmentary finds in the Great Lakes region, but two skeletons of Scott's moose that were found in a bog in New Jersey have indicated that the extinct form had longer legs and more complex antlers than the modern moose. When only pieces of antlers are found (fig. 80), Scott's moose may be distinguished from the modern moose on the basis that the branches of the antlers are longer and thinner.

It is believed that Scott's moose inhabited sphagnum bogs and that vegetational changes along with competition with the modern moose probably led to its extinction. This fossil moose has been found in the Sangamonian interglacial age Don Formation in the Toronto region and the early Wisconsinan Pottery Road Formation, also near Toronto. Scott's moose has been identified on the basis of very fragmentary material from late Wisconsinan postglacial sites in the southwestern and southeastern Lower Peninsula of Michigan as well as from the

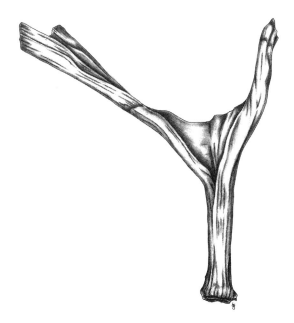

Fig. 80. Portion of a Scott's moose (*Cervalces scotti*) antler from the late Pleistocene of the Lower Peninsula of Michigan. (From J. A. Holman, *Michigan's Fossil Vertebrates* [East Lansing: Michigan State University Museum, 1975].)

Indian Trail Caverns late Pleistocene postglacial site in northwestern Ohio.

Today the familiar white-tailed deer (*Odocoileus virginianus*) occurs throughout most of the United States except for the western two tiers of states, then down into Mexico and Central America. It is a much smaller animal than its relative the elk, and males only reach a height of about three and one-half feet at the shoulder and a weight of about 275 pounds. A tiny white-tailed deer (Key deer) occurs in the Florida Keys. This deer weighs only about fifty pounds.

The antlers of male white-tailed deer are formed from a main "beam" that has prongs branching from it. In the Great Lakes region, fossils of this species are known from the Sangamonian interglacial age Don Formation near Toronto as well as the early Wisconsinan Pottery Road Formation, also near Toronto. White-tailed deer fossils are known from localities from late Wisconsinan postglacial sites in the southern part of the Lower Peninsula of Michigan as well as from the Indian Trail Caverns late Pleistocene postglacial site in northwestern Ohio. One of the Michigan deer specimens was found in association with a masto-dont and a giant beaver.

In 1982 an exciting discovery was announced in a Canadian scientific publication. The Toronto deer (*Torontoceros hypogaeus*) was described on the basis of a fragmentary skull that had parts of antler beams attached. This discovery was made during the digging of a tunnel for the Toronto subway. The deposits that yielded the deer were determined as late Wisconsinan postglacial lake deposits, and a carbon 14 date of approximately 11,300 years before the present was obtained on a portion of the antler beam.

Pollen from the site indicates that a mixed conifer hardwood forest existed in the area at the time the Toronto deer lived. The Toronto deer was about the size of a caribou but differed from both the white-tailed deer and the caribou in having very heavy antlers and in details of the structure of the antlers. The scientific name of the new deer has an interesting derivation. *Torontoceros* is from the Iroquois word *tarantou,* which means "meeting place," and the Greek word *ceros,* which means horn or antler. The species name is from the Greek word *hypo,* which means under or beneath and the Greek *geos,* which means "earth,"thus alluding to the subway.

Whenever a new extinct species is discovered, it becomes the object of intense scientific scrutiny. To make sure the new specimen was really new, it was taken to two consecutive yearly meetings of the Society of Vertebrate Paleontology to be examined by its members, who had seen nothing like it. Then, photographic illustrations of the specimen showing the peculiarities of *Torontoceros* were circulated to North American and European mammalogists who were deer antler specialists, and this group also had seen nothing like it. Thus, a new genus and species was born. One lovely thing about the science of paleontology, unlike some other branches of science where animals have to be sacrificed, is that "new life" is given to extinct things.

Today, two races (subspecies) of caribou (*Rangifer tarandus*) are recognized; the barren ground caribou, which occurs in the tundra regions of Canada, Alaska, and Greenland; and the woodland caribou, which occurs in the boreal forests south of the tundra. The woodland caribou reaches the Great Lakes region just north of Lake Superior. Caribou reach a height at the shoulder of about 4 feet in the woodland race, with the barren ground race being somewhat shorter. The woodland race also is somewhat heavier than the barren ground form, reaching a weight of about 400 pounds. Both sexes of both races of caribou have antlers that are somewhat mooselike (semipalmate branches), but they have one tine that reaches over the nose.

Sites in New York state outside of the Great Lakes region have yielded remains of caribou that were associated with late Wisconsinan Paleo-Indian artifacts. One site in southeastern lower Michigan has yielded caribou bones in association with a fluted Paleo-Indian point. Finally, sites in western Ontario near Lake Huron have yielded caribou bones from the late Wisconsinan, at the same time Paleo-Indians occurred there.

Thus, it has been postulated that caribou were possibly an important game animal for early humans in the latest part of the postglacial Pleistocene. The caribou has also been reported from the Indian Trail Caverns late Pleistocene postglacial site in northwestern Ohio. But thus far, there is no evidence that Paleo-Indians killed any animals in the cave.

Bovidae (bovids)

Cowlike artiodactyls are very numerous large herbivores and include such distinct species as the huge water buffalo of tropical regions and the small muskoxen of the tundra. It is also the family to which our domestic cattle, sheep, and goats belong. The domestic cow is a bovid thought to have been domesticated somewhere in southeast Asia. The members of this family have horns that are unbranched and are never shed. Three bovids that are known as fossils in the Great Lakes region are the bison (*Bison* sp.), the extinct woodland muskox (*Bootherium bombifrons*), and the barren ground muskox (*Ovibos moschatus*).

Modern bison (*Bison* sp.) were extremely abundant in North America when the European settlers arrived, but they were driven to near extinction by white hunters in the nineteenth century. Now bison have been reestablished in Oklahoma and some of the northern plains states, where they do well on special reservations. Bison have a huge head and a massive shoulder-hump as well as shaggy hair on the shoulders and on the front legs. The bison reaches about 6 feet in height at the shoulder. Yet with all of these distinctive characteristics, the bones and teeth of the skeleton are very difficult to distinguish from the closely related domestic cow, and some controversial identifications of "bison" have been made from time to time in the Great Lakes region.

Several extinct Pleistocene species of bison have been named, and some of these had much larger and longer sets of horns than does the modern species. It has been suggested that more extinct bison species have been named than really existed. Bison bones not identified to the specific level have been identified from the Sangamonian interglacial stage Don Formation near Toronto, the early Wisconsinan Pottery Road Formation near Toronto, and from late Wisconsinan Two Creeks sub-stage sites, also in the Toronto area.

Two muskoxen lived in the Great Lakes region during the Pleisto-cene, the extinct woodland muskox (*Bootherium bombifrons*) and the barren ground muskox that still survives. The woodland muskox (fig. 81 [color]) was taller and slimmer than the barren ground muskox and had a strange pitted basin on the skull between the horns (Fig. 82) that is not present in the modern barren ground muskox. The extinct wood-land muskox was known for many years as *Symbos cavifrons* before it was given its present name based on the rules of scientific name prior-ity.

The overall differences in the skull and skeleton of the two muskoxen has led scientists to suggest that the two animals are more distinct from one another than was originally believed. The woodland muskox is thought to have been a woodland grazer that inhabited both plains and woodlands. Based on pollen studies at a Michigan site, however, it has been suggested that it could have lived in either pine- or spruce-domi-nated forests.

Modern muskoxen form protective rings around their young to guard them from predators, but it is not known if this behavior occurred in the woodland muskox. Even though there is no paleontological evi-dence for this behavior, we have depicted the extinct animal as forming such protective rings (fig. 81). Muskoxen fossils are known from several localities from late Wisconsinan postglacial sites in the southern part of the Lower Peninsula of Michigan. Two of these finds were in bottom sediments of existing lakes. This is very unusual, as most finds of extinct vertebrates in the Great Lakes region are from the sediments of lakes that have been long extinct.

The barren ground muskoxen (*Ovibos moschatus*) are found today in the very far north in tundra regions in Alaska, Canada, and Green-land. The modern muskox is a small bovid that reaches a height of about 5 feet at the shoulder in very large individuals. The horns are broad and flat, are close to the skull, and have the curved tips pointing forward. Horns occur in both sexes. Barren ground muskoxen form protective rings around the young and stand their ground when preda-

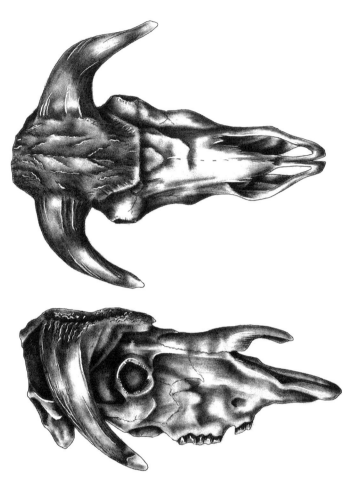

Fig. 82. Woodland muskox (*Bootherium bombifrons*) skull from the late Pleistocene of the Lower Peninsula of Michigan. *Upper,* top view; *lower,* side view. (From J. A. Holman, *Michigan's Fossil Vertebrates* [East Lansing: Michigan State University Museum, 1975].)

tors approach. This has led to pitiful slaughter of muskoxen by hunters. In the Great Lakes region barren ground muskoxen have been found as fossils from the early Wisconsinan Pottery Road Formation near Toronto and from the late Wisconsinan Two Creeks substage, also near Toronto, as well as from late Wisconsinan sites in northern Ohio.

Pleistocene Whales and Walruses

Whale and walrus remains have been found in Michigan that have been allegedly associated with ancient Pleistocene deposits. These remains have sparked great enthusiasm and controversy.

Whales

The presence of whales remains allegedly buried in glacial lake beach sands or supposedly associated with these sands in Michigan has been a cause of interest and controversy ever since the middle of the nineteenth century, when the Michigan geologist Alexander Winchell (father of the Mississippian geological period) mentioned such remains in an official report. In 1931, another well-known Michigan geologist, R. C. Hussey, published a report announcing that whale bones had been found in Lenawee and Oscoda County in the Lower Peninsula. Hussey speculated that 20,000 or 30,000 years ago, the whales swam inland by way of the St. Lawrence or the Hudson waterway into the ancient glacial lakes and into shallow rivers adjacent to those lakes. Here, he believed, they died of starvation, and their bones washed up onto the ancient lake beaches.

Other people suggested that whale bones might have been carried into the Great Lakes region from elsewhere. But several scientists in the 1950s and 1960s reviewed previous reports, believed that there were three valid whale records in the state, and suggested that these were all associated somehow with beach sands of ancient glacial lakes.

The three records were of a finback whale (*Balaenoptera*, fig. 83a), a sperm whale (*Physeter*, fig. 83b), and a right whale (*Balaena*, fig. 83c). These announcements sparked the imaginations of people, for whales are the largest animals that have ever lived, and they only accidentally enter freshwater from time to time.

In the 1970s routes of entry into the Great Lakes were speculated upon. It was suggested that both the sperm whale and the finback whale entered the glacial Great Lakes by a southern route up the Mississippi River and then entered Michigan by either the Illinois or the Wabash Rivers. This means that these huge animals would have had to cross the state of Michigan, moving east toward the glacial lakes. One would have to imagine a mightily swollen interior river system for this to have occurred.

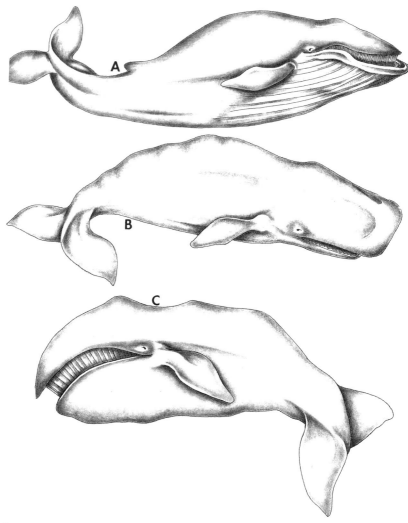

Fig. 83. Problematic Quaternary whales. *A*, finback whale (*Balaenoptera*); *B*, sperm whale (*Physeter*); and *C*, right whale (*Balaena*) have been reported from the Pleistocene of Michigan, but radiocarbon dates indicate that they existed much later in the Quaternary. (From J. A. Holman, *Michigan's Fossil Vertebrates* [East Lansing: Michigan State University Museum, 1975].)

It was postulated that the right whale entered the Great Lakes by two possible northern routes. They suggested either a trip from the sea into the Hudson and Mohawk river systems, thence into Lake Ontario and Lake Erie, with a sharp bend northward into glacial Lake Nipissing; or more likely, a route from the St. Lawrence system through either the Trent Valley or Ottawa River into Lake Nipissing.

Recently, the whale problem was addressed by Canadian paleontologists, who used sophisticated carbon 14 techniques to date bone cores taken from the Michigan whale specimens. Modern bone dates are much more reliable than they were in the 1960s and 1970s when dates could be up to 2,000 years off. These dates were shocking. The sperm whale was dated as less than 190 years old. The finback whale was dated as being between 790 and 650 years old. The right whale was dated as being between 810 and 690 years old. It was concluded from these dates that the whales represented by the Michigan specimens did not live in the Great Lakes because there would not have been enough high water during these times to have allowed these huge beasts to have entered.

The alternative hypothesis then was that the older whale bones were brought into Michigan at the same time that artifacts made from marine shells were brought into the state by Hopewell culture people from the Atlantic. Many whale bones and teeth continue to turn up in Michigan. Most of these are surface finds that cannot be stratigraphically placed. Sperm whale teeth have been found by people walking Michigan beaches. An especially intriguing new find is an undated sperm whale tooth that was found on the bottom of the Pine River near Mesick, Michigan, where the river was cutting through a deposit of organic material and wood about 40,000 years old!

It is the view of this book that many questions remain to be answered about whale bones and teeth in the Great Lakes region and that a riddle of the whales still exists. An intriguing aspect of this is that several interesting marine mammals have been reported from the Pleistocene Champlain Sea, which reached its eastern limits where the city of Quebec is presently located. These remains mainly represent white whales (also called belugas). But other fossils of harbor porpoises, humpback whales, finback whales, and right whales are also reported from the Champlain Sea. Recent radiocarbon dates indicate that the white whales inhabited the Champlain Sea about 10,500 years ago, whereas

Fig. 84. Walrus (*Odobenus*) scene. Walrus skull remains were reported from an "elevated glacial lake beach" on Mackinac Island, Michigan, but the age of these bones has been questioned. (From J. A. Holman, *Michigan's Fossil Vertebrates* [East Lansing: Michigan State University Museum, 1975].)

the finback whales lived there about 11,500 years ago. Five different species of seals have also been reported from this sea!

Walrus

Two finds of walrus (*Odobenus*) (figs. 84 and 85) first reported in the early 1950s have been considered to be authentic by several scientists in the 1960s and 1970s. One is the front portion of a skull that was found on Mackinac Island, Michigan, in an "elevated glacial lake beach." The other is of a *baculum* (penis bone) that was found in a gravel pit near Gaylord, Michigan. The modern consensus of opinion is that these "fossils" appeared to have been worked (whittled) by humans. Moreover, they were found extremely far from the nearest known historical range of walruses. It has been suggested that these Michigan walrus specimens should also be carbon dated.

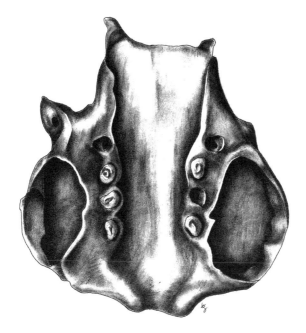

Fig. 85. Palatal portion of the skull of a walrus (*Odobenus*) found on an "elevated glacial lake beach" on Mackinac Island, Michigan. The age of this find has been questioned. (From J. A. Holman, *Michigan's Fossil Vertebrates* [East Lansing: Michigan State University Museum, 1975].)

Order Proboscidea (elephantlike mammals)

Proboscideans are first known from skull remains from the early Eocene of Algeria. This earliest ancestor is thought to have had a trunk, but the animal was much smaller than elephants of today or the mammoths and mastodonts of the Ice Age. Later, in the Oligocene epoch, a form called *Palaeomastodon* that had moderately well-developed tusks in both the upper and the lower jaws is thought to have given rise to the main branches of the proboscidean family tree.

The animals that eventually evolved from *Palaeomastodon* tended to develop their main set of tusks in the upper jaw. But one odd Miocene form developed a downwardly curving set of sharp tusks that occurred only in the lower jaw; and another Miocene form developed a long pair of spatula-shaped tusks in the lower jaw for mud grubbing. The two major groups that evolved from *Palaeomastodon* were the *gomphotheres* that eventually gave rise to the mammoths and elephants and the *mammutoids* that gave rise to the mastodonts. The mammoths are placed in the family Elephantidae with the elephants, whereas the mastodonts are placed in their own family, the Mammutidae.

Elephant Family
   Extinct Mammoths and Extinct and Modern Elephants
Mastodont Family
   Extinct Mastodonts

We shall discuss some of the characteristics that all of the elephants, mammoths, and mastodonts share, and then we shall discuss some of the individual differences in the fossil mammoths and mastodonts. All of these animals have a trunk that not only detects scents like a normal nose is supposed to do but also functions like a hand. This allows them to pull up plants and transfer them to their mouths, to grab each other by their tails as they amble along, or even to pick up relatively tiny objects such as peanuts. Moreover, these animals all drink through their trunks by sucking up water and spraying it in their mouths.

Elephants, mammoths, and mastodonts all have pillarlike limbs that support the body on an essentially horizontal vertebral column. The rounded feet have flattened pads on the bottom to support the essentially vertical limbs and short, thick nails. When modern elephants move fast, their legs do not bend much at the knee joints, and they never reach a stage where all of the legs are off the ground at the same time, as occurs in many smaller mammals.

The head of elephants, mammoths, and mastodonts is huge, but the skull is short because the rostrum (muzzle) has essentially been replaced by the trunk and tusks. In fact, tusk sheaths make up a significant part of the skull. Even though the part of the skull behind the tusk sheaths is large, it is relatively light and filled with sinuses (open spaces). The tusks are modified incisors, the canines are lost, and the cheek teeth are very broad and massive.

Tooth replacement is unique in these proboscideans in that the teeth are replaced in series from the back to the front of the jaw. The milk teeth appear and are worn down first, and then they are replaced from behind by a series of permanent teeth. As these permanent teeth are worn down at the front of the mouth, they are in turn replaced by teeth from behind, until all of the teeth are worn out. In both mammoths and mastodonts the last teeth to appear are longer and have more ridges or knobs on them.

Mammoths, mastodonts, and all of the other extinct vertebrates of the Great Lakes region became extinct *everywhere* about 10,000 years ago. We will discuss the fascinating and controversial subject of this sudden mass extinction later in this book.

Mammoths (*Mammuthus*) were widely distributed in North America during the Pleistocene, but the greatest number of finds have been in Alaska, the prairies of Canada, and the central and southern plains of the United States. Nevertheless, records are rather common in the Great Lakes region, the Atlantic Coast (especially Florida), and Mexico. There is even one record from El Salvador.

There are two views about the names of North American mammoths. One view is that there are five species. The other view is that the characters that distinguish the five species merge together in time and space, so that only one variable species is represented. Here we will accept the concept of several species of mammoth in North America with the idea in mind that they may represent stages in evolutionary development. But first we need to discuss a common misconception concerning mammoths and mastodonts.

As Different as Dogs and Cats! Many people think that the terms mammoth and mastodont are different words for the same giant Ice Age animal that looks like a shaggy elephant. Actually mammoths and mastodonts are as different from one another as dogs from cats or horses from rhinos (figs. 86 and 87). Some of the major differences between these huge beasts are as follows.

The skull of mammoths is domed on top and both the skull, and its tusk sheaths are oriented almost vertically (fig. 86b). In the mastodont the skull is flat on top, and both the skull and its tusk sheaths are almost horizontally oriented (fig. 87a). The jaws of the mammoth are short and directed vertically, whereas the jaws of the mastodont are longer and are almost horizontally directed. The tusks of mammoths exit the skull nearly vertically and then curve downward and outward, whereas the tusks of mastodonts exit the skull horizontally and then curve outward and inward. Some mastodonts grow a pair of smaller lower tusks.

The teeth of mammoths and mastodonts are the most identifiable single parts of these animals. The surfaces of mammoth teeth are composed of a series of thin, transverse rows of enamel (fig. 86a). The surfaces of mastodont teeth are composed of a series of large knobs,

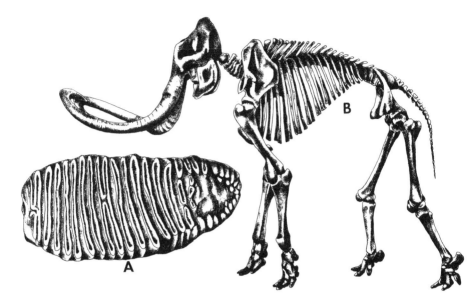

Fig. 86. Mammoth skeletal material. *A,* surface view of the tooth of a Jefferson mammoth (*Mammuthus jeffersoni*). *B,* skeleton of a Jefferson mammoth. (Modified from J. A. Holman, *Michigan's Fossil Vertebrates* [East Lansing: Michigan State University Museum, 1975].)

usually in two parallel rows (fig. 87b). The teeth, jaws, and muscles of mammoths and mastodonts function differently to produce two separate kinds of chewing motions. In mammoths the lower jaw moves back and forth on the upper jaw so that a grinding type of chewing occurs. In mastodonts the lower jaw moves up and down against the upper jaw so that a crushing type of chewing occurs between the knobby surfaces of the teeth.

The differences in the tooth, jaw, and muscle structure were reflected in the food habits of the two animals. Mammoths ground up grasses with the parallel ridges of their cheek teeth, and mastodonts crushed up mast and other browse with the bumpy surfaces of their cheek teeth. In fact, because of these differences, Ice Age mammoths greatly outnumbered mastodonts in the prairie states, where grasses were abundant, and mastodonts greatly outnumbered mammoths in the eastern states, where woodlands produced trees, shrubs, and mast to browse upon.

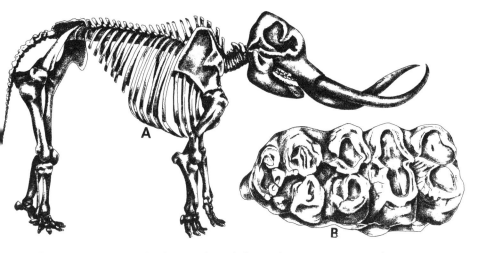

Fig. 87. Mastodont skeletal material. *A,* skeleton of an American mastodont (*Mammut americanum*). *B,* surface view of a tooth of an American mastodont. (Modified from J. A. Holman, *Michigan's Fossil Vertebrates* [East Lansing: Michigan State University Museum, 1975].)

The body plan of the region behind the skull is also very different in mammoths and mastodonts. The mammoth skeleton (fig. 86b) is lightly built in this region, whereas the mastodont has a stout heavy frame. The mammoth has longer front legs, the rear end is low to the ground, and the body arches upward to a hump behind the neck. Mastodonts (fig. 87a) have a more piglike body, with shorter legs, and with the rear end at about the same level as the front end. Thus, if we were able to see these two animals standing side by side, they would look quite different from one another.

Some paleontologists have suggested that the mammoth was a more intelligent animal than the mastodont. This is based, in part, on the relative size of the brains of the two animals. Other workers are not convinced of this.

Mammoths

The wooly mammoth (*Mammuthus primigenius*) inhabited the cold northern regions of Europe, Asia, and North America in the Pleistocene.

At present there is controversy about whether the "wooly mammoth" that has been reported from Ontario in the Great Lakes region was a hybrid between the wooly mammoth and the Jefferson mammoth, or if something else complicated was going on. Nevertheless, the wooly mammoth is the best known of any of the fossil proboscideans because of the thousands of bones and tusks, weighing hundreds of tons, and several spectacular frozen carcasses that have been found in Siberia.

Because of these frozen carcasses, we now have a better idea how the wooly mammoth really looked than perhaps any other extinct Pleistocene mammal. This animal had the general appearance of a shaggy elephant, but there were several important differences. It was rather small as elephants and mammoths go, reaching a maximum height of about 10 feet at the shoulders.

The skull had a very high dome, as is characteristic of all mammoths. The ears, however, were very small and unelephantlike. Moreover, the trunk was short compared to modern elephants, and the fingerlike projections on the tip of the trunk differed from those in both the African and the Indian elephant. The wooly mammoth had two "fingers" at the tip of its trunk, one in front and one in back. The African elephant has a finger in the front of the trunk, but it has a thick "thumb" in the back. The Indian elephant has just one finger on the front of the tip of the trunk. The tusks of mammoths were huge, and in some individuals the ends of the tusks became so twisted that they sometimes pointed at each other. The wooly mammoth fed on grasses and small tundra plants and had teeth with the thinnest and most numerous enamel plates of any known species.

The long, shaggy coat of the wooly mammoth is another characteristic feature, and this luxuriant growth of hair was the topic of several beautiful Paleolithic cave paintings in Europe. The entire coat consisted of an outer coat of long hair and an inner coat of short hair. Reddish-colored long hairs of mammoths have been found as well as darker hair; thus it may be that they had a change of hair color at the onset of the summer season as occurs in many Arctic mammals today. On the other hand, it has been suggested that fossil mammoth hair becomes bleached out during the long burial and that the long, shaggy outer hairs were probably black.

Wooly mammoth fossils are extraordinarily abundant in some areas of northern Siberia, where the ground has been deeply frozen since the

Ice Age! Mammoth tusks from this region have been so abundant and finely preserved that fossil ivory has been an important commercial product that has been exported to several other countries. Moreover, local people have made combs, knives, rings, and even caskets from this ivory. Other Siberian people have made houses out of wooly mammoth bones, sometimes using the jaw bones for units of the foundation.

Among the most fascinating fossils in the world are the carcasses of wooly mammoths that from time to time have been found buried in the permafrost. The flesh of some of these finds has been fed in frozen chunks to sled dogs. Moreover, from time to time, courageous humans have nibbled on cooked wooly mammoth meat and have found it swallowable but somewhat "freezer burned."

One of the most publicized fossils in the world is that of Dima, the frozen baby wooly mammoth. Dima was found by gold miners who were thawing out permafrost with hoses in 1977. Dima was only about 46 inches long and 41 inches high. She had a little trunk, little ears that were similar to the ones depicted in cave paintings, and ginger-colored hair.

Wooly mammoths have been reported as far south in the Great Lakes region as Toronto in the late Pleistocene, but evidently they never made it to Michigan. The Toronto remains have been reported from the late middle Wisconsinan Port Talbot substage and from the late Wisconsinan Two Creeks substage. However, these and other finds of Ontario mammoths have been reported of late merely as "*Mammuthus* sp." because of the nomenclatorial controversy we have previously discussed.

The mammoth that occurred in North America south of the ice in the Sangamonian interglacial age and also in Wisconsinan postglacial times has been called the Jefferson mammoth (*Mammuthus jeffersoni*) (figs. 86 and 88 [color]). We recognize here that some authors consider the Jefferson mammoth to be the northern equivalent of the more southern form, the Columbian mammoth (*Mammuthus columbi*). However, we will retain the name Jefferson mammoth until it is proven without doubt that the Jefferson and the Columbian mammoth are the same species.

The Jefferson mammoth was named in recognition of former United States president Thomas Jefferson, who kept fossil proboscidean bones in the White House and corresponded with famous European scientists about their significance. The Jefferson mammoth, contrary to popular opinion, was bigger than the wooly mammoth and got to be about 11 feet high at the shoulders.

The Jefferson mammoth, like the wooly mammoth, had huge tusks that often curved inwardly. It also had the domed skull; the short, down-turned lower jaw; and the highly arched body form of the wooly mammoth. The main difference between the two animals appears to be in the teeth, where the Jefferson mammoth had fewer enamel plates than the wooly mammoth. The tooth that has mainly been used to distinguish these animals has been the third molar. Unfortunately, no frozen carcasses of Jefferson mammoths have been found. Thus, we are not sure about whether it was a shaggy beast or not. Usually, the Jefferson mammoth is pictured as having shorter hair than its wooly relative; but this has been based on the speculation that it lived in a warmer climate.

Evidence indicates that the Jefferson mammoth and the related Columbian mammoth were killed for food by human hunters in the late Pleistocene. Well-established kill sites in the western United States indicate that groups of people hunted mammoths and killed them with spears. Evidence for human mammoth hunters is not as well established in the Great Lakes region, and we will discuss this in greater detail later in this book.

The Jefferson mammoth has been found in all of the states of the Great Lakes region near the end of the last Wisconsinan age. It is difficult to get the exact number of mammoth sites that occur in each of these states, for some finds have been counted more than once in published reports. A recent exhaustive study of the literature in Michigan shows (after several repeated records were eliminated) that there are 49 distinct mammoth sites in the state.

Most mammoth sites in the Great Lakes region are associated with sediments that fill in shallow basins or kettlelike depressions. We have discussed the ecostratigraphic zones that develop in these features in chapter 5. Mammoth fossils usually occur somewhere in the contact zone between muck or peat and the grayish, shelly marl below. The muck and peat represents a former mat of unstable vegetation (quaking bog), and it is believed that these heavy-bodied animals broke through these mats and became stuck in the sticky sediments below. It has been suggested that this occurred when these bogs were covered by light snow in the spring or in the fall. These trapped animals probably either drowned, starved to death, or were killed by late Pleistocene hunters. It might be added that the acid conditions of these bogs would prevent decay and favor the fossilization process.

Occasionally, mammoths have been found buried in ancient glacial lake sediments, probably when the animals were feeding in grasslands near the lakeshore. Even less frequently, mammoth fossils have been reported from streambed sediments in the Great Lakes region.

The mammoth situation in Ontario is unsettled at present because of the present controversy about mammoth names. Twenty-seven mammoth sites are known in Ontario, most of which occur in well-drained upland situations, especially on former glacial lake beaches. All of these records are referred to as "*Mammuthus* sp.," including the previous records of "*Mammuthus primigenius*" (wooly mammoth) from the Wisconsinan deposits of the Toronto area. Thus, these records might represent the wooly mammoth, the Jefferson mammoth, or both; or they might represent forms that are intermediate between the two.

Michigan's Mason-Quimby Line

A line frequently drawn across maps of Michigan when mammoths and mastodonts are discussed is called the Mason-Quimby Line (fig 89). This line reflects the provocative writings and maps of R. J. Mason and G. I. Quimby, archaeologists who were interested in Paleo-Indians and their food-gathering activities in Michigan. Mason questioned why there were no fluted points (points similar to the ones that were used in the West to kill mammoths) north of counties in the southern third of the Lower Peninsula of Michigan, and he suggested ecological reasons for the limited distribution of these finds.

Quimby noted the relationships between humans, vegetation, and proboscideans; and both Mason and Quimby believed that the Paleo-Indians of the entire Great Lakes region hunted mastodonts. This was based on the fact that many of the fluted points of the region were very similar to the Clovis points used by mammoth hunters in the West. Later, Quimby stated that the distribution of fluted points and known mastodont remains in the state was related to the probability that Paleo-Indians hunted these animals. The term *Mason-Quimby line* began to appear in the literature on the subject and is now commonly published

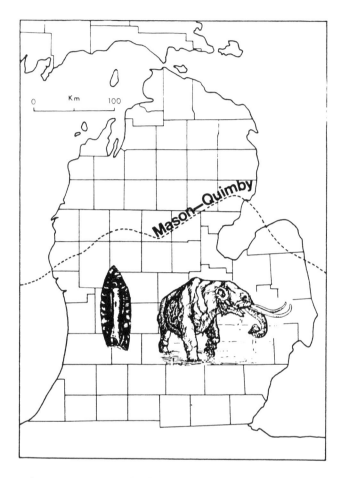

Fig. 89. Michigan's Mason-Quimby line. This line was originally set up to depict the northernmost occurrences of Paleo-Indian artifacts and proboscidean (mammoth and mastodont) remains in the state. Now, it is considered to depict the northernmost occurrence of most, if not all, of the Pleistocene vertebrates in the state.

in writings and used in classroom teaching. In fact, the term is so common that abbreviated references such as "north or south of the MQ" are understood by most archaeologists and paleontologists in the area.

It has recently been suggested that another important paleontological aspect of the MQ is that all of the previously reported records of extinct Pleistocene vertebrates from Michigan lie south of it. Thus, whatever factors restricted the distribution of mammoths and mastodonts in the late Pleistocene of Michigan must have also restricted the distribution of the extinct Pleistocene vertebrates (and probably other Pleistocene vertebrates as well).

The best explanation for this probably has to do with the positions of the ice margins in Michigan during the last episodes of deglaciation (see fig. 13b). Fourteen thousand years ago the end of the ice was about 35 miles south of the Mason-Quimby line; and 13,000 years ago it was about 70 miles north of the line. As the ice retreated between these intervals, it left a mass of sterile mud, sand, and gravel in its wake that had to be recolonized by plants and animals. Therefore, the Mason-Quimby line probably represents a *tension zone* between the biologically sterile zone to the north and the land that was being recolonized and organized into viable biological communities to the south.

Since extinct vertebrates died out about 10,000 years ago, it seems probable that the vegetational communities in this tension zone never developed the proper plant species to support these animals north of the line we call the Mason-Quimby. The distribution of mastodonts and mammoths in Ontario relative to the glacial boundaries is mainly an extension of the pattern seen in Michigan; and the Mason-Quimby line could well be looped over the northern extent of the ranges of Ontario proboscideans.

Mastodonts

Mastodonts have been known in North America since the middle Miocene about 12 million years ago. The North American late Pleistocene species is the American mastodont (*Mammut americanum,* figs. 87, 90 [color], and 91 [color]), and it ranged from Alaska to Florida. This species was most common in the eastern forests of North America and was a very common species in the southern part of the Great Lakes region. Mastodonts were about 10 feet high at the shoulder and, as we have previously discussed, had a heavier, more piglike body than mammoths. They also differed from mammoths in having a flatter head, a longer and horizontal lower jaw, and teeth with knobby surfaces.

The tusks of mastodonts normally were not as curved as those of mammoths, and male mastodonts often developed small lower tusks. Mastodonts are either right-tusked or left-tusked, just as humans are either right- or left-handed. When a pair of tusks belonging to the same individual are found, one is always more worn at the end than the other. Mastodonts use their tusks as tools, to break limbs off of trees, root in the soil, and in other endeavors.

Mastodonts ate twigs, conifer cones, tree leaves, and small swamp plants. It has been suggested that in the Great Lakes region the mastodont was a forest animal that browsed along streams and bogs. This would have ecologically separated it from the mammoths, which were grassland grazers. It is interesting to note that mastodont and mammoth fossils are seldom found together.

Mastodonts have been aged on the basis of growth lines that form in the dentine layers of their molar teeth and tusks. Growth lines in the tusks record lunar month intervals, two-week intervals, and daily intervals that may be seen upon microscopic examination of fine sections of the tusks. Thus, one may determine not only the age the animal died, but also the time of the year that it exited the surface of the earth to become a fossil.

Mastodonts may also be sexed on the basis of their bones, so that it might be determined that a specimen came from a female who died early in the spring when she was 32 years old. Older mastodonts became arthritic, and the type and extent of the condition may be determined by studying the skeleton. Thus a statement that an aging 50-year-old male with a bad hip and a chronically stiff neck got stuck in a bog late in the fall can also be made.

Mastodont sites in the Great Lakes region are usually similar to mammoth sites in that mastodont bones tend to be found between muck or peat and marl zones in kettlelike depressions or shallow basins. Mastodonts are also occasionally found in ancient glacial lake bed sediments, and less frequently in streambeds.

Mastodont records, like mammoth records, have sometimes been repeated in the literature, so that it appears there are more mastodont sites than really exist. But in Michigan and Ontario these sites have recently been evaluated, and the numbers are probably as correct as they are ever going to be. In Michigan there are 211 mastodont and 49 mammoth sites on record, all from south of the Mason-Quimby line. In Ontario there are 61 mastodont sites and 27 mammoth sites. Most Ontario mastodont sites are found on poorly drained areas near Lake Erie, where it is believed that they fed on forest vegetation.

It has been suggested that Paleo-Indians hunted mastodonts as well as mammoths in the Great Lakes region, but direct association between these proboscideans and humans has never been demonstrated. Nevertheless, there is considerable indirect evidence that humans killed, butchered, stored, and ate proboscideans in the Great Lakes region. Mastodonts, like mammoths, became extinct everywhere about 10,000 years ago. We will discuss the indirect evidence of human-proboscidean interaction and this sudden mass extinction later in this book.

Mammoths, Mastodonts, and Salt

It was recently suggested that the large concentration of proboscideans in the southern part of the Lower Peninsula of Michigan during the very late Pleistocene might be due to the occurrence of widespread salt licks and shallow saline waters (fig. 91 [color]). It was further suggested that salt-related studies might give information about movements of these animals and possibly even about their abrupt extinction.

The reasoning behind this hypothesis is as follows. There is an unusually large number of records of mammoths and mastodonts (49 mammoth and 211 mastodonts) in the southern two-thirds of Michigan's Lower Peninsula during a very short time period from about 12,000 to 10,000 years ago. Yet there are very few individual records of other mammals. In fact, in a twenty-year period, from about 1976 to 1986, 77 percent of all of the vertebrate fossils collected in Michigan were proboscideans. Yet the climate in the area during the time of the existence of these beasts is considered to have been a cold, harsh, proglacial climate.

The question is then, "Why should so many huge animals, so demanding on the biological resources of the ecosystem, be so abundant in such a severe environment?" The answer may be related to the following information on modern elephants. It is common knowledge that modern elephants crave salt and will often travel a long way to get it. This is because salt contains sodium and elephants have very high sodium requirements. In fact, the distribution of elephants in Africa is based on their access to salt. The animals drink at salt-rich water holes or may use their tusks to loosen salt-rich soil, which is then eaten.

Modern elephants often travel great distances seasonally to salty areas to build up their salt reserves and then trek back to their feeding and calving grounds. Without salt they can develop serious illnesses and die. Michigan's salt deposits, as we have seen, accumulated in shallow, evaporative seas during Silurian and Devonian times in the Michigan Basin. Upward crustal movement of the basin exposed one of the largest salt deposits in the world. Thus, it is hypothesized that salt may have been an important limiting factor in Pleistocene proboscidean distribution, and that the large concentration of these animals in southern Michigan might be associated with the existence of a readily available salt supply.

If proboscideans made seasonal trips from relatively saltless areas in Ohio, Indiana, and Illinois to Michigan to obtain salt, it should be possible to get radioactively targeted evidence of migrations. Thus far such evidence has not been obtained.

Mammoth and mastodont concentrations at Big Bone Lick in Kentucky, where the Cincinnati Arch brought salt near the surface, produced such large concentrations of proboscideans that some of the bones found their way to the White House in Washington, where they were studied by President Thomas Jefferson.

In the Atlantic states, many proboscidean localities are near the seashore. So it may be that salt was a very important factor in the lives of Pleistocene mammoths and mastodonts and that conditions at the end of the Ice Age that may have altered the availability of salt might have been critical to the animals.

We have completed our systematic review of important fossils of the Great Lakes region and are now ready for a historical summary.

Chapter 10
History of Life in the Great Lakes Basin

This chapter is a chronological account of the ancient life of the Great Lakes region. It looks at the broad picture of the development and extinction of biological communities from the Precambrian to the Pleistocene. Finally, the arrival of humans in the Great Lakes region and their possible impact on the large mammals of the area is discussed.

The Precambrian Era

The Precambrian era is estimated to have encompassed about seven-eighths of the time that has elapsed since the earth was formed! This is a time span of about 4,000 million years, a period of time difficult for humans to comprehend. Living things are first recorded from Precambrian rocks about 3,500 million years ago, and these life-forms remained simple for about the next 2,950 million years, until the beginning of the Cambrian.

The first organisms consist of bacteria preserved in chert and cabbage-like structures called stromatolites that were by-products of cyanobacteria (formerly called blue-green algae). These organisms are still the simplest of life-forms. They existed as cells, but they lacked a nucleus and are thus called *prokaryotic cells*. Some of them could exist without oxygen, but others needed oxygen to survive. The first ones could not manufacture their own food and merely absorbed organic materials from their environment.

Later on, these simple cellular forms evolved the process of photosynthesis, whereby carbon dioxide and water in the atmosphere were transformed into food materials with the release of oxygen. This was facilitated by a substance called chlorophyll and was driven by the energy from sunlight. The release of oxygen by this process caused a revolution in the earth's atmosphere, and the simple photosynthesizing cells became the producer organisms for a very simple ecological system.

In the Great Lakes region, the Precambrian Gunflint Chert of Ontario and Minnesota produced fine examples of bacteria and cyanobacteria as well as what has been interpreted as the hyphae of fungi. If the fungal identification is correct, then multicellular organisms as well as cells with nuclei (eukaryotes) had evolved by 2 billion years ago. Trace fossils that appear to represent burrows and trails occur in the late Precambrian, but the actual fossils of these animals have never been found. It is reckoned that this is because these animals were wormlike forms with soft bodies.

Time capsule to the Precambrian. Most people have had daydreams about being able to travel back to ancient scenes in a time capsule to get an idea of what the plants and animals represented by fossils really looked like. Let's board an imaginary time capsule and journey 2 billion years back in time to what is now the north shore of Lake Superior.

We alight from the capsule on the shore of an ancient sea. The sun is beating down unmercifully through the thin atmosphere. There are low, dark-colored mountains in the background (fig. 92 [color]). Some wispy clouds hang over the mountains, but the sky over the sea is cloudless and bright blue. The tide is out, and cabbagelike piles of stromatolites mark the boundary between the shore and sea. The land is composed of piles of broken rocks and sand.

The sea is a bluish green color. We can detect no evidence of life anywhere. Nothing is flying in the air or moving over the barren land. Then we detect something that looks like a giant, slimy oil slick that is moving in with the tide. It is a mass of dead organic sludge produced by billions of bacterial cells that were killed by a newly evolved strain of virus. As the bacterial oil slick moves in, we are overwhelmed by the odor of decay. If we lingered to watch the outcome we might see the stromatolite-producing "blue-green algae" colony smothered by this amorphous Precambrian "sea monster."

The Cambrian Period

The Cambrian period lasted about 50 million years and saw the origin of all of the major phyla of animals as well as the fragmentary remains of the first vertebrates. Although many groups are known, fossils of only three kinds of animals are really abundant in the Cambrian; a primitive group of invertebrates called the plesiosponges, the brachiopods, and the trilobites.

The plesiosponges probably deserve to be recognized as separate phylum, as they have characteristics that resemble both sponges and corals. These animals have a calcareous skeleton that is often cup shaped and consists of two walls that are porous and separated by radial septa. Attached to the bottom, these primitive animals built up small moundlike reefs in some of the early Cambrian seas. As the Cambrian wore on, the plesiosponges became rare and finally extinct by the end of the period. They are not common fossils in the Great Lakes Basin.

Brachiopods and trilobites are more common than plesiosponges in the Great Lakes region, but for some reason they are not very abundant in the rocks of the Michigan Basin. Most of the Cambrian brachiopods are of the inarticulate type and lack the structure that locks the two valves together. Some articulate brachiopods were around in the Cambrian, in fact they appeared in the early part of the period. But they really did not reach their heyday until the Ordovician period that followed.

One-third of all of the fossils that are found in the Cambrian are trilobites (see fig. 47). These interesting animals began to reach the apex of their abundance in the late Cambrian and then began a decline in the late Ordovician. The trilobites evolved from bottom crawlers to a diversity of forms, including burrowers, swimmers, and free floaters during the Cambrian.

One cannot write about the Cambrian without mentioning the middle Cambrian Burgess Shale of Alberta, which has yielded marvelous fossils of primitive soft-bodied animals—some of which have body plans unknown in other animal phyla—as well as other more familiar animals such as worms, crustaceans, and trilobites along with their internal organs and delicate external structures.

By late Cambrian times, the first vertebrates appeared, as we may judge on the basis of phosphatic plates from Wyoming. Undoubtedly the earliest vertebrate ancestors existed in middle Cambrian times, but they were soft bodied as was the chordate *Pikaia* from the Burgess Shale.

Time capsule to the Cambrian. Let's imagine that the time capsule has dropped us off in the Michigan Basin in about the middle of the Cambrian period. Before we wade into the sea with our scuba gear, we survey the terrain around us. The land is flat, and there are no mountain ranges. Because of a denser Cambrian atmosphere the sun is warm, rather than terribly hot as in our Precambrian experience. The land is barren of vegetation, at least as far as we can observe.

The first thing we see when we enter the water is a group of trilobites slowly crawling along the bottom. Two of them quickly burrow into the mud as we approach. A miniforest of brachiopods sways gently back and forth as gentle waves move in. Several kinds of wormlike creatures are disturbed by our presence and swim away in a rather aimless and disorganized way.

Then we notice a school of tiny, almost transparent creatures, not much more than an inch in length, swimming through the miniforest of brachiopods. The school suddenly moves en masse to the seafloor, where they burrow very quickly into the sand. If we had better eyes we would soon notice tiny ciliated "heads" poking out of the sand to filter-feed on minute particles of food.

One of the creatures wriggles out of the sand to look for better feeding grounds. A predaceous worm with snapping jaws swims errati-cally toward the tiny creature, which darts away in a straight line, leaving worms, creeping trilobites, and stalked brachiopods behind (fig. 93 [color]). It's a long road from *Amphioxus* (or an amphioxus-like creature) to vertebrates and ultimately to humans, but the beginning of this evolutionary sequence must have occurred in the Cambrian.

The Ordovician Period

The Ordovician period lasted for about 60 million years, from about 500 million to about 440 million years ago. When the Cambrian ended, all of the major phyla had evolved, but only a few of them were abundant. During the Ordovician marine animals began to flourish in the shallow seas that now were teeming with invertebrate life. Ordovician habitats were quite varied, and new food sources enabled new creatures to evolve. Calcium carbonate was the major shell-building material of the Ordovician, and in some of the seas calcareous shells became so abundant that they formed entire geological formations.

Bryozoans, rare in the Cambrian, increased significantly in the Ordovician and began to encrust many kinds of bottom structures, as well as the shells of other organisms. Graptolites became more important in the Ordovician, and brachiopods continued to expand. The beautiful crinoids also diversified in Ordovician times, as trilobites reached the pinnacle of their development. During much of the Ordovician the Michigan Basin was covered by seas. However, the seas were subject to fluctuation during this period, so that some sediments were laid down in nearshore situations, while other sediments reflect deeper, offshore deposition.

Time capsule to the Ordovician. This time the time capsule will deposit us on the shore of a shallow Ordovician sea in what is now the Lower Peninsula of Michigan. We adjust our flippers and goggles and begin paddling around in the tepid sea, where life is abundant and varied.

Trilobites are everywhere. Some are creeping along on the bottom, others are burrowing into the muddy sand, while still others are slowly swimming along in loose formation. Rocks and other objects on the bottom are encrusted with limy bryozoans. In some areas we see small forests of brachiopods, but in other areas we notice taller forests of stemmed crinoids, some of them brilliantly colored. Cup- and vase-shaped corals, some nicely colored, add beauty to the structure of the seafloor.

One lone animal, however, particularly strikes our eyes. It looks like a fish in some ways, but not quite. This ostracoderm is almost enclosed in a somewhat barrel-shaped bony box composed of several large plates, has no constantly moving bony operculum, as do fish, and has two tiny eyes that glint from the head part of the box. The tail section is composed of smaller plates, and the tail itself has the larger of its two fin lobes turned downward.

If we could examine the plates themselves with a magnifying glass, we would see that they were covered with tiny tubercles, each with a series of grooves down its side. Near the head of this animal we can see tiny puffs as it filter-feeds on tiny organic particles in the muddy sand. When we paddle too close to the animal, it moves upward and away with a few flicks of its tail. It settles down only a few feet away, and soon we see the little puffs again, which means it has begun the process of filter feeding again. Well-defined vertebrates now have finally secured a minor place among the hordes of invertebrate species of the Ordovician.

The Silurian Period

The Silurian is a short period (as geological periods go) that lasted from about 440 to about 410 million years ago. Shallow continental seas were extensive in North America, and the earliest known freshwater deposits occurred in northwestern Europe. The shallow seas in North America provided ideal habitats for the ever-expanding life-forms there.

The major invertebrate groups were brachiopods, trilobites (which were locally common), and graptolites. However, the mollusk fauna was expanding rapidly, and this included gastropods, bivalves, and cephalopods. Bryozoans continued to diversify, and they encrusted almost everything solid. Corals, stromatoporids, and crinoids increased in numbers and in kinds. During middle and late Silurian times the eurypterids or sea scorpions were the top predators.

Freshwater Beds

We have not discussed freshwater beds thus far in our historical account because freshwater sediments and fossils are almost nonexistent in the early Paleozoic fossil record. But toward the end of the Silurian period, freshwater beds became common in some areas, especially in northwestern Europe. With the onset of these freshwater deposits we get our first clear picture of early fishlike vertebrates.

Now there are numerous fossil specimens of whole fishes, mainly ostracoderms, plus the earliest remnants of all of the other classes of fishlike vertebrates, such as placoderms, sharklike fishes, and bony fishes (including the acanthodians). It appears that most of the early evolution of fishes occurred in early Paleozoic freshwater habitats and that this history has been largely hidden from us because of the lack of freshwater deposits during these countless millions of years.

The ostracoderms (see fig. 50) were highly developed by late Silurian times. There were flat-bodied bottom feeders with upthrusting tails and complex water-sensing devices on the top and sides of their heads. There were blind mud grubbers and other forms that sat on top of the mud by means of sledlike runners. Other types of ostracoderms were compressed "minnows" that fed on tiny organisms and bits of debris in the surface tension at the water-air interface. All of them were armored, possibly as a defense against the predatory eurypterids.

However, eurypterids themselves are thought to have had ostracoderm problems. One ostracoderm called *Jaymoitius* supposedly bored holes into eurypterids and sucked out their vital juices, much as modern sea lampreys do when they attack lake trout in the Great Lakes. Acanthodians are known by good fossils in late Silurian times and fragmentary remains of placoderms also appear then. Fossil scales announce the presence of both sharks and bony fishes in late Silurian times.

Silurian Reefs

In Silurian times, the inland seas of the Great Lakes region were warm and tropical, and a system of great pinnacle reefs built up around the Michigan Basin. Outlying reefs were more patchy. These reefs were built mainly by corals and stromatoporoids and were reinforced by calcareous algal plants and sponges. The cracks and holes in the reefs were at least partially filled in by bits and pieces of the shells of other invertebrate animals that lived nearby, such as bivalves, gastropods, brachiopods, and crinoids. Near the end of the Silurian, the great inland seas of the Michigan Basin began to dry up, and massive evaporative deposits of salt accumulated.

Time capsule to the Silurian. The time capsule now takes us back to the middle Silurian in what is now north central New York, near the southern shore of Lake Ontario. Here the reefs were low and patchy rather than the towering pinnacle type that surrounded the Michigan Basin. There were extensive tidal flats, and some of these may have had influxes of freshwater from time to time.

Upon arrival, we walk down the beach of a tidal flat. There are muddy as well as sandy portions. We notice that the sandy portions are littered with the shells of bivalves and gastropods very much like modern Florida beaches, as well as with parts of crinoid stems and a few beautiful cephalopod shells. The seawater is a slightly milky green.

We wade cautiously into the tidal flat, not really knowing what to expect. What we see reminds us of similar tidal flats that occur near some of the modern Florida keys. Small patches of nonliving corals, killed in earlier times by temporary withdrawals of the sea, make up part of the bottom structure. Living coral patches occur in deeper portions of the bay. Most of the shallow bottom is composed of a whitish, limy mud. Bivalves and gastropods churn through the mud, and a few trilobites scuttle along the bottom as well.

Suddenly we are startled by a dark shape about five feet long. It looks like a gigantic, flattened scorpion, and it has a pair of pincers at the end of long appendages. The monster crawls slowly along the top of the mud, its antennae waving slowly back and forth, its pincers probing into the milky ooze for prey. We watch in fascination as it pulls up a large worm tube, passes the tube up to its mouth, and then, using its complicated mouth parts, extracts a foot-long, wriggling sea worm. The marine worm soon is eaten, and the eurypterid continues to forage for food.

This time it pulls up a different object, an armored, somewhat fish-like creature about a foot long. The ostracoderm is duly transferred by the pincers to the mouth parts, which rasp away at the hard skeletal plates, but to no avail (fig. 94 [color]). Finally, this hard creature is dropped, the eurypterid returns to search the ooze for more soft-bodied prey, and the ostracoderm returns to its life of filtering mud.

The Devonian Period

The Devonian was a rather long and important period that lasted for about 50 million years, from about 410 million to about 360 million years ago. The Devonian has appropriately been called the Age of Fishes because of the continued radiation and modernization of the classes of fishes that were present at the end of the Silurian period. By the end of the Devonian the first tetrapods had made their appearance.

Marine invertebrates were even more abundant in the warm shallow seas of the Devonian than they were in Silurian times. Coral reefs continued to be built in many places, including the Great Lakes region. Both horn and tabulate corals as well as stromatoporoids were active reef builders. Some of the horn corals got to be over two feet high, and some coral heads were more than eight feet across. Brachiopods and crinoids were abundant, and algal seaweeds formed underwater forests.

Mollusks became very abundant in the Devonian period, and the bivalved pelecypods were more numerous than they ever had been. Gastropods were locally common, including some parts of the Great Lakes region. Among the cephalopods, the first ammonoids are known from the Devonian and were to become very dominant shellfish later in the Paleozoic.

Trilobites continued to decline in the Devonian, yet some very large species still prowled ocean waters, including *Dalmanites,* which was over 2 1/2 feet long. Eurypterids continued to produce some giant species; but as a group, eurypterids were also to decline during the period because they lost their top-predator role to the upcoming fishes. Among the echinoderm phylum, starfishes became abundant for the first time. Deposits in New York State are known where starfishes were trapped by sediments and fossilized in the process of taking apart clams, as they still do today.

As progressive jawed-fish groups began to radiate in the Devonian, the jawless ostracoderms began to decline and finally became extinct by the end of the period. Placoderms were very important Devonian vertebrates: They were mainly freshwater forms in the early Devonian, but by the late Devonian had fully invaded the sea, and huge forms like *Dunkleosteus* became the top predators. *Dunkleosteus* could have crushed the largest of the eurypterids like humans eating peanut brittle.

Some of the oldest sharklike fishes are known by cladodus-type teeth in middle Devonian times and then are represented by splendid specimens from the Cleveland Shales by late in the period. Acanthodian bony fishes elaborated new structures in the Devonian, and both primitive rayfinned and lobe-finned fishes were common, especially in freshwater. By the end of the Devonian, specialized crossopterygian lobe-finned fishes had given rise to the earliest tetrapods, some with extra "fingers" and "toes," and these were to ultimately become the first land animals. In addition, several primitive plants invaded the land to set the stage for later well-developed terrestrial communities.

Time capsule to the Devonian. This visit in the time capsule drops us in a bathosphere into a shallow late Devonian sea near what is now Cleveland, Ohio. We slowly descend to the seafloor about 30 feet down. Both algal seaweed and crinoid forests sway with the waves and tidal currents. The first vertebrate life we notice is a large school of small, primitive rayfinned fishes. They somewhat resemble a school of herring, except that the scales are bony, shiny, and diamond shaped, and their heads are too long. The school moves into the forest of seaweeds and begins feeding frantically on clouds of small invertebrate creatures moving vertically among the plants.

Adjacent to the algal forest is a small forest of brachiopods. They are anchored by their stalks to large flat objects that represent worn-down remnants of previously existing coral heads. Some of these "fossil" coral heads are covered with encrusting algal and bryozoan colonies. Feeding on these colonies are very small placoderms called antiarchs. They have peaky thoracic shields, small heads, and tiny nibbling jaws. They work their way up and down the extinct coral heads with their armlike "pectoral fins" rasping away at algal plants and bryozoan colonies.

But our attention is now attracted to the school of rayfinned fishes feeding in the algal forest. A cladoselachian shark has moved in after them, pushing algal plants aside and scattering the school into smaller units (fig. 95 [color]). Then a large form appears in the window of our bathosphere, inches from our faces—a huge head with half-opened mouth and round, black, lifeless-looking eyes staring! The mouth is ridged with jagged, rootless teeth. *Dunkleosteus*, it turns out, is territorial, and its tiny brain has received a message that some huge globular creature has invaded its domain and is about to attack its nest of placoderm eggs. In seconds we could be butted and crunched to smithereens by the angry arthrodire! The school of rayfinned fishes and the sharks have whisked away, and even the little antiarchs have scuttled off.

"Carboniferous Times"

The Mississippian Period

The Mississippian period represents approximately the lower half of what is recognized as the Carboniferous period in Europe. The Mississippian period lasted from about 360 to about 320 million years ago.

Limestone deposits characterize the Mississippian period in North America. But most of these deposits lie south of the Great Lakes region, where the local Mississippian rocks consist mainly of shales, siltstones, and sandstones.

The time of the great Paleozoic reef formations ended with the Devonian. Shallow seas were present in the Michigan Basin during most of the Mississippian, but in the very late part of the period the basin was uplifted, and parts of the earlier deposits were eroded away. The marine invertebrates of the Mississippian formed mainly a transitional fauna between the Devonian and the Pennsylvanian. The tiny protistan forams that were known since the Ordovician became very important as rock builders for the first time in the Mississippian. Some of these tiny protists, only the size of pinheads, built up great formations of rocks almost by themselves. These occur in the form of the so-called oolitic rocks that lie south of the Great Lakes region and that are used as building stones in southern Indiana.

Bryozoans of lacy structure were important, and crinoids were abundant and formed what were probably the most brilliantly colored seafloors ever known before or since. Blastoid echinoderms became common and varied during Mississippian times. All of these groups are known in the Great Lakes region, but they never became as large or as brilliant as they did in places like central and southern Indiana.

In freshwater swamps, primitive tetrapod stock such as *Ichthyostega* evolved into two basal groups known as the *temnospondyls* and the *anthracosaurs*. The temnospondyls had a history we will discuss in the following discussion of the Pennsylvanian period. The anthracosaurs ultimately gave rise to the true land animals, the reptiles. Unfortunately, few of these animals are known as fossils in the Great Lakes region.

The Pennsylvanian Period

The Pennsylvanian period corresponds to about the upper one-half of the Carboniferous period of Britain and Europe. The Pennsylvanian lasted for about 30 million years, from about 320 to about 290 million years ago. Pennsylvanian rocks occur nearest to the surface in the center of the Michigan Basin, but fossiliferous outcrops tend to be rather limited. The Pennsylvanian was a time when the sea in the Michigan

Basin came in and then went out again in a cyclic pattern. When the sea was in, marine communities produced invertebrate fossils. When the sea was out, coal-swamp communities produced mainly fossils of large, primitive, treelike plants.

Invertebrate animals in the encroaching seas were abundant and very diversified during the Pennsylvanian. Large fusilinid foraminiferans appeared during the Pennsylvanian and were exceedingly abundant in some limestone formations. Brachiopods were common on seafloors with hard bottoms, and gastropods and bivalves were abundant on seafloors with soft, muddy bottoms. The early nautiloid cephalopods declined, but primitive ammonoid cephalopods began to increase in variety. Among the echinoderms the blastoids were abundant in the early Pennsylvanian but declined later in the period.

The first true forests with treelike plants came into being when the sea had retreated in the Pennsylvanian. The "trees" in these forests were made up of primitive plants related to our modern ground pines and horsetails. These plants grew very fast and had more soft tissues than the true trees of today. The swamp forests composed of these plants provided the fossil material for the great coal deposits of the earth.

As the Pennsylvanian forests flourished, insects began to diversify and become abundant. Many of these early insect species reached a very large size in the warm, moist coal-swamp environment. Scorpions, centipedes, millipedes (some reaching very large size), spiders, and freshwater clams also became abundant and varied. Palaeoniscoid fishes and lungfishes inhabited the pools of the coal swamps, and the lungfishes burrowed into the mud to escape drought conditions. Large amphibians became abundant. The elongate embolomeres were aquatic predators, and some of the other labyrinthodonts took on the appearance of squatty alligators with short tails and huge flattened heads.

Smaller amphibians also swarmed in some of the coal-swamp forests and pools. Some had boomerang-shaped heads that probably made it difficult for the alligator-like predators to swallow them. Other small amphibians were limbless and had long snakelike bodies. One small group of coal-swamp amphibians called *microsaurs* evolved into insect-eating species that looked very much like small reptiles. Then, during the early part of the middle Pennsylvanian, the first small reptiles, also insect-eating forms, made their appearance.

Time capsule to the Pennsylvanian. The time capsule carries us now to an early Pennsylvanian coal swamp (fig. 96 [color]) in what is now about the center of the lower third of the Lower Peninsula of Michigan, near Lansing. We need to put our waders on before leaving the capsule because the land is wet and swampy. As we take our first soggy steps out of the capsule, we are confronted by a very warm, muggy, greenhouse atmosphere.

Huge lycopod trees are the dominant plants in the forest, and sphenopsids and seed ferns make up the smaller plants of the understory. The forest smells pungent and pithy, not at all like the crisp smell one gets in a modern oak forest, or the cool smell of pines one gets in more northern areas of the Great Lakes region.

We slog down to a forest pool to look for creatures. Before long we notice a school of small fish feeding in the vegetation at the edge of the pool. They are deep-bodied fish a few inches long that would somewhat resemble bluegills or sunfish if it were not for the shiny, thick, rhomboidal scales that cover their bodies. Suddenly, a huge water beetle grabs one of the fish and scuttles down into the vegetation with its prey.

We wander back into the forest, which is now droning with the sound of insects. A huge dragonfly with a wingspan of nearly three feet chases a smaller flying insect, causing us to duck as the monstrous insect buzzes by our heads. We notice a particularly large lycopod log on the forest floor and decide to roll it over to see if there are any small microsaurs or other amphibians hiding under it.

Over goes the log, but instead of small amphibians we see three huge cockroaches with waving antennae. The cockroaches scuttle away to take refuge under a fallen sphenopsid tree. We decide to try one more fallen log for amphibians. As this log goes over, we are startled by a foot-long centipede resting beneath it. As this creature crawls away on its horde of legs, we decide that a Pennsylvanian coal swamp takes a lot of getting used to!

The Lost Interval Reconsidered

We have already discussed the geological reasons behind the great Lost Interval that spanned about 290 million years of time in the Great Lakes region, from the end of the Pennsylvanian to almost the end of the Ice Age. During this interval many important groups we have discussed flourished and became extinct, and other important groups evolved to take their place.

Many significant marine invertebrate groups did not make it into the Mesozoic, as a particularly important crisis occurred between the Permian and the Triassic. Some of the groups that were left behind in the Paleozoic include the plesiosponges, stromatoporoids, and trilobites, as well as several important groups of corals, bryozoans, brachiopods, and echinoderms.

Another important time of marine invertebrate extinction occurred at the end of the Cretaceous and particularly impacted the shelled cephalopods. All of the ammonoids, a very dominant group in the Mesozoic, died out, and only a few nautiloids survived into the Tertiary.

Among the plants, lycopod and sphenopsid trees declined and seed fern trees became extinct during the Mesozoic, as ferns, cycads, ginkgos, and conifers flourished. By the early Cretaceous, flowering plants made their appearance and became dominant by late Cretaceous times. Grasslands became very important on a worldwide basis during the middle part of the Tertiary.

The vertebrate story became very complex during the Lost Interval. Primitive fish groups gave rise to modern sharks and rayfinned fishes during the latter part of the Mesozoic, and the rayfinned fishes underwent an enormous adaptive radiation in the Tertiary. Amphibians declined in importance in the early part of the Lost Interval as reptiles diversified. Primitive reptile groups expanded greatly in the Permian, and several mammal-like reptiles were very important parts of the terrestrial community.

In Triassic times the thecodont reptiles became very important animals and contained within them the ancestors of the dinosaurs. Dinosaurs and the earliest mammals both appeared near the end of the Triassic. The dinosaurs absolutely dominated the Jurassic and Cretaceous periods, a time span that lasted for about 145 million years. During the reign of the dinosaurs the mammals, small and furtive, hid during the daytime and came out to hunt insects at night, when the majority of dinosaurs were sleeping. They also quietly evolved into the basal groups that nourished the mammalian explosion in the Tertiary, after the extinction of the dinosaurs at the end of the Cretaceous.

Pterodactyls, flying cousins of the dinosaurs, dominated the skies for much of the Mesozoic, and the earliest birds evolved from small bipedal dinosaurs by late Jurassic times, perhaps earlier. Birds dominated the skies during the Tertiary, after the pterodactyls died out at the end of the Cretaceous.

Many modern orders of mammals arose in the Eocene epoch, replacing some early "experimental" groups, and a great radiation of hoofed mammals occurred during Miocene times, coincident with the widespread occurrence of grasslands. Snakes, perching birds, and grass-eating rodents also had a vigorous adaptive radiation during Miocene times. In the Pliocene some of these mammalian groups began to falter, and we will see later on that there was a major mammalian extinction at the end of the Pleistocene.

Time capsule to the Lost Interval? Thus far we have taken imaginary time capsule trips to specific places in the Great Lakes region, where we have fantasized about the animals and plants that would be found there. Since no fossil record (other than some Jurassic pollen and spores) exists in the Great Lakes region during the Lost Interval, we can only speculate broadly about what might have happened.

For instance, let's look at the Jurassic and Cretaceous. We know that the Great Lakes Basin was a rather well-drained upland during the Jurassic and the Cretaceous periods. Thus one might speculate that different kinds of communities developed in uplands compared to those of lowlands, as we know that this is what occurs everywhere on earth today. Moreover, we have every reason to believe that the Great Lakes area had an equable semitropical climate during most of the Mesozoic.

Contrast, for example, modern semitropical or tropical communities that develop along river swamps, to those of dry, sandy tablelands, and you'll get an idea of the differences there might have been between Mesozoic communities in the swamps of what is now Wyoming and Montana and the "tablelands" of the Great Lakes region. Mammals might have been more abundant in the tablelands and in some cases they might have been somewhat larger than the swamp forms. Unknown types of dinosaurs—more adapted to higher regions—might have existed in the Great Lakes Basin; and even the insects, pterodactyls, and early birds might have been different.

The Great Ice Age

The great Ice Age (Pleistocene) lasted from about 1.9 million years ago until about 10,000 years ago, when Recent (Holocene) times began. Glaciers of the Ice Age sculptured the modern topography of the Great Lakes area as well as that of many other places in the world in northern latitudes. Glaciers also formed in the mountains of some relatively southern areas of the world. We realize that the advance and retreat of the glaciers in the north had a great effect on the plant and animal life in northern areas and in the mountains; but there were other effects in southern areas that many people in northern latitudes do not appreciate. For instance, during glacial times, much atmospheric water was bound up in the continental ice; thus the global sea level (as well as the large-lake levels) were lower during these periods of time.

On the other hand, during interglacial times, when water from melting ice sheets flowed into the oceans, the sea level was higher. It is believed that the state of Florida was an island during some interglacial times, with the so-called Suwannee Straits cutting off peninsular Florida from the mainland. During glacial times Florida was not only connected to mainland but had more extensive shoreline than at present as the sea flow became depressed. The fact that sea shorelines were more extensive in Pleistocene times is demonstrated in the New England area by the discovery today of mastodont bones from the sediments at the bottom of the sea.

Ice Age Climate

We have already discussed the fact that interglacial temperate times occurred between glacial episodes in the Pleistocene. It is now known that the glacial ages were generally much longer than the interglacial ages. The Sangamonian interglacial age in North America, for instance, lasted for about 10,000 years; whereas the Wisconsinan glacial age lasted for about 100,000 years.

The same situation exists in Britain, where the Ipswichian interglacial age (equivalent to the North American Sangamonian) lasted 10,000 years and the Devensian glacial age (equivalent to the Wisconsinan) about 100,000 years. The time lines of earlier glacial and interglacial ages are not well established in either country; but it is generally believed that glacials were much longer than interglacials in these ages as well.

Ideas about the North American climate during the Ice Age have been greatly revised in the last decades. It was formerly believed that when the ice sheet extended into southern regions it pushed animal and plant communities southward ahead of it in bands. This is presently known as the "stripe hypothesis."

For instance, the last push of the Laurentide ice sheet in the late Wisconsinan, at its maximum extent, reached almost identical latitudes in central Illinois, Indiana, and Ohio. It thus seemed logical to reason that arctic tundra with short herbs and grasses would lie in a band south of the end of the ice sheet; that south of the tundra we should find a band of coniferous forest; and that south of the coniferous forest we should find a band of temperate deciduous forest. It was believed that the animals that were characteristic of these plant communities would also be pushed down with them.

It turns out that the situation is much more complicated than that. Studies of scores of North American Pleistocene vertebrate fossil faunas have indicated that, although there appears to have been a cold zone near the edge of the glacier, vertebrate populations of the middle latitudes in North America tended to be mixtures of northern and southern species.

In northwest Georgia, for instance, in the very late Wisconsinan, we find jaguars, pigsized armadillos, and giant tortoises the size of those that occur in the Galapagos Islands today existing along with northern spruce grouse, northern voles, and northern turtles. This association of northern and southern vertebrate species in Pleistocene faunas is common in many other midlatitude and southern states.

The modern explanation may be called the *plaid hypothesis* and is associated with a concept called the Pleistocene Climatic Equability Model. The plaid hypothesis recognizes that there are often mixed communities of northern and southern plants and animals well south of the glacial boundary. The explanation for these mixed communities involves the commonsense notion that plant and animal species respond to climatic changes (such as those that beset them during the southward thrust of the ice sheets) in their own individual ways, not as bands of plants and animals marching southward in a regular fashion in front of the advancing glacier.

In other words, some animals and plants, displaced from their northern homes by the glacier, would be able to adjust to more southern conditions, whereas others would not be able to do so. Thus, "plaid" or mozaic communities would exist south of the glacier and would be mainly composed of southern species as well as a few successful northern immigrants.

To answer the question of how these northern and southern animals could exist together, the Pleistocene Climatic Equability Model was proposed. This model suggests that the northern animals are present because of the cooler summers that exist in an equable climate; and that the southern animals such as the giant tortoises could exist because of the warmer winters in such a climate.

But during the entire Pleistocene the southern Great Lakes Basin was either buried under a mile or so of ice during glacial advances, or was close to the edge of the ice during glacial retreats. Thus, this area had a cold, *proglacial* climate during the Pleistocene, unlike midlatitude and southern regions in North America, which had an equable climate. For this reason, the southern Great Lakes area is a perfect place to search late Pleistocene and Holocene sites for evidence of reinvading species; for the flora and fauna of most of the region is the product of a reinvasion of plant and animal species that took place from about 14,000 to perhaps only a few thousand years ago.

The Pleistocene of Britain contrasts sharply with that of North America. There is not much suggestion of an equable Pleistocene climate there; in fact quite the contrary seems to be true. Interglacial faunas are composed of vertebrate assemblages that contain macaque monkeys, African lions, African hippos, and hyenas; whereas glacial faunas have arctic rodents, polar bears, and reindeer! This difference has been explained on the basis that the northern seas froze around the top of Britain, whereas in North America the Gulf of Mexico and South Atlantic Ocean generated warm air that moved northward at least as far as the midlatitudes.

Megavertebrate Communities in the Pleistocene

The Pleistocene vertebrate fauna was the product of millions of years of evolution during the Tertiary period. The major type of terrestrial community during the Tertiary was similar to the dinosaur communities in many ways. The most important animals were megaherbivores (huge herbivores) that ate large quantities of vegetation, including trees and ground shrubs. This activity allowed the various kinds of grasses to grow that became the food of smaller herbivorous species. Even the dung that the megaherbivores put back into the environment in large amounts was important as fertilizer. Smaller herbivores and the carnivores and the scavengers that fed upon them were all dependent on these megaherbivores for their existence.

It has recently been shown in Africa that elephants and rhinos are megaherbivores in the communities where they live; and if these animals became extinct a domino effect would lead to the disruption and probable extinction of much of the community. In the Great Lakes region and the rest of North America the mammoths and mastodonts were the megaherbivores of the Pleistocene and thus played a pivotal role in biotic communities from Michigan to Florida.

Other Important Extinct North American Pleistocene Vertebrates

We have already discussed the Pleistocene vertebrates of the Great Lakes region and will discuss them again later in relation to specific problems in the interpretation of the Ice Age. But we should mention several other important beasts that became extinct in North America to get an idea of how much the world lost by the devastating extinction that occurred about 10,000 years ago.

Giant land tortoises ranged from Florida north to southwestern Indiana, central Illinois, and northwestern Georgia during one time or another during the Pleistocene. Giant condors occurred in the western states. Packs of dire wolves roamed throughout much of North America and cave bears existed in the areas where caves occurred. An American lion that was larger and had longer legs than the African lion existed in the western United States. The saber-toothed "cat" was thought to be an important predator on young proboscideans.

Several species of horses, some of them striped like zebras, occurred in areas well south of the glacial margin. Camels, tapirs, several kinds of peccaries, and mammoths and mastodonts occurred. A giant bison, much larger than the modern bison, existed in the plains and western states.

Edentate mammals were important. The giant ground sloth stood over 15 feet high, and the glyptodont had a shell that was over 6 feet long. Clearly, the Pleistocene fauna was spectacular compared to the modern one. In fact, the former vertebrate paleontologist George Gaylord Simpson once stated that the Pleistocene mammalian fauna of Florida compares in richness with the modern one in Africa.

The Great Pleistocene Extinction

During most of the Tertiary and up to the end of the Ice Age, the major vertebrate populations of the world depended upon grasslands and megaherbivore-dominated communities. Human expansion at the close of the Pleistocene, coupled with the mass extinction of most of the large herbivorous genera, sparked the beginning of events that led to the world as we know it today. In this human-dominated world, domestic animals such as cattle, sheep, goats, and pigs have taken the place of extinct herbivores; and the grass cereals such as corn, wheat, oats, barley, and rice have largely replaced natural grasslands.

The extinction at the end of the Pleistocene has been termed "the extinction of the mammalian megafauna." But although the extinction struck mainly the large terrestrial herbivores, it also struck the carnivores and scavengers that were dependent upon them. At the famous Rancho La Brea tar pits in Los Angeles, for example, we see the extinction of not only the mammalian megaherbivores and other large herbivores, but also the extinction of dire wolves, sabertooths, and the huge American lion. Among scavengers we see the extinction of the huge condors as well as several dung beetles that fed on the droppings of the herbivores and probably were specialists on specific kinds of dung.

This Pleistocene extinction was generally worldwide. Smaller animals were largely spared. Relatively few rabbits and rodents became extinct; and other than the giant tortoises, very few reptiles became extinct, at least in the mainlands of the northern hemisphere. Practically no extinction is known among amphibians, fishes, and invertebrates, unless they were associated in some direct ecological way with the large herbivorous mammals.

Many scientific papers, magazine articles, books, and at least two international meetings of scientists have been devoted to the why of this extinction. The extinction of the dinosaurs at the end of the Cretaceous is of great academic interest, but it did not affect humankind directly. On the other hand, humans were present at the end of the

Pleistocene, and the extinction that occurred at that time greatly affected people.

Many hypotheses have been formulated to explain this extinction, and we shall consider a few of the major ones in the following paragraphs.

The Pleistocene overkill hypothesis. The Pleistocene overkill hypothesis has for decades been championed by Paul Martin of the University of Arizona. It is pointed out that Pleistocene vertebrates survived several periods of climatic change during the Pleistocene, yet the time of the major extinction came at the end of the Pleistocene. Martin's hypothesis suggests that the extinction follows the chronology of the spread of humans and their development as hunters of big game.

Martin reasons that when humans reached North America by the way of the land bridge that connected Siberia and Alaska they found herds of animals that were very vulnerable to human predation because they had never been confronted by humans before. Moreover, the invading humans had become skilled at hunting animals that were afraid of them. Thus, humans are thought to have spread rapidly through North America to the tip of South America, killing off the large herbivorous mammals as they went, in what has been termed a "Blitzkrieg."

Opponents to the overkill hypothesis point out that human kill sites are known from only a relatively few places and that human populations were too small at the time to have caused such a mass extinction. It is an intriguing hypothesis, however, for otherwise it is difficult to explain why so few of the smaller vertebrates became extinct. If one considers the reptiles of the Pleistocene, for instance, the only significant extinction that took place was that of the giant tortoises; and these large reptiles would have been extremely vulnerable to human predation. In fact, a giant Pleistocene tortoise that had been cooked over a fire and had either been killed by a wooden spear or manipulated over the fire by the spear, was found in a sinkhole in southwestern Florida.

The Pleistocene climatic equability hypothesis. This hypothesis has been discussed previously with regard to Pleistocene climates. It states that the climate in North America south of the glaciers must have been more equable than today with cooler summers and milder winters. The logical assumption is that the mild summers allow for the presence of the northern animals found in North American Pleistocene sites and that mild winters allow for the presence of the southern animals.

It is then further reasoned that our modern climate with colder winters and hotter summers must have originated about 10,000 years ago, and that this somehow must have affected the mammalian megafauna in such a negative way that it initiated a mass extinction. A second hypothesis associated with the Pleistocene climatic equability hypothesis attempts to explain how the changing climates could affect the megaherbivore community. This has been termed the out-of-step mating hypothesis.

The out-of-step mating hypothesis. This hypothesis assumes that the equable Pleistocene climate changed to the modern one of extremes about 10,000 years ago. It correlates the extinction of many large mammals with the onset of severe climates in the following way. Many large ungulates have gestation periods that are in step with existing climatic patterns. In other words, breeding in the fall is timed so that the young are born in the spring when new green vegetation is available.

Let us imagine that we have an equable climate, say in Nebraska in the plains region, and that in-step mating allows the young to be born in early March. There would be plenty of grass available, since moisture would be available at this time. But what if the modern climate of Nebraska arrived suddenly? The young would be born with a foot of snow on the ground and probably would not survive. Severe feeding stress would also occur in the parents, already weakened by reproductive stress. It seems unlikely that the proper genetic changes to bring about in-step breeding in the new climate would occur fast enough to save the large ungulates and their dependent carnivores.

Still another hypothesis suggests that a general drought and lowering of the water table at the end of the Pleistocene may be partially responsible for the great extinction. This hypothesis also takes into account the fact that small animals are capable of existing and reproducing in much smaller tracts of land than large ones; when conditions such as a major drought eliminates large portions of habitat, small animals are more likely to survive. It takes many acres to support a megaherbivore, but only a few square feet to support a mouse.

Some hypotheses have been joined together to form theoretical models for the late Pleistocene extinction and involve several aspects of interaction between climatic changes and plants and animals during the Pleistocene. An example of one of these follows.

Coevolutionary disequilibrium model. Coevolution is the concept that the evolution of one group of organisms affects the evolution of another group of organisms. Thus, it is suggested that when the communities are in coevolutionary equilibrium they evolve together in a harmonious way and that relatively few extinctions occur. But when these coevolutionary communities begin to evolve in a disharmonious way (e.g., vegetational communities evolve in a different way than the megaherbivores that depend upon them), large scale extinctions, such as the one that occurred at the end of the Pleistocene, may happen. Thus, environmental changes at the end of the Pleistocene are believed to have caused a major biotic reorganization, in which individual species responded to these changes in their own way, creating a disequilibrium in the system that led to a massive extinction.

Late Wisconsinan Postglacial Reinvasion and Extinction in the Great Lakes Basin

When the vast Laurentide ice sheet began its final retreat in the Great Lakes region about 15,000 years ago, it left a mass of sterile gravel, sand, and silt in its wake (see fig. 11). The retreat of this ice sheet probably was not an orderly one, so that the proglacial zone south of the glacier was probably in turmoil for long periods of time. This turmoil likely produced a lag time in the recolonization of the proglacial zone by stable plant and animal communities. This proglacial area might well be termed a tension zone, and it would explain the lack of vertebrate fossils north of the Mason-Quimby line (see fig. 89) in Michigan.

Tundra-tolerant animals probably began to colonize the southern Great Lakes region about 13,000 years ago. This group would include grizzly and black bears, caribou, modern muskoxen, lemmings, yellow-cheeked vole, heather vole, pikas, and wooly mammoths. During the time between 13,000 and 12,500 years ago these animals would have encountered a tundralike vegetation, but there were scattered clumps of trees such as juniper, aspen, ash, and spruce as well as shrubs such as willow, silverberry, and crowberry.

Several of these early tundra-tolerant mammals must have invaded the Great Lakes region from the far northwest through the unglaciated corridor that went through Alaska down into the United States and eastward almost to Lake Superior. At some point in time, this corridor must have existed north of the glacial lakes to allow these far north-western animals to reach the Toronto area and southwestward into Ohio.

From about 12,500 years ago to about 11,800 years ago the southern Great Lakes region consisted mainly of boreal forest dominated by spruce trees. There were also open woodlands and parklands available for colonization. The animals and plants of this interval obviously pushed into the area from the south. We know that frogs and a painted turtle reached southern Michigan during this time span, as well as frogs and Blanding's and snapping turtles in northwestern Ohio.

Important mammals that invaded the area during this time include giant beavers, flat-headed peccaries, Scott's moose, and woodland muskoxen. Jefferson mammoth, and the American mastodont also be-came very abundant in the region during this time, especially in south-ern Michigan. These animals were big game herds in the area for about the next 2,500 years. It has been suggested that mammoths and masto-donts were attracted to southern Michigan because of the numerous salt seeps and sources of shallow saline water, and therefore these mammals might have been migratory.

About 10,000 years ago the widespread worldwide extinction of large mammalian herbivores took its toll in the Great Lakes region as well as everywhere else. The following mammals became extinct in the Great Lakes Basin as well as in the rest of the world.

Short-faced bear *Arctodus simus*
Giant beaver *Castoroides ohioensis*
Flat-headed peccary *Platygonus compressus*
Scott's moose *Cervalces scotti*
Toronto deer *Torontoceros hypogaeus*
Woodland muskox *Bootherium bombifrons*
Wooly mammoth *Mammuthus primigenius*
Jefferson mammoth *Mammuthus jeffersoni*
American mastodont *Mammut americanum*

Animals that became extinct in the Great Lakes Basin but that survive in other areas today include the following:

Grizzly bear *Ursus arctos*
Caribou *Rangifer tarandus*

Bison *Bison* sp.
Barren ground muskox *Ovibos moschatus*
Pika *Ochotona* sp.
Greenland collared lemming *Dicrostonyx groenlandicus*
Yellow-cheeked vole *Microtus xanthognathus*
Heather vole *Phenacomys intermedius*
Northern bog lemming *Synaptomys borealis*

These mammals (with the exception of the bison) are extinct in the area today because they retreated to the north and northwest as the Great Lakes region became increasingly warmer from the end of the Pleistocene through the Holocene. We have discussed some of the hypotheses for the worldwide extinction of the large herbivorous mammals and their dependent carnivores and scavengers at the end of the Pleistocene. Actually, any or all of these hypotheses could be either directly or indirectly applied to the Great Lakes region. Even the out-of-step mating hypothesis could be applied if the big game animals migrated southward to have their young.

We have pointed out that each of these hypotheses has its champions. But another viewpoint is that perhaps all sudden extinctions reflect those odd points in time when several things go wrong at once. Let's use the analogy of a major highway accident. A single factor such as faulty or impaired driving, bad road conditions, bad weather conditions, or a faulty vehicle might result in a close call or a minor accident. But if all of these factors occurred at once, a major disaster is very likely to occur.

Perhaps several of the events suggested by the various extinction hypotheses occurred at once at the end of the Pleistocene about 10,000 years ago. Let us say that (1) the climate changed from equable to inequable, causing many large herbivores to have out-of-step mating, (2) the water table dropped, causing not only a shortage of drinking water but also of essential shallow saline water for megaherbivores, (3) human hunters arrived to confront inexperienced big game herds that already existed in a disharmonious ecological mosaic of species, and (4) new diseases were introduced by species that immigrated across the Bering Straits. Each of these changes would be especially hard on the large herbivores because of their large demands on the ecosystem as well as their low reproductive rates. Together, they would have been disastrous.

Humans in the Pleistocene of the Great Lakes Region

Humans lived in Europe and Asia almost a half million years ago, but they did not immigrate to North America until near the end of the Pleistocene, as the last ice sheet was retreating. Traveling humans are believed to have reached the northern part of North America by means of a complete or partial land bridge that connected Siberia and Alaska. They then migrated down through the unglaciated region in Alaska and Canada, through the United States, across the Central American land bridge, and finally, all of the way to the southern tip of South America.

These early Americans were not "cave men," and if they were still around and wore modern clothes, they would not look any different from people of today with similar genetic backgrounds. When these people arrived in the Great Lakes region near the end of the Ice Age, they left some of their spear points and tools behind. The scattered spear points are solid evidence that Paleo-Indian big game hunters dwelled in the region, but the relatively few occupation sites known are thought to have been only briefly inhabited.

Paleo-Indian spear points are called *fluted points* (fig. 97) and are easily distinguished from the small triangular points and other points that are notched at the base (much more common in the Great Lakes region) left behind by peoples who lived in the region much later. Fluted points do not have a notch at the base, and they are shaped somewhat like elongated leaves. These paleopoints have a groove down the middle of one or both sides called a flute, which is thought to have acted like the groove on a bayonet and promoted bleeding to weaken large game. The fluted point formed the business end of the spear. The wooden shaft of the spear was notched to house the point, which was bound to the shaft by hide made into twine.

Some archaeologists believe that there were few bands of paleohunters in the Great Lakes region, but others think they may have been more numerous, considering the number of finds of fluted points in all of the states and provinces in the region. For instance, there are more than 100 records of fluted points in the state of Michigan, and many private collectors have additional specimens, some as many as 30 or more. Other tools of Paleohunters include stone hide-scrapers, stone knives, and small pointed tools called *gravers* used to poke holes in hides.

Fig. 97. Artist's conception of Paleo-Indians attacking a bogged-down mastodont in the late Pleistocene of the Great Lakes Basin. The two spear points on the left side of the picture represent fluted points of the type left behind by Paleo-Indians in Michigan. The three points on the right represent those that occurred much later in time.

Michigan fluted points occurred at the same time that mammoths and mastodonts roamed the state in large numbers. Some of the Michigan points are called *Gainey* points and are very similar to the *Clovis* points of the plains states and southwestern United States that were made by the people who lived there about 11,500 to 11,000 years ago. Some fluted points in other states of the Great Lakes region, during the same time interval as above, are generally similar to Gainey and Clovis points. Still other fluted points found in the Great Lakes region are believed to have been perhaps two thousand years younger than the Clovis-like points and to have been used for hunting different kinds of game.

In the plains and Southwest, Clovis points are often found near mammoth skeletons. One mammoth in Arizona wandered off to die with eight clovis points in its body. This may indicate that several spearmen participated in the hunt. The Clovis-point people camped on ridges and terraces next to rivers and streams where big game came to eat or drink. Scientists have experimented with Clovis points on dead African elephants and they have shown that the spears easily could have produced fatal wounds. It has been suggested that Clovis-point people hunted in pairs, and that one person would attract the animals's attention while the other one either hurled a spear at the animal or jabbed it with a spear.

It is the Clovis-point people (including the Great Lakes region "look-alike-point people") who have been suggested as the culprits in the overkill hypothesis previously discussed. The idea is that the large mammals did not particularly fear these people who had sharpened their skills for thousands of years on more wary Eurasian game. Why should a behemoth run away from a relatively small two-legged primate with a stick in its hand?

Based on the limited occupation time indicated by the rather small number of Paleo-Indian occupation sites studied in the Great Lakes region, it may be that the hunters migrated into the area with the mammoths and mastodonts, stayed long enough to kill and butcher the animals, and then moved out with enough meat for the winter to more southern areas.

Actually, evidence that mammoths and mastodonts were significantly diminished by paleohunters in the Great Lakes region is inconclusive. For instance, there are as yet no sites in either Ontario or Michigan where mammoths or mastodonts are directly associated with any Paleo-Indian fluted points or stone tools! However, some paleontologists have pointed out that stone tools were not expendable for Paleo-Indian hunters in the Great Lakes region and that both stone tools and Clovis-type spear points were not casually parted with. This would account for the lack of such objects associated with mammoth or mastodont skeletons.

There are other kinds of evidence that humans killed and ate mastodonts, at least in Michigan. Evidence presented includes cut marks on mastodont bones believed to have been made when the meat was removed from the dead animal. Other marks have been found on the ends of mastodont bones that have been interpreted as having been made when the animals were taken apart during the butchering process.

Still other mastodont bones have been interpreted as having been fire blackened, perhaps indicating that the meat had been cooked and eaten. It has been suggested that certain mastodont bones taken from the kill itself were used as tools for stripping off hides. One bone in the tongue skeleton of mastodonts (the *stylohyoid* bone) is shaped somewhat like a probe, and some of these bones at mastodont sites appear to have been worn smooth by use.

These assertions have been backed up by the examination of the bone alterations by scanning electron microscopy, which seems to distinguish nonhuman from human alterations. The microscope shows that the cut marks have a different microscopic appearance than those made by the forces of nature or by the modern tools that were used to dig the fossils out of the ground.

Certain mastodont bones appear to have been broken as if the marrow had been extracted for food, and other important parts of the skeleton are missing, as if they had been carried away. Recently, materials have been found that have been interpreted as evidence that mastodont meat was cached in mastodont intestines under the ice for storage and that the caches were marked by stones.

Although the evidence is very intriguing, many Michigan archaeologists remain somewhat skeptical, and they will continue to worry until stone tools or spear points are found in association with either mammoth or mastodont burials. Unfortunately such associations are very rare in the Great Lakes region.

So, the challenge exists. Somewhere, some absent-minded paleohunter in Michigan or Ontario must have forgotton to retrieve his spear point from his mammoth or mastodont carcass, or perhaps he left a tool or two by the kill. The discovery of such a site will take a lot of the worry out of Michigan and Ontario archaeologists and get a lot of media attention for the discoverer.

Time capsule to the late Pleistocene. Now our time capsule whisks us back 11,000 years to southern Michigan. We alight on a teardrop-shaped hill called a drumlin. The hill is nearly covered by spruce trees but has a prominent stand of jack pine in an area where lightning started a small fire several years before. At the bottom of the hill is a small, shallow lake surrounded by shrubby willows.

The small lake is fed by a tiny stream that carries saline water from ancient evaporative Silurian rocks brought near the surface by uplift eons ago. Suddenly, some huge, elephantlike (but also somewhat piglike) animals crash through the trees. Some of the mastodonts begin eating willow plants, while others drink the mildly salty water, which is sucked up into the trunks and then sprayed into their mouths. Still others spray themselves with water in an attempt to discourage the thousands of deerflies that are pestering them.

One of the group departs from the eating-drinking routine to worry over something on a flat depression near the edge of the pond. It picks it up with its trunk and then gently lays it down again. Others in the mastodont troop also show interest in the object, which is the skull of another mastodont killed that spring by hunters. The skull had originally been discovered near a quaking bog by the mastodont group several weeks ago, and one of them carried it carefully to the salt-procuring site.

Human hunters had found the animal belonging to the skull stuck in the sediments of the bog that spring; and after many thrown spears (fig. 97) the mastodont was struck with enough points that it began to slowly bleed to death. The hunters fled when other mastodonts approached to gaze on their fatally wounded relative. Later, the dead animal was approached by two family groups of humans, who butchered it and carried away all of the parts except for the skull, which had had the brain and tongue removed. Three spears that penetrated the carcass and broke during the animal's torment were removed and the spear points saved.

The present mastodonts catch our scent and begin to move nervously about. Trunks are lifted and warning guttural grunts are given. Large females gather around the young mastodonts, while the bulls lumber restlessly back and forth, trying to focus their black, piggish eyes on possible enemies. In 11,000 years the only evidence that these great mammals ever existed in the spot will be a skull dug out of the low part of a cornfield by a farmer's plow.

Chapter 11
Living Fossils

There are no records of dinosaur finds in the entire Great Lakes region, but "living fossils" whose ancestors lived with the dinosaurs occur in the region today. We often take these animals for granted, or sometimes they are not well treated because they do not quite measure up to our idea of what a respectable fish, bird, or mammal should look like. Nevertheless, all of them should be admired for their adaptability and survivability.

Scientists have come up with several somewhat different definitions of living fossils, but the best one is probably this: A living fossil is a life-form that has not changed morphologically for an extremely long geological time. All of the Great Lakes animals discussed here have existed in essentially the same form since the late Cretaceous period well over 60 million years ago, and each of these animals has special adaptations for such a long geological existence.

Club Mosses (Ground Pines)

The little club mosses, commonly called "ground pines" in the Great Lakes region, are lycopod remnants of the Paleozoic, when their huge, treelike relatives were a dominant part of the great coal-swamp forests of the Pennsylvanian period. Today, there are only four genera of club mosses left, and all of them consist of small herbaceous plants. In the Great Lakes area, little club mosses called *Lycopodium* are common ground-cover plants in moist woodland situations. People often think they are "baby pine trees," but they have soft leaves rather than the hard needles of pine.

Lycopodium plants (see fig. 20a) are typically encountered in clusters along moist forest paths. A *Lycopodium* plant is usually observed in the field as a group of small stems bearing compound leaves with tiny leaflets emerging from the ground. Observation will reveal that these leaf-bearing bodies emerge from a horizontal or *prostrate* stem from which small roots emerge. During the reproductive season leafless upright stems bearing elongate cones emerge from the leafy sections.

These small plants have little economic importance for humans, except that they are sometimes used for Christmas decorations, but they are of great interest to those of us that like to see and touch living fossils whose ancestors sheltered the ancient amphibians of the Paleozoic.

Horsetails

Horsetails of the genus *Equisetum* (see fig. 20b) are common plants of open, moist, usually sandy areas in the Great Lakes region. They are living fossils that are also remnants of the vast Paleozoic coal-swamp forests. Most of us recognize horsetails as plants that we can pull apart in little sections that may be refitted again. What we usually see in the field are the upright, jointed stems of these plants, sometimes capped with somewhat elongate cones.

The slender leaves of *Equisetum* occur in whorls visible around the areas where the joints occur. The upright, jointed stems emerge from a horizontal stem from which small roots emerge. Probably the best place to find horsetails in the Great Lakes region is on moist, sandy banks, often in disturbed areas. The hardy nature of horsetails has enabled them to escape the extinction that befell their larger relatives eons ago.

Garfishes

The garfishes extend far back in the fossil record. In fact, the very same genus (*Lepisosteus*) that occurs in the Great Lakes region today lived with the dinosaurs back in the late Cretaceous. Garfishes, sometimes called garpike, have long bodies covered by thick, diamond-shaped scales, and they have a long toothy snout.

One of the most common fossils that vertebrate paleontologists find are garfish scales. Their diamond shape and shiny surfaces make them easy to recognize. These scales look very much like the scales covering some of the palaeoniscoid fishes of the Paleozoic era found in a few Pennsylvanian age deposits in the region. Judging from the number of gar scales that occur in fossil collections, it appears that these fishes were quite abundant in their ancient habitats. Garfish vertebrae are also very numerous in the fossil record. These vertebrae have concentric growth rings similar to tree rings in that they indicate how old the fossil fishes were when they died.

Today, garfishes occur only in North America, and paleontologists from other countries love to observe these living fossils in the wild. The Great Lakes area has two common species of garfishes that occur in the southern part of the region, the spotted gar and the longnose gar. Both of these fish prefer quiet water with soft bottoms and ample vegetation. Garfish are usually not eaten, and they sometimes are accused of being voracious predators of game fish. However, the small diameter of their toothy snout shows that gars are mainly specialized for catching minnows.

Gars prefer to lie near the surface of the water, where they catch their prey by making short lunges. If they bite on a hook and line they are hard to hook because of their bony mouths. In warm weather garfishes tend to rise to the top of the water and take gulps of air. This air goes to an *air bladder* in the body of the fish that acts as a lung to supplement gill breathing.

Garfishes are not as common in the Great Lakes waterways as they are in the more southern states, but when they are caught in the region they are usually considered "junk fish" and are sometimes thrown up on the bank to die—an example of the attitude of some people toward living fossils.

The Bowfin

The bowfin (see fig. 64b) is another example of a living fossil fish. The same genus (*Amia*) that lives in the Great Lakes region today also goes back to the late Cretaceous, when bowfins coexisted with the dinosaurs. These fish are another delight for foreign paleontologists. Bowfins occur only in eastern North America today but lived in Africa, Asia, Europe, and South America during ancient times.

The bowfin is represented by a single species (*Amia calva*) that may have more common names than any other American fish. They are called dogfish, mudfish, grindles, and cypress trout; they also have some colorful names deriving from their cylindrical shape and dark brown coloration.

The bowfin may be recognized by its cylindrical body, long wavy top fin, and the large head that bears many large pointed teeth. Like the garfishes, the bowfin has an air bladder that enables it to supplement its gill breathing; and bowfins may also be seen gulping air at the surface of the water on hot summer days. This habit allows bowfins to live in water where the oxygen content becomes too low to support many other kinds of Great Lakes fishes. The fossil parts of bowfins that are usually found consist of vertebrae and skull parts. It is easy to recognize their sculptured skull bones and toothy jaws.

The bowfin likes quiet water, such as backwaters of rivers and lakes and swamps. Bowfins may be very common in small bog lakes that are filling in in the southern part of the Great Lakes region. Like the gars, the bowfin is seldom eaten in the region, but the soft flesh is used for making very tasty fish salads in some of the southern states.

The bowfin is truly voracious and can swallow larger prey than can garfishes of equal size. Fishermen in the region tend to be hard on bowfins and garfishes, but there is really no reason to abuse either of them. Certainly their long geological age should give them some respect! How did garfishes and bowfins survive so long with so little change? Probably their survival is based upon their perfect set of adaptions for life in quiet, shallow, water, enhanced by their ability to use their air bladders as lungs when oxygen is in short supply.

Softshell Turtles

Softshell turtles (genus *Apalone,* see fig. 70b) go back at least to the Cretaceous and possibly even into the Jurassic age. These are unique turtles with soft, leathery shells supported by an underlying bony shell. They have a long neck, a nose that looks like a snorkel, and very powerfully webbed feet. Softshell turtles occurred almost worldwide in ancient times and swam around in quiet waters among garfishes, bowfins, and crocodiles, while dinosaurs stalked the shoreline.

Softshell turtle fossils are abundant in many ancient sediments and usually consist of pieces of the bony shell that support the leathery part. These bones are sculptured with pits and ridges and are very easy to identify. Three species of softshell occur in the eastern United States, but only one species, the spiny softshell (*Apalone spinifera*) occurs in the Great Lakes region. These animals may be locally common, especially in slow-flowing rivers with muddy or sandy banks in the southern part of the region.

The strongly webbed feet and pancake shape of softshells make them outstanding swimmers. They love crayfish and also eat small fishes and an occasional frog. Softshells are shy of humans and will rapidly swim away from waders, but they will bite what grabs them. Softshell turtles are often used for food, and their flesh is said to be delicious. Sometimes these flattened animals are battered and then fried like pancakes. They are only locally common in the Great Lakes region; and because of their unique appearance and ancient vintage they should be treated kindly.

Few freshwater turtles in the world can approach the swimming speed and underwater dexterity of the softshells; so it may be the combination of the protective shell as well as swimming ability that fitted them for such a long existence. Being able to breathe with only the tiny tip of the snorkel nose breaking the water also makes them difficult for enemies to locate.

Loons

An exciting development in paleontology was the discovery that loons existed in the late Cretaceous along with the dinosaurs. Actually, it took many years for all of the details of this find to come to light. In the early 1900s a bird fossil was discovered in the late Cretaceous of Chile. This fossil was first identified as a loonlike ancient bird and put in a box in a museum case.

Then recently, a true loon skeleton was discovered in late Cretaceous deposits from Seymour Island in Antarctica. This caused a renewed interest in the Chilean fossil; when paleontologists reexamined the South American bird, they found out that it also represented a true loon rather than an ancient loonlike bird. The fact that loons appear to have occurred widely in the late Cretaceous has been a vital discovery in paleo-ornithology. One gets goose bumps imagining the characteristic tremulo calls and haunting wails of the loon song echoing over the lakes and swamps of the Cretaceous over 60 million years ago.

Today, loons nest in the Great Lakes; but with the onset of fall they fly south to winter in the shallow bays of the Gulf of Mexico or the Atlantic Coast, where they become fishing partners of pelicans, cormorants, anhingas, and other semitropical birds. Yet, with all of its primitive greatness, the common loon has been threatened in parts of the Great Lakes region. The reasons for the loon decline are varied. But excessive shoreline development, boating disturbances, and botulism die-offs in Lake Michigan have hurt them. Moreover, the presence of toxins in their winter grounds may have adverse effects. It would be heartbreaking if this ancient bird—with more than 60 million years behind it—were to become extinct due to human habitat encroachments and pollutants.

Why is the loon a living fossil? This seems more difficult to answer than in the previously discussed animals. Nevertheless, the loon has very dense bones, a sturdy skeleton, and other structures that make it well adapted for diving for fish or for escaping from its predators. There certainly must have been many dangerous predators for loons in the ancient Cretaceous lakes and seas.

The Opossum

The opossum, commonly called "possum," is quite a primitive mammal. The name comes from the Algonquian Native American language and was written *apasum* by the early colonists. Opossums (fig. 98) lived in the late Cretaceous in North America and probably in South America and likely had the same basic habits they have today.

Opossums are marsupials, which means that they are mammals with a pouch on their bellies. When young opossums are born, they are about the size of a honey bee and almost, larval in form; but they somehow manage to crawl into the mother's pouch, where they attach themselves orally to a teat. After they mature enough to look like real opossums, they ride around on the female for a time, clinging to her sparse hair.

Opossums have a more "reptilian" skeleton than other North American mammals. They have very toothy jaws, and the skull narrows considerably in the area where the brain occurs. They have an oddly

Fig. 98. Scene depicting a Cretaceous opossum between the feet of a bipedal dinosaur. Opossums are living fossils that have been expanding their ranges in the Great Lakes Basin during modern times.

inflected process on the back parts of their lower jaws, and they have extra bones in the belly region that support the pouch. Male opossums have very enlarged canine teeth.

Despite their primitive skeleton and small brains, opossums have been quite successful in North America and have steadily moved northward for the past ninety years, so that they now live in the "land of the porcupines" and have even invaded the Upper Peninsula of Michigan. Opossums use the burrows of other animals to escape the cold Great Lakes winters, but they often get frostbitten ears and lose parts of their bristly, nearly naked tails to cold weather. They are opportunistic feeders and will eat about anything digestible. They have been known to occupy the carcasses of large, long-dead mammals, used for both food and shelter. It is tempting to suggest that opossums also found temporary food and shelters in dinosaur carcasses in the Cretaceous.

Opossums have a remarkable ability to play dead, even when shaken or otherwise abused by dogs or other predators. This "reptilian" behavior probably allows them to survive rambunctious attacks by predators that are more stimulated by the struggle of their prey than by their hunger for it. If an opossum is approached by humans or other large animals, the opossum may stand its ground, not being exceptionally fleet of foot, turn its head aside, bare its teeth, and hiss like a reptile. On the other hand, young opossums in captivity emit plaintive whistles and squeaks that tend to endear them to their human captors.

Opossum meat is rich and fatty, but few of them are eaten in the Great Lakes region. The biggest enemies of opossums appear to be automobiles, which run over many animals, especially during the spring and the fall. The humble opposum with its small brain and flat-footed gait seems to have survived for these millions of years by being generalized structurally, being able to eat and digest a wide variety of food, and being successful reproductively.

It is interesting that among the Great Lakes region living fossils only the loon is considered to be a noble animal. But garfish, bowfins, softshell turtles, and opossums are fascinating from structural, behavioral, and evolutionary standpoints. Through them we can see what animals represented by these modern "fossils" really looked like and acted like.

Epilogue

We have examined changes that have taken place through time as documented by the fossil record in the Great Lakes region. Though parts of the fossil record are missing, we have seen evidence of many earthly events: primitive cells 3.5 billion years ago; Paleozoic seas teeming with invertebrate life and strange fishes; great coal-swamp forests of primitive treelike plants; essentially lifeless glacial ages; reinvasion of previously glaciated areas by plant and animal communities dominated by megaherbivores; the appearance of humans late in the Ice Age; and finally, the extinction of most of the mammalian megafauna at the end of the Ice Age.

What can the past tell us about the future? The fossil record tells us that humans as well as all living species will either become extinct or evolve into new species. It also tells us that evolution over the long haul is rather progressive, at least to human eyes. The fossil record tells us that world climates change from time to time, and that lush tropical communities can become harsh cold ones. It tells us that sea levels rise and fall and that if a glacial age returns, Chicago may be under a mile of ice and Miami, Florida, may be an inland city without a beach! The fossil record also tells us that mass extinctions occur from time to time, but there always seem to be enough surviving species to establish thriving biological communities.

Some people believe that humans have enough brains and technology to modify the course of future events and extinctions. Only time will tell.

Where to Learn More

One of the main purposes of this book is to get people interested in the ancient life of the Great Lakes region. Thus, information follows on institutions that have fossil collections and/or exhibits on fossils of the area.

Museums and Other Institutions

If you are interested in fossils from specific areas in the Great Lakes region, you may wish to contact persons at one of the following museums university departments or state geological surveys for additional information.

New York

American Museum of Natural History
Central Park West at 79th Street
New York, NY 10024

Buffalo Museum of Science
Humboldt Parkway
Buffalo, NY 14211

New York State Museum
State Geological Survey
Cultural and Educational Center, Empire State Plaza
Albany, NY 12230

Paleontological Research Institution
Ithaca, NY 14850

Vassar College Geology Museum
Poughkeepsie, NY 12600

Ohio

Cincinnati Museum of Natural History
1301 Western Avenue
Cincinnati, OH 45203

Cleveland Museum of Natural History
Wade Oval, University Circle
Cleveland, OH 44106

Dayton Museum of Natural History
De Weese Parkway
Dayton, OH 45414

Ohio Division of Geological Survey
Fountain Square, Building B
Columbus, OH 43224

Michigan

Center for Cultural and Natural History
124 Rowe Hall
Central Michigan University
Mount Pleasant, MI 48859

Cranbrook Institute of Science
500 Lone Pine Road
Bloomfield Hills, MI 48303

Great Lakes Area Paleontological Museum
381 South Long Lake Road
Traverse City, MI 49643

Kingman Museum of Natural History
West Michigan Avenue at 20th Street
Battle Creek, MI 49017

Michigan State University Museum
West Circle Drive
East Lansing, MI 48824

Museum of Paleontology
University of Michigan
Ann Arbor, MI 48109

Public Museum of Grand Rapids
54 Jefferson SE
Grand Rapids, MI 49503

Wayne State University Museum of Natural History
Biology Building
Wayne State University
Detroit, MI 48202

Indiana

Children's Museum
3000 N Meridian Street
Indianapolis, IN 46204

Indiana Geological Survey
611 North Walnut Grove
University of Indiana
Bloomington, IN 47405

Indiana State Museum
202 N Alabama Street
Indianapolis, IN 46204

Joseph Moore Museum
Earlham College
Richmond, IN 47374

Illinois

Field Museum of Natural History
Roosevelt Road at Lakeshore Drive
Chicago, IL 60605

Fryxell Geological Museum
Augustana College
Rock Island, IL 61201

Illinois State Geological Survey
Natural Resources Building
615 East Peabody Drive
Champaign, IL 61820

Illinois State Museum
Springfield and Edwards Streets
Springfield, IL 62706

Museum of the Chicago Academy of Sciences
2001 N Clark Street
Chicago, IL 60614

Wheaton College
Wheaton, IL 60187
(Whole Mammoth Exhibit)

Wisconsin

Geology Museum
University of Wisconsin—Milwaukee
3367 North Downer Avenue
Milwaukee, WI 53211

Green Memorial Museum
Milwaukee, WI 53200

Milwaukee Public Museum
1800 Wells Street
Milwaukee, WI 53233

University of Wisconsin Zoological Museum
Lowell Noland Building
Madison, WI 53706

Wisconsin Geological and Natural History Survey
1815 University Avenue
Madison, WI 53706

Minnesota

James Ford Bell Museum of Natural History
10 Church Street SE
Minneapolis, MN 55455

Geology Museum
University of Minnesota, Duluth
Duluth, MN 55800

Minnesota Geological Survey
1633 Eustis Street
St. Paul, MN 55108

Ontario

Department of Geology
University of Ontario
Toronto, Ontario M5S 2C6

National Museum of Natural Sciences
Ottawa, Ontario K1A OMB

Royal Ontario Museum
Toronto, Ontario M5S 2C6

Bibliography

The following is a list of selected references that deal with the topics of this book on a chapter-by-chapter basis.

Chapter 1

Beerbower, J. R. 1968. *Search for the Past.* 2d ed. Englewood Cliffs, N.J.: Prentice-Hall.

Dunbar, C. O., and K. M. Waage. 1969. *Historical Geology.* 3d ed. New York: John Wiley and Sons.

Gould, S. J., and T. J. M. Schopf, eds. 1980. *The History of Paleontology.* 43 vols. New York: Arno Press.

Harlan, W. B. 1990. *A Geologic Time Scale.* Cambridge: Cambridge University Press.

Marvin, U. B. 1973. *Continental Drift: The Evolution of a Concept.* Washington, D.C.: Smithsonian Institution Press.

Raup, D. M., and S. M. Stanley. 1978. *Principles of Paleontology.* San Francisco: W. H. Freeman.

Stearn, C. W., and R. L. Carroll. 1989. *Paleontology: The Record of Life.* New York: Wiley and Sons.

Stokes, W. L. 1982. *Essentials of Earth History.* 4th ed. Englewood Cliffs, N.J.: Prentice-Hall.

Wilson, J. T., ed. 1976. *Continents Adrift and Continents Around.* San Francisco: W. H. Freeman.

Chapter 2

Chapman, L. J., and D. F. Putnam. 1984. *The Physiography of Southern Ontario.* Toronto: Ontario Geological Survey.

Daniel, G., and J. Sullivan. 1981. *The North Woods.* San Francisco: Sierra Club Books.

Dapples, E. C., and M. E. Hopkins, eds. 1969. *Environments of Coal Deposition.* Geological Society of America Special Papers 114.

Dorr, J. A., and D. F. Eschman. 1970. *Geology of Michigan.* Ann Arbor: University of Michigan Press.

Fisher, J. H., ed. 1977. *Reefs and Environments—Concepts and Depositional Models.* American Association of Petroleum Geologists Studies 5.

Hough, J. L. 1958. *Geology of the Great Lakes.* Urbana: University of Illinois Press.

King, P. B. 1976. *Precambrian Geology of the United States: An Explanatory Text to Accompany the Geologic Map of the United States.* United States Geological Survey Professional Paper 902.

Leverett, F., and F. B. Taylor. 1915. *Pleistocene of Indiana and Michigan and the History of the Great Lakes.* United States Geological Survey Monograph 53.

Mesolella, K. J., J. D. Robinson, L. M. McCormick, and A. R. Ormiston. 1975. *Cyclic Deposition of Silurian Carbonates and Evaporites in Michigan Basin.* American Association of Petroleum Geologists Bulletin 58.

Ojakangas, R. W., and C. L. Matsch. 1982. *Minnesota's Geology.* Minneapolis: University of Minnesota Press.

Paull, R. K., and R. A. Paull. 1977. *Geology of Wisconsin and Upper Michigan.* Dubuque, Iowa: Kandall-Hunt.

Stearn, C. W., R. L. Carroll, and T. H. Clark. 1979. *Geological Evolution of North America.* 3d ed. New York: John Wiley and Sons.

Chapter 3

Arnold, C. A. 1949. Fossil Flora of the Michigan Coal Basin. *The University of Michigan Museum of Paleontology Contributions* 7:131–269.

Barnes, R. 1980. *Invertebrate Zoology.* 4th ed. Philadelphia: Saunders.

Diener, T. 1981. Viroids. *Scientific American* 244(1): 66–73.

Fay, P., and C. Van Baalen, eds. 1987. *The Cyanobacteria.* Oxford: Blackwell.

Moore-Landecker, E. 1982. *Fundamentals of the Fungi.* Englewood Cliffs, N. J.: Prentice-Hall.

Pough, F. H., J. B. Heiser, and W. N. McFarland. 1989. *Vertebrate Life*. 3d ed. New York: Macmillan.

Raven, P., R. Evert, and S. Eichorn. 1986. *Biology of Plants*. 4th ed. New York: Worth.

Russell, H. 1979. *A Life of Invertebrates*. New York: Macmillan.

Sagan, D., and L. Margulis. 1988. *Garden of Microbial Delights*. New York: Harcourt Brace Jovanovich.

Starr, C., and R. Taggart. 1987. *Biology: The Unity and Diversity of Life*. Belmont, Calif.: Wadsworth.

Taylor, T. 1981. *Paleobotany*. New York: McGraw-Hill.

Wallace, R. A. 1987. *Biology, the World of Life*. Glenview, Ill.: Scott-Foresman.

Chapter 4

Ager, D. V. 1963. *Principles of Paleoecology*. New York: McGraw-Hill.

Behrensmeyer, A. K., and S. M. Kidwell. 1985. Taphonomy's contribution to paleobiology. *Paleobiology* 11(1): 105–119.

Graham, R. J., J. A. Holman, and P. W. Parmalee. 1983. *Taphonomy and Paleoecology of the Christensen Bog Bone Bed, Hancock County, Indiana*. Illinois State Museum Reports of Investigations 38.

Hecker, R. F. 1965. *Introduction to Paleoecology*. New York: Elsevier.

Imbrie, J., and N. D. Newell. 1964. *Approaches to Paleoecology*. New York: Wiley.

Laporte, L. F. 1968. *Ancient Environments*. Englewood Cliffs, N.J.: Prentice-Hall.

McKerrow, W. S., ed. 1978. *The Ecology of Fossils*. London: Gerald Duckworth.

Raup, D. M., and S. M. Stanley. 1978. *Principles of Paleontology*. San Francisco: W. H. Freeman.

Chapters 5 and 6

Case, G. R. 1982. *A Pictorial Guide to Fossils*. New York: Van Nostrand Reinhold.

Holman, J. A. 1975. *Michigan's Fossil Vertebrates*. East Lansing: Michigan State University Museum.

Kapp, R. O., S. G. Beld, and J. A. Holman. 1990. Paleontological resources in Michigan: An overview. In, R. W. Stoffle, ed., *Cultural and Paleontological Effects of Siting a Low-Level Radioactive Waste Storage Facility in Michigan*. Ann Arbor: Institute for Social Research.

La Plante, L. 1977. *The Weekend Fossil Hunter.* New York: Drake.
MacFall, R. P., and J. Wollin. 1983. *Fossils for Amateurs.* 2d ed. New York: Van Nostrand Reinhold.
Murray, M. 1967. *Hunting for Fossils.* New York: Macmillan.
Parker, S., and R. L. Berner. 1990. *The Practical Paleontologist.* New York: Simon and Schuster.
Raup, D. M., and S. M. Stanley. 1978. *Principles of Paleontology.* San Francisco: W. H. Freeman.
Shrock, R. R., and W. H. Twenhofel. 1953. *Principles of Invertebrate Paleontology.* 2d ed. New York: McGraw-Hill.

Chapters 7, 8, and 9

Andrews, H. N. 1961. *Studies in Paleobotany.* New York: Wiley.
Banks, R. C., R. W. McDiarmid, and A. L. Gardner. 1987. Checklist of Vertebrates of the United States, the U.S. Territories, and Canada. *United States Department of the Interior Fish and Wildlife Service Resource Publication 66.*
Canright, J. E. 1959. *Fossil Plants of Indiana.* Bloomington: Indiana Geological Survey.
Carroll, R. L. 1988. *Vertebrate Paleontology and Evolution.* New York: W. H. Freeman.
Dorr, J. A., and D. F. Eschman. 1970. *Geology of Michigan.* Ann Arbor: University of Michigan Press.
Douglass, D. 1971. *Midwest Fossils.* Colorado Springs: Earth Science Publishing.
Fairbridge, R. W., and D. Jablonski. 1979. *The Encyclopedia of Paleontology.* New York: Academic Press.
Fenton, C., and M. Fenton. 1959. *The Fossil Book.* New York: Doubleday.
Goldring, W. 1958. *Handbook of Paleontology for Beginners and Amateurs.* Ithaca: Paleontological Research Labs.
Holman, J. A. 1975. *Michigan's Fossil Vertebrates.* East Lansing: Michigan State University Museum.
Hoskins, D. M. 1964. *Fossil Collecting in Pennsylvania.* Harrisburg: Topographic and Geologic Survey Publication.
La Roque, A. 1955. *Ohio Fossils.* Columbus: Ohio Geological Survey.
Moodie, R. L. 1933. *Popular Guide to the Nature and Environment of the Fossil Vertebrates of New York.* Albany: State Museum
Moore, R. C., C. G. Lalicker, and A. G. Fisher. 1952. *Invertebrate Fossils.* New York: McGraw-Hill.

Murray, M. 1967. *Hunting for Fossils.* New York: Macmillan.

Ojakangas, R. W., and C. L. Matsch. 1982. *Minnesota's Geology.* Minneapolis: University of Minnesota Press.

Ostrow, M. E. 1961. *Fossil Collecting in Wisconsin.* Madison: Geological Survey.

Perry, T. G. 1959. *Fossils: Prehistoric Animals in Hoosier Rocks.* Bloomington: Indiana Geological Survey.

Ransom, J. E. 1964. *Fossils in America.* New York: Harper.

Raup, D. R., et al. 1987. *Paleontological Collecting.* Washington D. C.: National Academy Press.

Romer, A. S. 1966. *Vertebrate Paleontology.* Chicago: University of Chicago Press.

Shimer, H. W., and R. R. Shrock. 1944. *Index Fossils of North America.* Cambridge: MIT Press.

Shrock, R. R., and W. H. Twenhofel. 1953. *Principles of Invertebrate Paleontology.* 2d ed. New York: McGraw-Hill.

Taylor, T. 1981. *Paleobotany.* New York: McGraw-Hill.

Waddington, J. 1979. *An Introduction to Ontario Fossils.* Toronto: Royal Ontario Museum.

West, R. W. 1989. State Regulation of Geological, Paleontological, and Archaeological Collecting. *Curator* 32(4): 281–319.

West, R. W. 1991. State Regulation of Geological, Paleontological, and Archaeological Collecting. *Curator* 34(3):199–209.

Wilson, R. L. 1967. The Pleistocene vertebrates of Michigan. *Papers of the Michigan Academy of Science, Arts and Letters* 52:197–234.

Chapter 10

Dorr, J. A., and D. F. Eschman. 1970. *Geology of Michigan.* Ann Arbor: University of Michigan Press.

Dunbar, C. O., and K. M. Waage. 1969. *Historical Geology.* 3d ed. New York: John Wiley and Sons.

Eicher, D. L., and A. L. McAlester. 1980. *History of the Earth.* Englewood Cliffs, N. J.: Prentice-Hall.

Hibbard, C. W. 1951. Animal life in Michigan during the Ice Age. *Michigan Alumnus Quarterly Review* 57: 200–208.

Holman, J. A. 1975. *Michigan's Fossil Vertebrates.* East Lansing: Michigan State University Museum.

Holman, J. A. 1988. Michigan's mastodonts and mammoths revisited. *Midwest Friends of the Pleistocene Field Conference Field Guide.* Michigan State University Department of Geology.

Holman, J. A., D. C. Fisher, and R. O. Kapp. 1986. Recent discoveries of fossil vertebrates in Michigan. *Michigan Academician* 18:431–63.

Holman, J. A., and M. B. Holman. 1991. Mysteries of our past. *Michigan Natural Resources Magazine,* September–October, 16–21.

Kapp, R. O., S. G. Beld, and J. A. Holman. 1990. Paleontological resources in Michigan: an overview. In, R. W. Stoffle, ed., *Cultural and Paleontological Effects on Siting a Low-Level Radioactive Waste Storage Facility in Michigan.* Ann Arbor: Institute for Social Research.

Laub, R. S., N. G. Miller, and D. W. Steadman, eds. 1988. *Late Pleistocene and Early Holocene Paleontology and Archeology of the Eastern Great Lakes Region.* Buffalo: Buffalo Society of Natural Sciences.

Martin, P. S., and R. Klein, eds. 1984. *Quaternary Extinctions: A Prehistoric Revolution.* Tucson: University of Arizona Press.

Mason, R. J. 1958. Late Pleistocene geochronology and the Paleo-Indian penetration of the Lower Michigan Peninsula. *University of Michigan Museum of Anthropology, Anthropological Papers* 11:1–48.

McAlester, A. L. 1977. *The History of Life.* Englewood Cliffs, N.J.: Prentice-Hall.

Stearn, C. W., and R. L. Carroll. 1989. *Paleontology: The Record of Life.* New York: Wiley and Sons.

Stearn, C. W., R. L. Carroll, and T. H. Clark. 1979. *Geological Evolution of North America.* 3d ed. New York: John Wiley and Sons.

Stokes, W. L. 1982. *Essentials of Earth History.* 4th ed. Englewood Cliffs, N.J.: Prentice-Hall.

Chapter 11

Beerbower, J. R. 1968. *Search for the Past.* 2d ed. Englewood Cliffs, N.J.: Prentice-Hall.

Bretsky, P. W., and D. M. Lorenz. 1972. Adaptive responses to environmental stability. *Proceedings of the North American Paleontological Convention.* 1:522–50.

Carroll, R. L. 1988. *Vertebrate Paleontology and Evolution.* New York: W. H. Freeman.

Darwin, C. 1859. *On the Origin of Species by Means of Natural Selection.* London: John Murray.

Holman, J. A. 1992. Michigan's living fossils. *Michigan Natural Resources Magazine,* September–October, 10–15.

Stearn, C. W., and R. L. Carroll. 1989. *Paleontology: The Record of Life.* New York: Wiley and Sons.

Index